The French Essay

Twayne's World Authors Series

French Literature

David O'Connell, Editor

University of Illinois

TWAS 775

The French Essay

By Theodore P. Fraser

College of the Holy Cross

Twayne Publishers • *Boston*

The French Essay

Theodore P. Fraser

Copyright © 1986 by G. K. Hall & Co.
All Rights Reserved
Published by Twayne Publishers
A Division of G. K. Hall & Co.
70 Lincoln Street
Boston, Massachusetts 02111

Copyediting supervised by Lewis DeSimone
Book production by Elizabeth Todesco
Book design by Barbara Anderson

Typeset in 11 pt. Garamond
by Compset, Inc., Beverly, Massachusetts

Printed on permanent/durable acid-free paper
and bound in the United States of America

Library of Congress Cataloging in Publication Data

Fraser, Theodore P.
  The French essay.

  (Twayne's world authors series; TWAS 775. French literature)
  Bibliography: p. 176
  Includes index.
  1. French essays—History and criticism.   I. Title.
II. Series: Twayne's world authors series; TWAS 775.
III. Series: Twayne's world authors series. French literature.
PQ731.F727   1986   844'.009   85-27218
ISBN 0-8057-6626-X

To my parents

Contents

119070

About the Author

Theodore P. Fraser received the B.A. from Fordham University and the M.A. and Ph.D. from Brown University. He was appointed French government assistant at the Collège Moderne de Garçons in Grenoble, where he taught from 1956 to 1957. After teaching at the Lawrenceville School, Tufts University, Bates College, and Bucknell University, he came to Holy Cross College in 1968. He was chairman of the Department of Modern Languages and Literatures from 1971 to 1980. He also founded and currently directs the college's studies in European literature program. In 1980, he was fellow in residence at the Fondation-Camargo, Cassis, France. He has published two books, *Le Duchat, First Editor of Rabelais* (1971) and *The Moralist Tradition in France* (1982); two language texts, *Readings in French Literature* (1975) and *Le Pot au feu* (1975); and a number of book reviews, principally on modern French authors.

Preface

Any study of the essay must initially come to grips with the thorny problem of defining both the structure and the limits of this most diverse of all literary genres. This task seems all the more difficult—and elusive—when applied to a study of the French essay, which, up to the present, has resisted any attempt at definition, or even classification. In fact, no general work on the French essay as a genre has yet been written; and a well-known American scholar, Richard Chadbourne, who in our own day has taken measure of the task, remarks that "No Brunetière has yet appeared to track the evolution of the French essay."[1] He further states that anyone attempting such an enterprise would find his task "bewildering" in the extreme. For though a Frenchman, Montaigne, created the familiar or "classical" form of the essay—"the artfully rambling attempt at self-definition"—there have been far more illustrious continuers of his tradition in England than in France during the past four hundred years. In fact, the development of the essay has virtually become synonymous with the brilliant works of such authors as Francis Bacon, Abraham Cowley, Joseph Addison and Richard Steele, Jonathan Swift, Charles Lamb, Leigh Hunt, Robert Louis Stevenson, G. K. Chesterton, and Virginia Woolf, who throughout the centuries have artfully perfected the form.

The French themselves seem to accept this general opinion and even appear to wonder if a viable tradition of the essay does indeed exist in French literature. Such a well-known vehicle for popular consumption as *La Grande Encyclopédie*, in its most recent edition, crystallizes this uncertainty in its entry for the *essai*.[2] After first providing a historical treatment of Montaigne's invention of the genre, the author remarks:

Indeed it has only been the English who, along with Montaigne, have discovered a means of expression that seems to have been destined to them from all eternity. In addition to the good sense dear to the author of the *Essais*, they have brought to the genre the qualities particular to their race.[3]

Among these national characteristics, the reviewer mentions a lack of rigid structure and ceremony, as well as a sense of humor that presents matter in a form of "admirable conversation for well educated people."

The article goes on to claim that "in France, Montaigne's *Essais* could almost be regarded as an accident. Our national temperament has rarely inclined our authors to the familiar essay, and the essay has never constituted a major part of the literary output of our authors."

While admitting that writers such as Voltaire (in the *Essay on Epic Poetry* and the *Essay on General History and Customs*), and Mauriac (in *Bloc-Notes* and *Of Myself and Others*) have maintained some kind of traditional use of the essay form, the article concludes that the hallmark of the French variety has always been a desire to be "intelligent and brilliant."[4] The French essay has ever remained the vehicle for dry reason (*la raison raisonnante*) even when it has sought to contest this very process. Hence, works such as Pascal's *Pensées* and La Rochefoucauld's *Maximes* soon brought to bear on Montaigne's personal form a taste for minute analysis, the famous *esprit de géométrie* defined by Pascal, which, in the reviewer's opinion, has consistently won out over that warmth of sentiment and penchant for self-revelation that so well characterize the English variety.

Inconclusive as is this article, it is richly expressive when compared with the curious entry dedicated to the matter of the essay in an edition of this same encyclopedia published at the end of the last century.[5] Significantly, the volume contains no entry for the word *essai,* and the reviewer introduces his remarks under the rubric "essayist", which he pointedly designates an English term. No allusion is made to Montaigne, to his *Essais,* or to the development of the essay form itself. Instead, the article constitutes a polemic against the many articles then written by a certain group of English essayists whose works were being proliferated in the many popular periodicals of the day.

The reviewer first defines the essayist as "every writer who in magazines and periodical reviews deals with short writings in a rapid style on such matters as manners, morality, science, and art." He makes a sharp distinction between the eighteenth-century essayists (Budgell, Pope, Gay, and Johnson) and those currently writing essays for popular consumption. He credits the former with maintaining the purity of the English language and with propagating good taste among the populace; for the latter, however, he seems to have only scorn. This crop of new essayists, mostly young women and products of the new English high schools, he claims, were currently filling provincial periodicals with all manner of insipid and maudlin ramblings and were even actively encouraged to do so by their educational system. Could anyone imagine, he concludes, "a more pernicious training for the future mothers of families?"

Despite the blatantly sexist prejudices of the writer and his apparent lack of critical acumen, the article serves as a valuable index as to how decidedly foreign the incidental and freewheeling nature of the British essay was to the French temperament of the last century, at least as regards its vogue in magazines and periodicals. It further indicates that the *essai* did not enjoy popular recognition as a distinct literary genre in French letters; and finally, we see that the term *essayist* had not as yet gained entry into the French language.

This term passed into the language just at the turn of the century, and at that time the essay technique was apparently regarded by critics as more or less synonymous with the growing tendency of writers to deal with their own personal views and problems, whether in novels or in nonfictional prose.

Yet major works of literary criticism written in the early decades of the twentieth century still did not include the essay form as a separate genre of French literature, but dealt with it only as it pertained to the fortunes of Montaigne's *Essais* and to the apparent eclipse that his project and art form had undergone in French letters. The great Montaigne scholar Pierre Villey claimed, for example, that in the seventeenth century the *Essais* soon became victim to the changing political and religious climate generated by the reign of Louis XVI and the triumph of the Counter Reformation.[6] Except in libertine circles, Montaigne's indulgent skepticism and exaltation of the individual were judged to be inimical to the renewed stress on religious orthodoxy and to the preference expressed by classical authors for universal statement in literary forms. Hence only in seventeenth-century England could the open-ended and nondoctrinary form of the essay find fertile soil and realize its authentic development in the writings of Sir Thomas Browne, Sir William Cornwallis, Sir William Temple, Ben Jonson, and others. Villey further stated that the essay returned to France only at the beginning of the eighteenth century, where, shorn of its association with Montaigne, it would assume a different identity and become a vehicle for serious studies on philosophical, literary, and political matters much in the style of such extended and scholarly treatises as Dryden's *Essay on Dramatic Poesy* (1688), and Locke's *Essay on Human Understanding* (1690), which had inspired the essay's reappearance on French soil.

The other great French critic who turned his attention to the fortune of the *essai* was Gustave Lanson. In his work on Montaigne, he dedicated one entire chapter, entitled "L'influence des *Essais*," to chart the manifestation of the genre both in France and England.[7] Concurring with Villey on the decline of the familiar essay in his own country,

Lanson went on to probe reasons for this phenomenon. He claimed that after the essay's return in the early eighteenth century, many French authors showed a reluctance to use the essay title for their works because of the term's obvious association with Montaigne. Clearly, Montaigne's universal reputation made the use of his title a risky venture, especially for personal pieces. Instead, writers preferred to employ the more traditional designations: *discours, traité, réflexions, considérations, pensées,* and *dialogue,* even if their works were of a personal or familiar nature. Although Lanson admitted that the *essai* has frequently been used by many French writers from the Enlightenment period up to modern times, he claimed that, after 1700, this cachet no longer implied an affinity with Montaigne's works, project, or style. Rather the term *essai* more often than not has been used to designate a well-knit, serious, often long, and personal study written in what could be called the "English manner." Hence, there has come to exist a curious dichotomy between the French use of the generic term *essai* and the particular cast and meaning that Montaigne gave to his artistic achievement—which for all intents and purposes has remained his own very special property in French literature.

Lanson's tacit recognition of some kind of essay tradition in French literature brings us to the knotty problem of definition of terms. For if one grants thst Montaigne's model did not thrive posthumously in France and that an imbalance manifestly exists between the English and French continuation of this particular form of the genre, what then can be said of the numerous nonfictional pieces entitled *essai,* or of the many *discours, traités, réflexions,* and other such works written from the seventeenth century to the present? Are they authentic forms of the essay that have taken different paths, or do they fall outside of this artistic designation? What can be said, moreover, of the rich profusion of moralist literature—such nonfictional works as Pascal's *Pensées,* La Rochefoucauld's *Maximes,* or La Bruyère's *Caractères,* which, like Montaigne's *Essais,* profoundly examine the wellspring of human conduct and motive? Are these examples of the essay as it has adapted itself to the classical preference for universal statement, or must they be regarded as distinctly different prose forms?

Unquestionably these perplexing problems of identification stem largely from a general and long-standing uncertainty as to how to define adequately the many manifestations that this elusive genre has assumed, not only in France but everywhere, in its long passage from Montaigne's period to our own day. An excellent case in point is provided by so standard a reference as *Cassell's Encyclopedia of Literature*. In the article on "Essay," the author first characterizes the genre as comprising "a moderately brief prose discussion of a restricted topic." He then candidly admits that "Because of the wide applicaton of the term, no satisfactory definition can be arrived at." He also states that the essay defies any attempt at classification as well, and some fifteen categories of essay types (aphoristic, descriptive, reflective, psychological, biographical, cosmical, etc.) are merely listed in passing.[8]

A very useful division that the article makes, and one that seems absolutely essential for any study of the essay in its diverse forms, is that between the "informal" and the "formal" essay. The "informal essay" includes all moderately brief aphoristic works like those of Francis Bacon, periodical essays in the manner of Addison and Steele, and personal or familiar essays associated with Montaigne, Cowley, Lamb, Chesterton, and a host of others. On the other hand, instead of crystallizing into a set literary form, the "formal essay" has tended to become more and more diversified in form, spirit, and length according to the theme and purpose of the author. Qualities of the formal essay include seriousness of purpose, dignity, tight logical organization, and generally more protracted length. Though the personal element is also present in the formal essay, it is usually subdued or limited to an exposition of the author's particular views without self-revelatory details being given for their own sake. Written from an admittedly Anglo-American point of view, the article offers as examples of the informal essay such pieces as Swift's "Meditations on a Broomstick," and Lamb's "Dissertation on Roast Pig," and for the formal, Carlyle's *Heroes and Hero-Worship*, and George Orwell's *Critical Essays*.[9]

Valuable as this article assuredly is in stating the complexity of definition and in providing a method to approach the study of the essay, it is ultimately too prosaic and does not deal sufficiently with the psychological and aesthetic dimensions that give the genre its distinctive coloration. This larger view is admirably presented by David Daiches in his excellent introduction to the anthology entitled *A Century of the Essay British and American*.[10] In this brief essay on the essay, he provides what is perhaps the best commentary presently available on the nature and limits of the genre as a prose form.

For Daiches, Montaigne's familiar essay constitutes the genre par excellence. With his "confessional discourses" the Frenchman established the form for all time as a literary genre and nurtured a tradition extending to our own day. Yet there is a more modern tradition that coexists with the familiar form. More serious in purpose and harkening back to the philosophical treatises of the Greeks and Romans, this other essay embodies a prose discussion "which can handle any subject, be of any length, and is often of interest only to those who have a previous interest in the subject handled."[11] The mass media publications of the modern age have, in fact, employed this essay form as their stock in trade to examine all manner of topics—political, social, scientific, medical, moral, and so forth.

This second form has a limit beyond which the essayist cannot venture. If any given piece is concerned only with the dissemination of knowledge in some specialized area, and that for its own sake, if elements of the author's personality are absent or virtually so, and if the relevance of the matter does not extend to embrace broader human concerns, then the author has not the right to grace his writing with the title "essay." His, instead, is the work of a technical expert, and much of what is printed in books and magazines (of today) falls into this domain.

As Daiches describes it, the art of the essay is very different from the method employed in technical works. Unlike the latter, an essay translates into prose the elements of refined conversation befitting educated people, and it expresses ideas forcefully without having to resort to the graceless and often hermetic language of technical experts. The essay, in the final analysis, remains the primary vehicle for extending the limits of human knowledge in specific areas. And it is not the technical expert, but the essayist, "who best integrates this knowledge with the pattern of the culture of his day, who airs it and demonstrates its relevance to our daily thinking and its general significance in the intellectual climate of our time."[12]

What ultimately characterizes the essay for Daiches is not its specific form or content, but rather the state of mind and the intention of its writer. Whether the prose work be "a loose sally of the mind, an undigested piece," to use Doctor Johnson's sobriquet, or a very serious prose discussion, it must fulfill the following conditions: first, the work must bear the stamp of the author's particular temperament; second, it should clearly reflect his fundamental thought patterns; and third, it should reveal his most personal feelings or convictions on any topic with which it deals. This cogent analysis fleshes out the dry delineation of the essay usually found in standard references, and it succinctly defines the characteristics that must be commonly shared by all forms of the genre; finally, it sets the limits beyond which the essay form cannot exist.

Armed with these considerations, we are therefore provided with a working definition that is both sufficiently precise yet broad enough to offer a panoply suitable to the extraordinary diversity of the genre. For example, forms traditionally attributed to it—the character sketch, the dialogue, and the aphoristic piece—though initially seeming to differ markedly one from the other—can, upon analysis, be regarded as sharing to varying degrees the essential characteristics of the genre, hence as different yet authentic manifestations of the essay form. And by using these valuable guidelines in our study, we can eschew rigid methods of categorization and pursue instead an analytic approach that respects the spirit, diversity, and the limits of this extremely rich genre.

Though the critical study of the essay form pursued up to this point has dealt primarily with the genre in the context of English literature, it can be immediately applied to French authors and prose works as well. In fact, anyone reasonably familiar with French literature should find no shortage of authors whose works fall within the guidelines of our working definition of the essay. Among the most obvious are writers universally acknowledged to be great essayists and consistently included in any universal survey of the genre: Montaigne, Voltaire, Diderot, Rousseau, Chateaubriand, Sainte-Beuve, Renan, Rémy de Gourmont, Alain, Gide, Henri Massis, Claudel, Julien Benda, Valéry, Bernanos, Camus, Sartre, and de Beauvoir, to mention perhaps the most important. Then there is the brilliant tradition of French critics who have created a distinctive art form in essays devoted to literature and criticism: Baudelaire, Mallarmé, Paul Bourget, Jules Lemaître, Gustave Lanson, Charles Du Bos, Jacques Maritain, Albert Saurès, Anatole France, Jean Paulhan; and more recently, Jean Starobinski, Roland Barthes, Georges Poulet, Nathalie Sarraute, and Alain Robbe-Grillet, to mention only a few.

Less certain and initially perplexing is the task of identifying forms of the French essay in the earlier period of French literature, spanning the seventeenth and even the eighteenth centuries. Indeed, it is the problems encountered in any investigation of this same period that have doubtless caused critics (both in France and elsewhere) to wonder if an authentic tradition for the essay can in fact be said to exist at all in French literature before the nineteenth century.

As far as I can determine, Professor Chadbourne is the first scholar to have made an initial probe regarding the presence of the essay in this earlier period, and his findings, though tentative, are extremely significant because they admirably put in context the problems besetting any general study of the French essay. He describes the manifestations of the essay in this time period as comprising a few works with the generic title, for example, "Pierre Nicole's popular *Essais de morale,* and in the eighteenth century, a number of gazettes imitative of Addison and Steele, and a profusion of unclassifiable opuscules, distant cousins of the Essay." He further mentions what he terms "the greater works": Saint Évremond's letters and dissertations, La Bruyère's *Caractères,* the letters of Mme de Sévigné, Voltaire's *Lettres philosophiques,* and others that "resemble the essay occasionally in spirit but seldom in form."[13]

Unquestionably, Professor Chadbourne has very well appraised the situation and has also posed what must be regarded as the major problem of interpretation for any investigation of the French essay. To put the question simply, are the major works that he cites and the more obscure opuscules to which he refers only "distant cousins" of the essay, and must it be said that their resemblance to this genre is marginal at best? Given the guidelines established above, I am inclined to take a larger view of what constitutes the essay form, and I do not feel that these prose forms should be peremptorily discarded merely because they initially appear to bear little resemblance to the "classical" form of the essay. And though I grant that Professor Chadbourne's contention has merit if, for this period, one limits the scope of the investigation to manifestations of the familiar or "informal" essay, I believe that this is ultimately too restrictive a method. I also contend that this judgment implicitly reflects the strong preference—even bias—commonly held by critics to regard the familiar essay as the only authentic form of the genre, or at the very least, as the only significant manifestation of the essay in this earlier period, and as such, to be found almost exclusively in English literature.

Certainly, if one adheres to a more restricted definition of the essay, then many earlier nonfictional prose works of French authors should automatically be discounted in this study simply because they fail to conform substantially to Montaigne's technique and intention. The moralist works already mentioned could well fall outside the definition as well as the letters and *Les Entretiens* of Guez de Balzac, and many of the incidental prose works of Saint Évremond. And for that matter, the many *essais* written by such important Enlightenment figures as Montesquieu, D'Alembert, D'Holbach, Rousseau, and perhaps even Voltaire might find difficult entry. And how should one regard Marivaux's numerous articles in the *Spectateur français, Indigent philosophe,* or

Cabinet du philosophe, Diderot's treatises and dialogues, and Rousseau's *Discours* and moral studies (*Emile* or *Lettre sur les spectacles*)? Though none of these works could claim to be imitative of Montaigne's model, or to be completely preoccupied with his process of inner questioning and self-revelation, might it not be said that they may very well nonetheless embody the essential characteristics of the essay (the disclosure of the author's temperament, his intimate patterns of thought, and his innermost thoughts and convictions)?

In any case, it would seem most unwise to exclude, at the outset, any or all of the authors or works mentioned above in a study of the French essay. For if they are taken in chronological order and viewed with respect to their reputation and importance in French literature, they offer strong preliminary indications that, despite hesitation or even reluctance on the part of critics to recognize it, the French may in fact possess a strong and valid tradition of the essay even for the earlier period.

No matter how this problem of interpretation is ultimately resolved, there obviously exists a compelling need to reevaluate these and other nonfictional prose works so as to determine how they relate to the development of the essay in France. In order to focus clearly on this matter and on the broader aspects of the topic, my study (unlike most works on the essay) begins with the premise that the essay is not a particularly English thing; and though the genre undergoes a brilliant evolution in English literature (particularly for the familiar form), the English essay is not necessarily paradigmatic for the genre as a whole, but is rather the product of only one tradition in the evolution of the essay form. Hence, though both the French and English models stem from a common source (Montaigne's *Essais*), the development of the essay in France must not be automatically identified with evolving manifestations of its English counterpart. Nor should it be surprising if one finds that, despite similarities, the two models diverge from a common path and ultimately even develop quite distinct forms of the same genre because of the particular tastes, needs, and temperament of the respective cultures that have nurtured them.

The approach that I take in this study will be to apply the concept of the essay developed in this preface to a number of French authors and works extending in time from Montaigne to the present. Because of the severe limitation of space that such a broad and somewhat unwieldy topic necessarily imposes on a one-volume work, I shall limit my attention only to the most important and representative examples of the essay taken in a century-to-century arrangement of chapters. While the categories of the informal and formal essay are useful as a general means of classification and will serve as parameters within which to pursue this investigation, I shall not attempt to construct any additional kind of taxonomy into which works might neatly fall. I shall instead attempt to examine the essay by using the characteristics described above in order to capture the spirit and psychology of the genre. As to method, I shall investigate the essay synchronically, as it evolves through the centuries, and diachronically, that is, how the essay can be described structurally as an enduring component of intellectual and artistic expression in French literature. Ultimately both considerations should converge to elucidate the particular structure and craft that can be said to exemplify the essay in France.

Theodore P. Fraser

College of the Holy Cross

Acknowledgments

A number of people have aided, directly or indirectly, in the writing of this book and I am happy to have this opportunity to express my deep gratitude: first to my parents, who through the years have given assistance of many kinds and whose generosity I can never adequately repay; then to David O'Connell, who first suggeted that I undertake a study of the French essay and who guided the work through all its lengthy phases; to Wallace Fowlie, Alfred Desautels, S.J., James Lawler, Reino Virtanen, and Charles Mackey, who offered much encouragement and valuable suggestions at critical moments along the way; to Holy Cross College for its generous faculty fellowship and to the Fondation Camargo (and the hospitality of Russell Young and Michael Pretina) for the opportunity to write much of the work at its inspiring site in Cassis, France; to my good friend and colleague Richard Kopp, whose reading of various parts of the text afforded me judicious and probing criticism; finally, to my good friend F. X. Slevin, whose expert reading of and extensive comments on the entire final draft made for considerable stylistic improvement.

Chronology

Chapter One
Montaigne and the Essay

Classical Antecedents

In the preface of the second edition of his *Essayes* (1597), Bacon gave the first written reference to the essay as a distinct prose genre by acknowledging the debt that the form owed to classical authors, and to Seneca in particular. Having just borrowed Montaigne's recently coined title for his own more aphoristic and didactic pieces, Bacon declared: "The word is late, but the thing is ancient: For Seneca's Epistles to Lucilius are essaies, that is dispersed meditacions."[1]

There is no question that he was correct; yet literary antecedents for the essay go back much farther in history than he had imagined. Though the essay is late to emerge in world literature and is manifestly preceded by poetry, drama, and the work of chroniclers, it nevertheless has its roots in the earliest forms of written expression. Such ancient works as the *Tao te Ching (The Way of Power),* composed sometime between the eighth and ninth centuries B.C. to teach Confucian tranquility of the mind, the Books of Proverbs and Ecclesiastes of the Bible, and the aphoristic pieces of Hipporates and Publilius Syrus (second and first centuries B.C.) were essentially composed of lapidary expressions to record the collective funds stored by earliest peoples and contain the wisdom and experience amassed by diverse civilizations.

Montaigne (in his earliest essays), Bacon, and a number of subsequent essayists did indeed construct their essays on a tissue or series of these "compendious sayins" and used them as points of departure on which to exercise their judgment or to clarify their particular views. Such aphorisms as "Do nothing and everything is done" (*Tao te Ching*), "A bad conscience often shelters us from danger but never from fear" (Publilius Syrus), or "Time and tide for no man bide" and "Be not penny wise and pound foolish" (both actually commented upon by Bacon himself in the appendix to his *Elements of Rhetoric*) were often the very stuff of which essays were made.[2] Hence, the basic building blocks of the essay were present in the earlier stages of man's literary endeavor. Furthermore, these essential components, which would one day be

fused into the essay, were from the start of a moral, didactic, and pre-
scriptive nature and were intended to pass on to posterity kernels of
wisdom gleaned through human experience.

Yet it is specifically by the literature of Greco-Roman antiquity that
the modern essay has been most strongly influenced in form and content. In his extremely valuable work on Montaigne, Professor Hugo
Friedrich has provided by far the best study presently available on the
question of the modern essay's roots in classical antiquity.[3] For Friedrich, the form of the modern essay was contained in germ and passed
on to Montaigne by means of two literary genres much cherished by
the ancients: the letter and the dialogue.[4] Both exemplified the "open
form" or *ordo neglectus,* and as such they were sufficiently supple to serve
as admirable vehicles for transmitting the various strains of moralist
literature that flourished in the late Hellenic and Roman periods. The
letter was most remarkably developed in such models as Cicero's *Letters
to Atticus* or Seneca's *Letters to Lucilius.* By its nature, this form simu-
lated a richly nuanced kind of chat in which the most personal expressions of speech could be used. It could also be filled with details that
presumably might be disclosed only to one's most intimate associates.
The dialogue offered even more artistic possibilities for the exposition
of ideas than the letter, which, after all, is only half a dialogue. Because
it was usually longer and would necessarily engage several different
personae in its development, the dialogue could bring multiple points
of view to bear on the topic and could presumably be more exhaustive
of the matter. Among the most important classical models of this genre
are Plato's *Dialogues,* the matrix of all philosophical and moral discourses. His system of maieutics, the famous Socratic method of posing
questions in order to advance in the knowledge of what one does not
know, lies at the very heart of the essay technique. Also important as
antecedents were the urbane and superbly composed dialogues of Cicero (*Of Friendship, Of Old Age,* and the longer *Tusculan Disputations*).
Of immense importance, finally, is the "diatribe" or narrative discourse, a mixed form of the dialogue that Plutarch brought to perfection in his *Moralia.* These literary discourses, which he composed on a
myriad of political, religious, moral, and scientific matters, would exert a profound influence on Montaigne, and it might even be said that
Plutarch, more than any other author, would inspire the form and
spirit that the *Essais* would assume.

It can therefore be held that because of a growing predilection for
the "open ended" format provided by these genres, a preliminary form

of the essay gradually came to be established about the close of the Augustan Age. Opposed to the constraints of philosophical systems, this literary form favored the free expression of moral probings to forward the ideal of the individual as the proper end of moral investigation. For Friedrich, the Stoic and Epicurean traditions of moral philosophy, despite differences in emphasis, had both gradually evolved the ideal of the sage, the man who wished to integrate his own quest for happiness with forms of universal truth, and who had therefore to assume his own identity and assert his own desires for happiness without recourse to any political or religious system.[5] Corresponding to this evolution of a personal ethic, the authors mentioned above and others (Horace, Lucretius, Marcus Aurelius, Titus Livy, Lucian, and Juvenal) initiated or perfected literary models that would become the stock components of the essay—the aphorism, apothegm, reflection, portraiture, philosophical dialogue, verse essay, satirical sketch, and historical biography. And what essentially bound together such a disparate grouping of literary forms was the moral emphasis either implied or fully expressed in the subject matter. The great moralist literature of the Augustan and post-Augustan periods therefore increasingly probed character, motive, human foibles, and virtue to the end of providing guidelines or precepts in the art of living. Hence they provided the essential literary forms and moral topics from which the essay would be created.

After this brief preliminary discussion of classical antecedents, we should now turn our attention to the important matter of Montaigne's knowledge and use of these authors and prose models in the creation of the essay.

Montaigne's Development of the Essay Genre

Michel de Montaigne was well acquainted through background and cultural formation with many of these classical authors and with the tradition that they represented. Born in 1533, he reached maturity during the first wave of French humanism, which was exemplified by such brilliant figures as Guillaume Budé, François Rabelais, Etienne Dolet, and Joachim du Bellay. His father, Pierre Eyquem de Montaigne, a rich Bordeaux merchant and himself an enthusiastic student of the Renaissance, provided the young boy with what on all counts was a truly remarkable education. During his earliest years, he was instructed by a tutor who taught him Latin as a living tongue before he even spoke his native tongue. When six years of age, Montaigne was sent to the Collège de Guyenne of Bordeaux, one of the most celebrated preparatory schools of the time in France and one where the new learning of the Renaissance was held in honor.

Despite the school's excellent reputation as a place of learning, Montaigne suffered a great deal while there. Later he would criticize the rigid, narrow attitudes of some of his teachers, as well as the harsh discipline and primitive hygienic conditions that prevailed. His father intervened and arranged for his son to receive a private education from tutors outside of the school. One of these, whom Montaigne remembered as "a man of greatest understanding," allowed the youth to cultivate his natural literary tastes, and he immersed himself in the works of Ovid, Horace, Cicero, Terence, and Plautus. When thirteen, he had completed his secondary education and began the study of law, probably at the University of Toulouse.

In his approach to the literature of the classical period, Montaigne differed markedly from earlier humanists. For one thing, he did not have a sufficient command of Greek to read with ease in this language, and his contact with the great authors of the Hellenist tradition was gained through translations in Latin and the vernacular, or through excerpts culled from Latin compilations.[6]

He never seemed to deplore to any great extent this lacuna in his background—an attitude unimaginable to a Rabelais or a Budé, who had regarded a thorough working knowledge of Greek as a sine qua non for all serious humanistic studies. For Montaigne, however, an emphasis on the mechanical learning of linguistic forms for their own sake was more the function of the philologist or specialist, which he assuredly was not and which he had not the slightest intention of becoming.

Montaigne also differed from his humanist predecessors in that he was not usually a systematic reader of the "complete works" of any given author, even if these were available to him. Instead he more often than not resorted to the compilations provided by Aulus Gellius, Valerius Maximus, or Ambrosius Macrobius, and other anthologists dating from the late Roman Empire, wherein he could find important extracts from Greek and Latin authors (Herodotus, Plato, Sextus Empiricus, Titus Livy, et al.) whom he either could not read in Greek, or whose works might not otherwise be accessible or were of only marginal interest to him. As a result, he developed a broad, eclectic method of reading and, consequently, did not read all that he could have among extant sources, but rather let himself be led by personal tastes and interests.

Yet it was not merely out of negligence or "nonchalance"—a term he himself used to describe his approach to study—that Montaigne pursued such a selective method of reading the ancients. We should remember that he belonged to that generation of humanists once removed (numbering Calvin, Agrippa d'Aubigné, Théodore de Bèze, the older Ronsard, and Henri Estienne) who no longer possessed the voracious appetite of a Petrarch, an Erasmus, or a Rabelais for all that could be culled from classical authors. Nor did Montaigne and his peers share the somewhat uncritical and unqualified veneration of the latter for classical authors simply as such. Chastened by the political and religious turmoil about them and disabused of the hope that the dissemination of the *bonae litterae* would usher in a new Golden or Saturnian Age, these latter-day humanists studied the ancients for more particular reasons and frequently related their findings to polemical and doctrinary ends. Though Montaigne resisted such a tendency and, in comparison with the fiercely partisan views of the Catholic Ronsard and the Protestants Calvin, de Bèze, or d'Aubigné, remained adamantly undogmatic—or uncommitted, as we should say today—he nevertheless insisted that the ancients be read critically and for a specific reason.

This relatively new attitude is succinctly demonstrated if we contrast Montaigne's ideas on how to educate the young with the earlier method presented in fictional form by Rabelais.[7] In his celebrated chapters on the education of the young prince Gargantua by the good Renaissance and evangelical tutor Ponocrate, Rabelais proposed an exacting program of study and physical exercise to form a vigorous mind and body. To foster this end he prescribed a regimen that wasted no minute of the day. When reading and memorizing a formidable list of readings from the Bible and the ancients, or when waiting to play sports or copiously sweating just afterwards, the young Gargantua was obliged to repeat and discuss what he had learned that day; and every attempt was made by the tutor to make this bookish content relevant to what the lad saw or experienced about him. In this way Rabelais hoped to develop a good courtier, a man for all seasons, and a jack of all trades, whose education had been based on a pedagogical system of rote learning and memorization not radically unlike that administered by the Medieval schoolmen.

In his essay, "On the Education of Children" (1:26), Montaigne is first concerned (as was Rabelais) with the proper choice of a tutor for his student. "I would," he declared, "also urge that care be given to choose a guide with a well-made, rather than a well-filled head."[8] He further regarded as harmful the imposing of an unassimilable number of classical texts on a young mind. Instead, he insisted that the entire process of education be bent to the aim of developing sound judgment and a refined sense of moral discrimination. Hence, only those texts that abetted such training should be used. His student should be encouraged, moreover, to submit what he read to his own critical evaluation. He should be led to accept or reject it, to apply or not apply it to his life, not because it bore the cachet of a Cicero or a Plato, but because he found it to be true. As the result of such a program, Montaigne envisaged the formation of a human being who, like his tutor, would have a "well-made head," one who could make moral decisions based on his own lights and translate them into action, and who would live usefully for himself and for others.

Though both authors shared a common concern for the formation of the whole man and of the obligation of any educational system to pursue that end vigorously and humanely, each gives an essentially different stress to priorities. Rabelais emphasizes learning as much as possible; Montaigne, on the other hand, is primarily concerned with forming critical judgment. Rabelais's product would no doubt be a useful, well-rounded gentleman; though less learned, Montaigne's charge would tend more to rely on his own judgment in conducting his affairs and in making his decisions.

In his work on Rabelais, the noted Montaigne scholar Donald M. Frame regards their difference on views on education to be largely the result of the different phases of humanism that each represents. He says: "Each one is representative of his moment: Rabelais of the excited wonder at the new Golden Age; Montaigne, of the late disillusionment at the sight of learned fools. Had their times been reversed, many of their emphases might have been as well."[9]

In this comparison are revealed Montaigne's most essential attitudes toward the proper use of classical literature and the end that it should serve in developing a genuinely human person. And we can also deduce from this philosophy his own personal approach as a humanist to the wisdom of antiquity. In general, he refused merely to transmit or imitate the teachings of the ancients but first subjected them to his own critical examination. Only then would he apply them or not to his own life. Such a process required a continuing program of meditation and reflection to which he was naturally disposed both by temperament and education. The *essai* technique was thus already present in germ in Montaigne's initial approach to the study and use of classical sources.

We should now turn our attention to Montaigne's initial period of apprenticeship as an essayist and to his earliest method of writing. Montaigne's literary career essentially began when he retired from active life in 1571, at the age of thirty-eight. Prior to that time, he had pursued a career in law, serving some thirteen years as counselor in the *Chambre des enquêtes* of the parliament of Bordeaux. Dissatisfaction with his own political career and revulsion at the strife and violence of religious wars that were tearing France apart had convinced him that his "waning" years should best be spent at his country estate of Montaigne—some sixty kilometers distant from Bordeaux. There he proposed to live "in quiet and reading."

In his now famous "tower" adjacent to a well-stocked library, Montaigne first devoted himself to study and reflection. He would leaf through favorite texts and jot comments down in the margins to serve as *aide-mémoires* in propping up what he claimed was his faulty memory. It was not long before a natural need not only to preserve his musings but also to clarify his reflections led him to set his thoughts to paper.

At first Montaigne's exercises in composition differed little from the practice used by humanists writing shortly before and even in hs own day. By the beginning of the sixteenth century, there had come into existence in nearly all of the countries touched by the Renaissance various types of works composed primarily to collect and disseminate the raw ideas of antiquity cast in classical forms of expressions: in "sentences," moral sayings, or apothegms. Of these, Erasmus's *Adagia and Apopthygms* (1500) were the most celebrated examples. A special kind of writing, in France known as *la leçon morale,* began to supplement the mere cataloging of sayings by grouping together in short dissertations on ethical topics celebrated apothegms, examples, and sentences drawn from the ancients. Pierre Villey cites as examples Caelius Rhodiginus's thirty volumes of compilations, the *Lectiones antiquae;* and in the vernacular, the Spaniard Guevara's *Golden Epistles,* and in France, Pierre Boyaustuau's *Theater of the World.*[10]

These authors whether writing in the vernacular or in Latin, had a practical goal: they wanted to collect and make accessible to their contemporaries the attitudes, observations, and discoveries of the ancients in all matters pertaining to the conduct of life. Though they seldom went beyond an impersonal and straightforward presentation of matter drawn from the "examples" and aphoristic sayings found in such compilations as Aulus Gellius's *Attic Nights* (second century A.D.), or Macrobius's *Saturnalia* (4th century A.D.), they nevertheless treated universal topics: man's paradoxical wretchedness and grandeur; moral virtues and dominant vices; attitudes on death and education; strange customs, singular happenings, fabulous tales from the animal world, etc.

When he began to write, Montaigne seems to have had no other aim than the compiling of similar *leçons morales* for his own edification, and he most certainly did not intend to write a book or to provide his self-portrait. Indeed, the first pieces written between 1572 and 1574 indicate as much, since they mainly consist of brief collections of anecdotes and "sentences" devoted to such common (and conventional) topics as "Parley Time Is Dangerous" (1:6); "The Intention Is Judge of Our Actions" (1:7); or "One Is Punished for Defending a Place Obstinately Without Reason" (1:15).

Other topics, such as "Our Feelings Reach Out Beyond Us" (1:3); "Of Constancy" (1:12); or "That the Taste of Good and Evil Depends on the Opinion We Have of Them" (1:14), provide a more elaborate format and even a few personal asides. Yet his method differed little from that of those writing just before him, especially as regards his reticence to reveal intimate attitudes or his own personal experiences in his writings.

In one early essay he indicates, however, that this method of compilation and limited commentary was not felicitous to his peace of mind but was sometimes, in fact, most unsettling. Writing on the topic "Of Idleness" (1:9) and the use he had made of it in this early period of retirement, he declares:

Lately when I retired to my home, determined to bother about nothing except spending the little life I have left in rest and seclusion, it seemed to me I could do my mind no greater favor than to let it entertain itself in full idleness and stay and settle in itself. . . . But I find . . . that, on the contrary, like a runaway horse, it gives itself a hundred times more trouble than it took for others, and gives birth to so many chimeras and fantastic monsters, that in order to contemplate their ineptitude and strangeness at my pleasure, I have begun to put them in writing. (21)

Clearly his artistic spirit was straining to be delivered from this somewhat sterile practice; and as an author, he was coming to grips with the question, "Why does one write?"

The reasons for Montaigne's turning away from this mode of composition soon after 1571 can be partially explained at least by what has already been said about his temperament and particular interests. He had already developed a relatively independent mind as regards the authors he was reading and he approached their works not with a worshipful attitude, but for the purpose of stimulating his own thought process. They were grist for his mill, and he found it only natural to compare his views on specific matters with those they presented. From the very start he had also possessed the frame of reference of a moralist, which his humanistic education had all the more refined. Intensely interested in everything relating to human conduct and motive, he had consistently used his reading to exercise and sharpen his own observations on human nature. It is therefore hardly surprising that his probings would gradually induce him to amplify his comments beyond the strictures of the *leçon morale*. After a time, this *leçon* would only serve as a point of departure for his own intimate reflections and commentary.

There were additional personal considerations that prompted him to turn inward to record his private thoughts. Not at home in his time and a stranger to the partisan strife that he witnessed all about him, he resorted to his writings as a means of consolation, a refuge that he constructed against the forces that threatened his peace of mind. Such a man would naturally turn to the consolation afforded by communing with the great minds of the past who, experiencing similar disillusionments, had embraced a like detachment and had used their writings to record their own private musings.

Finally, of more serious and immediate import was Montaigne's seemingly inconsolable grief at the recent loss of the two human beings whom he loved the best and who had most influenced his life: Etienne de La Boétie, the friend of his life, a young magistrate and promising writer like himself, died in 1563; and five years later, he lost "the best father that ever was," who had been sensitive to his every need. Isolated in a marriage that provided little consolation, tormented by persistent fears of death, and clinging to the Stoical views and example he had learned at the side of La Boétie, whose valiant last moments he would never forget, Montaigne turned to the consolation offered by the Roman author Seneca and entered the first major phase of his literary formation. At this point we should examine the major classical influences that would profoundly affect the development of Montaigne's still undefined project of the essay.

Any assessment of the primary influences exerted on Montaigne from Greek and Roman literature in his development of the essay form must forever be indebted to Pierre Villey's monumental work, *Les Sources et l'évolution des "Essais" de Montaigne,* which appeared in 1908.[11] Through his exhaustive and painstaking work on classical sources, Villey was able to identify Seneca, Plutarch, and Sextus Empiricus as the trio of ancient philosophers who most influenced the development of Montaigne's thought and the evolution of his essay project. Not systematic philosophers but moralists, they offered mental attitudes and views on the human condition that were congenial with his own temperament, range of interests, and habits of thought; and through prolonged reading and meditation on their works, he underwent a veritable intellectual and artistic transformation that enabled him to bring the familiar essay form into being. In fact, so important was their respective influence at crucial stages of the writing of the *essais* that Villey regarded them as major catalysts leading Montaigne through the major phases of the development of the genre: Seneca for the "Stoical" period (1571–72); Plutarch as a reaction to Stoical rigidity (1572–74); and Sextus Empiricus as the impetus for Montaigne's "skeptical" crisis (1576). And the enduring influence of all three provided an essentially symbiotic cultural formation that prepared Montaigne for the final phase of his literary creation: the "Epicurean" essays of book 3, the work of the mature artist that best exemplifies his thought and craft.[12]

Villey characterized the evolution as an essentially organic one, which is to say that Montaigne's final achievement—"the definitive philosophy of the essays, the art of thinking and the search for truth"—depends upon a substratum of attitudes and a cast of mind that he had possessed in germ from the very beginning.[13] Professor Donald M. Frame has provided excellent additional insights by stressing the psychological aspects of this process. According to him, Montaigne, "the apprehensive humanist," gradually succeeded in divesting himself of his early obsessive fears of meeting pain and death, for which he had first adopted as antidote Stoical indifference and the force of the will.[14] From the death-oriented attitudes of the early essays written between 1572 and 1574, Frame notes Montaigne's gradually downplaying the "heroics" of the sages before the vicissitudes of fortune (our common lot, after all) and his finally accepting the human condition by freely utilizing the natural means at our disposal to find pleasure and happiness in this life.

Since Montaigne's essay form is concretely linked to his project of self-study and is, in fact, the instrument by which he recorded his adventure of self-discovery, some attention must be given to the complex problem of intellectual development. Yet in a study primarily concerned with the essay as a literary genre, the matter of Montaigne's cultural evolution and ultimate assumption of a particular philosophy of life, though never absent, must be viewed as secondary and considered only in so far as it pertains to the creation of the essay itself. My intention is therefore not to retrace the path so well trodden by Montaigne experts—Villey, Frame, and Friedrich, and others—on the general matter of his intellectual and literary borrowings, but rather to concentrate on the organic growth of the essay form viewed in the corpus of the *essai* themselves. I can therefore give only passing mention at this stage of my study to a few of the many classical authors other than Seneca, Plutarch, and Sextus Empiricus who never ceased to provide major intellectual stimulation for Montaigne: Horace, the author most cited in the *essais* and a role model through his cultivation of the minor yet sure pleasures of life; Lucretius, whose frank naturalism and strong espousal of the pleasure principle Montaigne so well appreciated; and Plato, of immense value as the source of the priceless "life" of Socrates, whom Montaigne regarded as a high point in the evolution of the human soul.

More essential to this study is a brief review of Montaigne's apprenticeship under the tutelage of Seneca, Plutarch, and Sextus Empiricus, since through their example and influence he gradually perfected the familiar essay form in the pieces that he wrote from 1572–80 for the first two books. After this, a study will be made of Montaigne's full and conscious assumption of his craft as essayist, most clearly manifested in the works of book 3.

The work of Seneca that most captivated Montaigne was the *Letters to Lucilius,* often referred to not as a collection of letters but rather as essays.[15] They were written during the last two years of Seneca's life (63–65 A.D.) for a young Roman knight from Pompeii ostensibly to wean the youth from the "Epicurean" influences to which he was presumably attracted. Composed in an epistolary form, the letters (numbering 124 pieces) are filled with many personal, self-revelatory details drawn from their author's life and used as a springboard from which to address abstract matters on such "Stoical" topics as the stoutheartedness of the sage in the face of adversity, how to live with the discomfort and decline brought on by age, how to deal with pain, or on the nature of the supreme good.

Seneca couched these considerations in a style new to classical literature. He broke away from the stiffness of Cicero's oratorical rhetoric and dealt with his person in a psychological depth unknown till then. He feigned an unlabored style and invested his prose with short sentences, lively images, scenes of life around him, and many moral aphorisms on which to reflect.

Montaigne was deeply involved with Seneca in the essays he wrote up to 1572. The drama of Stoicism so attractively presented in the *Letters* obviously fascinated him by its lofty themes of self-possession and the ideal of the unperturbed wise man ever captain of his soul. Moreover, his natural fear of death, accentuated by the recent loss of his father and best friend, was allayed by Stoical professions of indifference to this and all forms of suffering and pain. He was also captivated by the genial and discursive tone of Seneca's letters, by their familiar yet polished literary style and the many aphorisms by which they captured the essence of Stoical attitudes and introduced so many other ideas.

Most of the dominant themes of the early essays were largely inspired by Seneca: the preoccupation with, and constant preparation for, death; the need to retire from the distractions of public life; the consolation of solitude; and necessity to distance oneself from "the common herd." Entire passages from the essay "To Philosophize Is to Learn to Die" (1:20), and "Of Solitude" (1:34) seem almost to have been taken whole, only slightly recast, and then inserted in the text. In "To Philosophize," for example, we read: "The advantage of living is not measured by length but by use; some men have lived long, and lived little; attend to it while you are in it. It lies in your will, not in the number of years, for you have lived long enough" (67). And in Seneca's epistle "On the Shortness of Life": "Show me that the good in life does not depend upon life's length but upon the use we make of it; also . . . that it is possible or rather usual, for a man who has lived long to have lived little."[16]

The well known exhortation from "Of Solitude" urging early retirement indicates an even stronger resemblance to Seneca's own counsel on the matter in his epistle "On Worldliness and Retirement." Montaigne declares:

We have lived enough for others, let us live at least this remaining bit of life for ourselves. Let us bring back our thoughts and plans to ourselves and our well-being. It is no small matter to arrange our retirement securely. . . . Since

God gives us leisure to make arrangements for moving out, let us make them; let us pack our bags; let us take an early leave of company. (178)

And we read in Seneca:

If possible withdraw yourself from all business of which you speak; and if you cannot do this, tear yourself away. We have dissipated enough of our time already; let us in old age begin to pack up our baggage. Surely there is nothing in this life that men can begrudge us. [17]

Noteworthy in this comparison of passages is not only Montaigne's close reliance on the wording of Seneca's text but also the striking similarity to be found in rhetorical forms—the exhortatory style, the magisterial "we" employed by both writers, and a somewhat haughty and elitist tone the writers use to distinguish themselves from the common herd. There is also present on the part of both a reserve in talking intimately about the self.

It is Villey's contention that, for precisely the reasons stated above, Montaigne soon became disaffected with the theatrical, somewhat arrogant and reserved tone of the *Letters*. [18] There is sufficient internal evidence in these early essays to indicate, moreover, that even in the process of utilizing Senecan themes, Montaigne was already adapting them to his own personal attitudes. In the two essays referred to, for example, he draws distinctly different conclusions from his own meditations on death and solitude. In the first, he turns from Seneca's emphasis on the moral resistence with which we should oppose death and, in a lengthy exhortation, counsels a tranquil acceptance for this final end that nature prepares all human beings to accept without rigid posturing. And to the Senecan concept of retirement as a means of gaining self-possession and of resisting the moral contamination of an unpure world, he opposes the ideal of an aesthetic and moral cultivation of the self gained through the pleasures of study and contemplation in a manner devoid of any rigid constraint.

We may conclude that if indeed Montaigne can be said to have undergone an authentic Stoical period (Friedrich denies it), it was characterized not by interior conviction but rather by fascination for this philosopher's themes and his discursive manner of writing. Even so, this early contact with Stoical ideas and doctrines is of extreme importance because, through it, Montaigne was challenged and motivated to sharpen his own moral attitudes and to strike out in his own direction as a writer. The *Letters* also provided a literary model that inspired him to refine his own prose style along personal lines and to expand the narrow scope of his writings beyond the limiting format of the *leçon morale*.

The watershed in Montaigne's artistic and intellectual development certainly occurred after 1572, when he was able to read Jacques Amyot's newly printed French translation of Plutarch's *Moralia*.[19] Indeed the appearance of this monumental translation of Plutarch's principal moral work was of immediate importance not only to Montaigne, but to the entire community of French scholars as well since it quickly became the principal source book from which the sixteenth (and seventeenth) century would draw its understanding of the history, culture, and moral doctrine of the ancients.[20]

Montaigne was already familiar with the rich store of biographical matter offered by Plutarch in the *Parallel Lives*. He deeply appreciated this work and had already included many salient anecdotes and moral examples drawn from it in his earlier *essais*. Yet the *Moralia*'s impact on him was to be far more decisive.

Composed probably toward the end of the first century when Plutarch was engaged in a diplomatic mission at Rome, the *Moralia* numbers eighty different titles. The first twenty articles were dedicated to specifically ethical topics; and though other titles of a more diverse nature were later added, the title, "Moral Works," was never altered.[21] These eighty extant pieces treat a multitude of daily incidents involving Plutarch's own life, family, personal memories, private concerns, or comments on persons he knew. To these Plutarch constantly applied his own insights and observations, couching them in the style of well-written lectures addressed to a circle of close friends and associates. The tone is warm and genial, and the form is not that of a systematic thesis but rather a flow of anecdotes, sayings, reflections, and images employed to render as clear as possible the ideas presented. The whole is woven together in an appealing tapestry of details that allowed the writer to use many levels of style and to reveal many facets of his personality and art. The wide-ranging topics contained in the work can be indicated by a partial listing of a few of the titles: "The Education of Children," "How to Tell a Flatterer from a Friend," "How to Study Poets," "How to Profit from One's Enemies," "Advice on Keeping Well," "Advice to Bride and Groom," and "Table Talk."

A few years later Montaigne would express in the *Essais* the preference he now had for Plutarch, over all other authors. In "Of Anger" (2:31, p. 539), written between 1578–80, he declared that "Plutarch is admirable throughout, but especially where he judges human actions," and in comparing the Roman Stoic to the Greek moralist, Montaigne held that "The first [Seneca] is full of witty points and sallies; Plutarch of things. The former heats you and moves you more, the latter contents you more and pays you better" ("Of Books," 2:10, p. 301). That this opinion endured, indeed that it became more marked, is attested to in the glowing tribute that he paid him in one of the later essays ("On Some Verses of Virgil," 3:5). Stating that now in old age he prefers to do without the aid of books when he writes, he comments:

> But it is harder for me to do without Plutarch. He is so universal and so full that on all occasions, and however eccentric the subject you have taken up, he makes his way into your work and offers you a liberal hand. . . . I cannot be with him even a little without taking out a drumstick or a wing. (666)

Montaigne did not simply admire Plutarch's acumen as a "judge of human actions," but he also introduced into the *Essais* views on moral conduct, human nature, and social and political problems that strongly resembled the latter's. One would be hard pressed to determine, in fact, if this similarity reposed upon views commonly shared initially or was a case of Montaigne's adopting, after reflection, some of the ideas of the Greek philosopher for his own. A comparison of the article "On the Education of Children" in the *Moralia* with the essay of the same title (1:26), for example, reveals striking parallels of thought.[22] Both writers place a heavy emphasis on the social background of parents as a most decisive factor in the child's development; both assert that philosophy, which they each describe as a discipline fostering sound judgment and character, is the linchpin of any educational system; and they are both adamant in their belief that any sound program of education should give adequate but not excessive attention to physical development through proper diet and exercise.

It is also important to note that in this essay (written in 1578), Montaigne provided one of his first personal criticisms of an existing social institution, and what is more significant, important autobiographical details drawn from his own educational experience as well: his early total immersion in the Latin language, his father's concern that he be wakened from sleep gently, with pleasant sounding instruments, to enhance his mental tranquility and the spectacle of the classroom as he remembered it—a place where cruel teachers often imposed a reign of terror on their tender victims. It would seem that Plutarch's practice of filling his writings with personal details drawn from his life and independent opinions formed through his own experience was already exerting a strong influence on Montaigne to do likewise.

What seems clear, then, is that Montaigne regarded Plutarch as a kindred spirit, and one whose philosophy on many aspects of life he found to be most compatible with his own evolving attitudes—a fact that is hardly surprising should one give even a cursory summation of Plutarch's essential views. His philosophical persuasion was that of a nondogmatic Platonist. As such, he consistently ridiculed the arrogance of the Stoics in disdaining or regarding only as neutral such good things as health, riches, and honors. He taught instead that such conditions should neither be overly praised nor rashly disdained. To a rigid and ascetic management of one's life he opposed a more human ideal, one that would accommodate man's natural inclinations to virtue without breaking his spirit. He espoused a tolerant attitude toward human foibles and viewed man as a perplexing mixture of good and evil tendencies.

Through his sustained encounter with Plutarch, Montaigne found an eloquent spokesman for his own disenchantment with Seneca and the Stoical doctrines that had previously intrigued him; he also found that Plutarch's essential view on man and human condition both corresponded with, and shored up, his own. In short, the eighty prose pieces of the *Moralia* can be regarded as a kind of textbook that encouraged Montaigne to liberate himself substantially from unquestioning adherence to any dogmatic moral system, to rely on his own personal observations and others in forming his attitudes and opinions, and to view with greater tolerance and sympathy the common run of humanity. In a word, Plutarch gave Montaigne the courage to assert his own individualism as a writer and a man.

In 1576, four years after he recorded his delight at receiving the Amyot translation, Montaigne had a medal struck in honor of another Greek philosopher who was to play a major role in his intellectual evolution and in the development of the essay, the skeptic Sextus Empiricus. Emblazoned on this medallion was a balance whose two scales rested in equal repose, and underneath them was engraved the motto *Que scay-je* (What do I know?). Villey recalls that about this same period Montaigne had the walls of his library adorned with a number of Greek "sentences" also drawn from Sextus's writings, which read, "I can decide nothing"; "I do not understand"; and "I remain in doubt."[23]

These were not the only inscriptions to grace the library walls (others from Scripture relating the theme *vanitas vanitatum,* stressing the brevity of life, were also prominently displayed); taken together, these maxims provide a good indication of the extreme state of mental perplexity that Montaigne was then undergoing.

That Sextus Empiricus played a commanding role during Montaigne's period of skeptical crisis is hardly surprising. A Greek physician of the second century B.C., he was the major source available to Renaissance humanists for the history and dogma of the skeptical school of philosophy. As such, he transmitted in his writings the essential doctrines of the movement as well as the basic teachings of its founder, Pyrrho of Elis (c. 360–270 B.C.).[24] Like Pyrrho, he adopted the attitude of an "inquirer" or investigator in evaluating any assumption that truth existed or that any knowledge of it was possible. He attacked the Stoic doctrine that sense perception was a sure avenue to knowledge, and he held that true intellectual freedom was to be found only in the cultivation of a neutral, noncommitted attitude toward the problems of thinking and living. He taught as the ultimate ideal the mental state of apathy, or *ataraxy,* which provided a kind of refuge within the self against the natural perturbations of body and mind.

In the polemical climate of the late Renaissance, the skeptical consolation afforded by such doctrines as the suspension of judgment and the refuge of "apathy" had great general appeal to French humanists, and to Montaigne in particular. He had lived with open eyes in a period during which religious, political, and moral tenets hitherto held to be inviolable were openly contested; and such earth-shaking experiences as the discovery of the New World and the Copernican revolution had further created a climate of uncertainty and relativism as regards the order and nature of the universe itself. Montaigne's study of Sextus simply led him to a recognition of the dubious premises upon which reposed so many so called human "truths"; and more importantly, it offered him a systematic means to suspend his judgment and effect his own tabula rasa of what could not be legitimately known by the human intellect.

That Montaigne had strong skeptical inclinations before his serious encounter with Sextus can be clearly observed in an earlier essay. In "It Is Folly to Measure the True and the False by Our Own Capacity" (1:27, p. 133), he states: "We must judge with true reverence the infinite power of nature, and with more consciousness of our ignorance and weakness. How many things of slight probability there are, testified to by trustworthy people, which if we cannot be convinced of them, we should at least leave in suspense." And using selected examples he goes on to counsel prudence in denying the truth of things that, though initially appearing incredible to our own lights, become even probable when more fully observed or explained.

Montaigne brilliantly demonstrated his mastery of skeptical methodology in a lengthy essay composed from 1576 to 1580, "Apology for Raymond Sebond" (2:12). This spirited defense of the Catalan theologian's *Natural Theology,* a huge tome that Montaigne had previously translated at his father's request, constitutes perhaps the most blistering attack ever mounted against the presumption that the human mind can, through its unaided light, know anything with certitude. In his very lengthy treatise, Montaigne took unabashed pleasure in ridiculing the mere suggestion that any school of philosophy had ever approximated certitude on such fundamental questions as the existence of God, the makeup of the physical universe, whether man's nature differs esentially from that of the animals, or what constitutes goodness and justice. He viewed human institutions as riddled with inconsistencies, corrupt, and operating on far less than rational principles. Only the mysteries of faith presented by Christian revelation escape exposure to doubt and ridicule in the essay.

Though in the main the work far more resembles the form of a philosophical treatise or disquisition than that of a personal essay, it nevertheless registers a dramatic breakthrough in that direction. In the "Apology" Montaigne no longer shows the slightest reticence in inserting throughout comments and asides that reveal his most personal opinions. He makes this process evident by the use of two literary personae: The magisterial "we" is employed when he presents commonly held observations on the inability of man to reason correctly and the false notions that result from such vain attempts. Alternating with the "we" is the use of the "I"—the private person, Montaigne the writer, who with the "I" introduces views, attitudes, or insights that may support the "we" statements or occasionally dissent from them, depending upon his own perceptions or experiences.

For example, to the general observation that "We see innumerable similar examples, not only false but inept and insistent (in the teachings of the older schools of philosophy. . . ," he adds, "For myself I prefer to believe that they [the philosophers] treated knowledge casually, like a toy to play around with, and amused themselves with reason as with a vain and frivolous instrument . . ." (408). And to reinforce the essay's central and sustained theme of the extreme change-ability of human nature—enunciated by the universal "we"—he adds at one point:

> I would hardly dare tell of the vanity and weakness that I find in myself. My footing is so unsteady and insecure, I find it so vacillating and ready to slip, and my sight is so unreliable, that on an empty stomach I find myself another man than after a meal. If my health smiles upon me, and the brightness of a beautiful day, I am a fine fellow; if I have a corn bothering my toe, I am surly, unpleasant, and unapproachable. (425)

This skeptical crisis so well crystallized in the "Apology" had far reaching and enduring effects on Montaigne's thought and literary project. From his skeptical bath he emerged with a more limited view of what he believed he knew or could know about the great questions relating to life and existence. As a result, he was now strongly imbued with the desire to place himself at the center of his literary cosmos. For if all philosophical certitude had been proved (to his satisfaction at least) to be faulty or inconclusive, the only fruitful topic remaining for study and to which some certitude could be attached was that of the self. Within these boundaries Montaigne was resolved to pursue a project that, amidst the collapse of universal certitude of any kind, alone seemed relevant. And though admittedly limited in its scope, such a laborious endeavor could cast sufficient light on the essential truths of an individual's makeup—his "essential pattern"—to be eminently worthwhile. Indeed, in the final analysis, Montaigne now believed that this was the most appropriate area of investigation not only for himself but for every human being as well.

After passing through the crucible of skeptical inquiry, the essay form had also been transformed into a more supple instrument to ex-plore this comprehensive though unsystematic process of self-study and discovery. As seen above, Montaigne had used it in the "Apology" to record a disparate yet artful accumulation of details gained through concrete observation and reflection to contest the synthetic constructs of all philosophical systems. Just as the skeptical spirit avoided any one classification or arrangement of data, so did the essay reject any one view to explain ultimate truth and reality. We can thus say that Mon-taigne had virtually fashioned the essay form into an excellent vehicle to express the language of skeptical analysis. It only remained for the essay to open itself to a deeper and subtle study of the very movements of the soul to become, as Professor Freidrich has termed it, "the poetic form that skepticism has assumed in literature."[25] But this final evolution could only be achieved after its author had fully and consciously realized his craft in the masterpieces written in the last phase of his literary career.

In summary, the cultural apprenticeship spent under the tutelage of Seneca, Plutarch, and Sextus Empiricus had a decisive effect on Montaigne as a writer. From them he had derived a wealth of subject matter, particular habits of thought, and a critical spirit of investigation to allow him to pursue his special project. In an essay between 1578 and 1580 ("Of Giving the Lie," 1:18), he indicated in the clearest of terms that he had his topic well in hand, and that the untamed horse, as he had previously described his early literary experiments, had finally been harnessed to a worthy end. He declares:

I have painted my inward self with colors clearer than my original one. I have no more made my book than my book has made me—a book consubstantial with its author, concerned with my own self, an integral part of my life, not concerned with some third-hand extraneous purpose like all other books. (499)

After such a succinct declaration by Montaigne on the method and worth of his project, it only remains for us to turn to an examination of the essay form itself. This final and most important consideration can best be structured by addressing the three following questions that go to the very heart of the matter: What did the term *essai* mean to Montaigne; what specific end or ends did he ascribe to its practice; and what essential changes or growth patterns did the essay undergo during the final phase of its development?

The French word *essai* has for its etymological root the Latin noun *exagium,* a term dating from the postclassical period and meaning a weight (*poids*) or an amount weighed at one time (*pesée*). In the sixteenth century *essai* had come to mean an exercise, test, trial, or food sample.[26] When Montaigne adopted this term to characterize his literary diversions is hard and perhaps even impossible to gauge. The first allusion that he makes to the term as a method occurs in the essay "Of Democritus and Heraclitus," written sometime between 1572 and 1580. Here he makes the term virtually synonymous with the intellectual operation of forming judgments: "Judgment is a tool to use on all subjects and comes in everywhere. Therefore in the tests [*essais*] that I made of it here, I use every sort of occasion" (1:50, p. 219). He goes on to state that all topics are indeed appropriate for an *essai* of judgment:

> If it is a subject I do not understand at all, even on that I essay my judgment, sounding the ford from a good distance; and then, finding it too deep for my height, I stick to the back. . . . Sometimes in a vain and nonexistent subject I try to see if it will find the wherewithal to give it body, prop it up, and support it. Sometimes I lead it to a noble and well-born subject in which it has nothing original. . . . (219)

For Montaigne the *essai* as a practice therefore means a test or exercise of the mental faculties in forming a judgment on any given subject. In this particular essay he illustrates how he uses it by letting his mind wander over a number of opinions on the question of how to confront the "vain" and "ridiculous" nature of man. He finally sides with the openly mocking attitude of Democritus, though he admits that it was not as congenial to him as the compassionate stance advocated by Heraclitus.

He further indicates in this very same passage that, given his particular cast of mind, the *essai* exercise only brings him to a tentative conclusion: "For I do not see the whole of anything; nor those who promise to show it to us." Hence the exercise implies a mental state favoring uncertainty and the tacit assumption that other points of view are ever equally tenable. In a later essay, "Of Repentance" (3:2, p. 611), he seems even more emphatic about the inconclusive nature of his judgments when he states: "If my mind could gain a firm footing, I would not make essays, I would make decisions; but it is always in apprenticeship and on trial."

Consistently throughout his writings, then, Montaigne would stress the tentative and experimental nature of the *essai* exercise. Whether or not any given "trial" would lead him to some kind of definitive understanding of the matter under study was relatively unimportant and, indeed, was not even to be expected. Rather, sufficient to itself was the challenge any *essai* offered to his mental powers as a means of sharpening his judgment.

At times Montaigne even seemed to refer to his *essais* in somewhat disparaging terms. On one occasion he likens the "human notions" arrived at in the essay to those "such as children set forth . . . to be instructed, not to instruct" ("Of Prayers," 1:56, p. 234); on another, he equates the practice to "this daydream of meddling with writing," resulting in "the argument and subject" of his work, "the only book in the world of its kind, a book with wild and eccentric plans" ("On the Affection of Fathers for Their Children," 2:8, p. 278). And in his very last essay ("Of Experience" [3:13, p. 826]), he even makes reference to the entire collection as "all this fricassee which records the *essais* of my life."

We should not infer from these remarks, however, that Montaigne ever personally called into question the usefulness of the *essai* practice for his own private ends or that he ever had to overcome serious doubts as to its validity. As several of the passages cited above have indicated, he was adamant on this score from the beginning. Yet when the project of self-study became the center and expressed the purpose of his writings, when, roughly after 1574, the *essais* shifted in content from the random assessment of general topics to take up a detailed examination of his own person, he naturally felt pressed to justify his methodology and his literary instrument. The question simply put was the following: Since it served as the underpinning of his entire project, could the *essai* be defended as an adequate vehicle first to probe and explore his intuitive reflections on the self, and then to fix them in literary form? More generally stated, could such a seemingly subjective, arbitrary, and even frivolous modus operandi serve to unearth the essential truths of his authentic self? Clearly some kind of test needed to be applied to determine its validity.

Montaigne squarely addressed these crucial questions in the essay "Of Presumption" (2:17), which he wrote sometime during the period 1578–80. Underlying his entire argument is his claim to be able to form "good and sound opinions" as part of his birthright as a human being; for, to the common run of mankind, to which he assuredly belonged, "the fairest division of her favors that nature has given us is that of sense" (499). As an average human being, Montaigne therefore insists on the essential validity of his own natural lights and on his share of common sense.

Next he declares that, unlike other men, he has been single-minded in the use of these attributes granted him by nature, that he has expended all his energies to a single end, the "business" of the self:

The world always looks straight ahead; as for me, I turn my gaze inward, I fix it there. Everyone looks in front of him; as for me, I look inside of me; I have no business but with myself; I continually observe myself, I take stock of myself, I taste myself. Others always go elsewhere . . . as for me, I roll about in myself. (499)

Montaigne also insists that he has conducted this enterprise to a worthy and virtuous end, that of relating the truth about himself. "Truth is the first and fundamental part of virtue. We must love it for itself . . . My soul by nature shuns lying and hates even to think a lie" (491). And he further claims that those truths that he has examined represent the deepest and most essential part of himself: "For the firmest and most general ideas I have are those which, in a manner of speaking, were born with me. They are natural and all mine." And though he has written them "crude and simple . . . but a little confused and imperfect," he has tested them through his reading: "Since then I have established and fortified them by the authority of others and the sound arguments of the ancients, with whom I found my judgment in agreement" (499).

For all these reasons, Montaigne is convinced that he has developed "the capacity for sifting truth," and this he owes to his own powers and to his exercise of the *essai.* Consequently, he now has not the least doubt about the validity of his plan, nor the slightest reticence in carrying forth his project. To his critics he exclaims: "Blame my project if you will, but not my procedure. I see well without others telling me, how little value and weight all this has and the folly of my plan." And he rests his case, saying: "It is enough that my judgment is not unshod, of which these are the essays" (499).

This text can be regarded as Montaigne's strongest and most explicit defense of his project and method, and never again would he feel obliged to justify either. Habitual, one might say daily, practice in the "sifting of truth" through his readings and their application to his "natural ideas" had led him to a mastery of the *essai* technique and to this vigorous assertion of its soundness.

The subject matter of "Of Presumption" gives ample evidence that, now the self-confident artist, Montaigne had finally succeeded in artfully combining the two disparate elements that had hitherto been unevenly developed and represented in the earlier essays. With the moral matter—the essential *leçon morale,* he now fused a rich outpouring of autobiographical detail to sketch a complete physical and moral portrait. With delightful understatement he describes himself as being of mediocre, even common, estate in most respects—physical stature, appearance, intelligence, memory, speech, writing skills, even his command of the French language: He claims to be barely capable of husbanding his own affairs and would, if left to his own devices, starve in a well-stocked kitchen. Yet he yields to no one as regards those two major qualities that recommend him as a writer—the soundness of his judgment and his enduring commitment to truth.

By artfully combining these two elements, Montaigne effectively clarified and broadened the scope of his project. Henceforth the personal depiction of an individual in all his dimensions would be directed to a moral study of man himself. The *essai* technique had therfore led Montaigne to pursue his project of self-study no longer as the isolated individual of the early years of his retirement, but as Montaigne, a microcosm of the human condition. And with this shift in emphasis he ushers his readers into the enlarged cosmos of the later essays.

The first edition of the *Essais* (books 1 and 2) appeared in 1580. In the next eight years leading to the publication of the thirteen essays of book 3, Montaigne's life was filled with many experiences that would nourish his final writings. For over a year he lived the life of a tourist, traveling through France and Germany and stopping at various thermal stations to take the waters for his persistent ailment of the kidney stone. He then resided in Rome for several months before being called back home, in 1581, to serve as mayor of Bordeaux. He very competently filled this post for two consecutive terms of four years, each with considerable success; and during his last year in office, he had to cope with a plague that killed nearly half of the citizens of his city. Not in residence at the time, he refused to enter the city's walls and instead convened the election of his successor from the environs—an action for which he has been severely criticized. Returning for a year to his family estate, he was caught up in the strife between extremist factions of Protestants and Catholics when the latter laid siege to Protestant Castillon, a few leagues distant. Then he was forced to flee with his family to avoid a fresh outbreak of plague at his very gates. For about six months he traveled in caravan and was finally able to return home in 1586. The next two years he probably spent in the steady composition of the last book and in supplying hundreds of revisions to the first two.

In these later *essais* the traits that had come to characterize the pieces written between 1578 and 1580 became even more pronounced.[27] The chapters are now much longer, more rambling and freewheeling. They no longer subordinate the tissue of personal experience to anecdotes or examples gleaned through reading. They instead bring to center Montaigne's many new experiences gained through travel and public office as a means of clarifying his ideas and enunciating his views. Everywhere in the text Montaigne now unabashedly "rolls" in himself as he regales his reader with all manner of things: incidents drawn from his youth and manhood, his habits of mind and body, his bout with the "stone," his dietary regime and digestive and evacuatory processes, his whims and prejudices, and his most deeply held personal convictions.

What most strikingly distinguishes the final essays from the earlier ones is the use that Montaigne was now determined to make of them. Building on the view that he had developed of himself as a microcosm of all that is human, he had finally gained the supreme self-confidence to assert that the example of his own life—"a life ordinary and without luster"—could readily (and profitably) be applied to that of every other human being. This precept he set forth in the clearest of terms in the celebrated passage from "Of Repentance," where he asserts:

I set forth a humble and inglorious life; that does not matter. You can tie up all moral philosophy with a common and private life just as well as with a life of richer stuff. Every man bears the entire stamp of the human condition. (611)

Once acknowledging this universal tie with the rest of humanity, Montaigne would no longer have any inhibition in discoursing on any and all problems central to the human condition and, hence, of vital concern to all human beings. Drawing from his most intimate reflections and experience, as a consummate moralist he was prepared, moreover, to offer counsel to all who would listen to him; and he was adamant about his right to do so because of the essential unity and solidarity he knew that he shared with all mankind.

As a consequence, the final book of *essais* presents an untrammeled flow of insights and counsels on many of our most deeply shared human experiences and problems. The following summation reveals only some of the most important: religious conversion and repentance ("Of Repentance," 3:2); a psychological and social study of human sexuality ("Some Verses of Virgil," 3:5); customs and mores of the peoples of the New World and what this reveals of customs and practices in general ("Of Coaches," 3:6); the advantages of travel and Montaigne's urbanity as a citizen of the world ("Of Vanity," 3:9); how to strike a delicate balance between what we owe to the social weal and to a legitimate cultivation of the self ("Of Husbanding Your Will," 3:10); witchcraft and man's enduring cruelty to his fellows because of intolerance and superstition ("Of Cripples," 3:11); and Montaigne's coming to terms with death finally gained through the example of the lowly and un-schooled, who meet it simply and naturally ("Of Physiognomy," 3:12).

Montaigne ultimately achieves a striking reconciliation of art and nature in the last essays. As he perfected the essay form, he also evolved, through a marvelous process of intellectual alchemy, a philos-ophy of nature that could accept without regret or recrimination the sum total of all that makes up the human person: his passions, foibles, virtues, vices, foolishness, wisdom, and good and bad intentions. For Montaigne man is ever an amalgam of all of these, and rather than ranting against the human conditon or trying to transcend it, he should instead bend his efforts to refine his judgment and moral sense. In this process, the universal desire for happiness is the goal, and the voice of nature, enlightened by moral discrimination, the guide.

This philosophy is most fully and eloquently stated in the last essay that Montaigne wrote. In "Of Experience" (3:13)—the magnificent coda of his artistic and intellectual achievement—he terminates his project of moral study and counsel with this glowing testimony to the incalculable beauty and worth of a life well lived:

It is an absolute perfection and virtually divine to know how to enjoy our being rightfully. We seek other conditions because we do not understand the use of our own, and go outside of ourselves because we do not know what it is like inside. . . . The most beautiful lives, to my mind, are those that con-form to the common human pattern, with order, but without miracle, and without eccentricity. (857)

The creation of the familiar essay was thus fortuitously linked to Montaigne's gradual elaboration of a personal philosophy of life gained through self-discovery. Beginning as a rather typical humanist of his day, he soon subjected the kernels of wisdom gleaned from his readings of the ancients to a searching analysis that allowed him to diverge markedly from their technique. Rather than regarding his intimate feelings as secondary, as they usually had done, he compared his deep-est opinions of the self with observations passed down to him; nor did he seek to conceal this process but made it the primary object of his writings. That is to say, these topics were reflected from and refracted through his particular and gifted temperament. Gradually he became convinced that not only did his views reflect himself alone but were truly representative and beneficial to humanity as a whole. It was by this psychological process of self-analysis through his musings and writings and their application to all mankind that he ultimately fathered the essay.

The importance of his creation as a means of literary expression is truly incalculable. As Professor Henri Peyre has described it:

With Montaigne, the essay achieved for the first time what it can achieve better than any other form of writing, except perhaps the epistolary one: a means of self-discovery. It gave the writer a way of reaching the secret springs of his behaviour, of seizing the man and the author at once in his contradictions, in his profound disunity, and in his mobility.[28]

Chapter Two

The Essay in Seventeenth-Century France: Transition and Change

After Montaigne's death, the essay form as he created it virtually vanished from the French literary scene. Only two works composed in the following century bear the title: Pierre Nicole's *Essais de morale* (1671), and Blaise Pascal's *Essai pour les coniques* (1640). Under his title the eminent Jansenist theologian Nicole compiled a collection of moral tracts that differed radically in style and content from the mode of self-study in which Montaigne had indulged. In fact, as shall be seen later, the latter's essay form had become for this stern moralist symptomatic of an approach to life and thought that was clearly sinful because of its emphasis on the individual ego. For his part, Pascal used the title for a work dedicated to mathematical enquiry, and in his later philosophical writings, he would fulminate against the *sot project,* or foolish project, which he considered Montaigne's study of the self to have been.

Despite the virtual disappearance of the essay title in French letters, Montaigne's popularity does not seem to have waned appreciably (there are some thirty-five editions of the *Essais* that appeared between 1616 and 1669). Moreover, his influence among scholars and scientists of a libertine or skeptical frame of mind (Gassendi, Guy Patin, Lamothe le Vayer, Théophile de Viau, and the Du Puy brothers, to name the most important) remained dominant throughout the century. Antoine Adam has observed that these thinkers and intellectuals agreed that "his [Montaigne's] *a priori* convictions could be used in a study of man, that he [man] is not controlled by rational forces but that his beliefs and customs are the result of education, received opinions, and habit."[1] And like their mentor, they were also inclined to suspend judgment on the question of whether man could through natural reason attain certitude on such matters as the immortality of the soul and the existence of God; and some of them—Théophile de Viau and Gassendi—

had gone far beyond this fideist position and were for all intents and purposes confirmed agnostics.

Though Montaigne's thought reigned supreme among intellectual dissidents and, as the evidence indicates, he was widely read as an author, how does one account for the virtual disappearance of the essay as title and project in the seventeenth century? Several factors need to be examined to account for this surprising phenomenon, all the more astonishing when contrasted with the extraordinary vogue that the *Essais* were enjoying in England during the same period.

First there is the consideration of the enormous and enduring posthumous prestige that Montaigne received in his own country as the creator of the personal essay. In the period immediately following his death it would seem that no Frenchman, out of respect to his memory and awed by his achievement, had the audacity to attempt to undertake a similar project or to use its title. Indeed, Montaigne's genius had a chilling effect even upon those who admired him the most. As an example, there is the case of Pierre Charron, an intimate friend and self-styled disciple. This celebrated theologian-preacher, whose own religious views eventually came to be highly suspect to religious authorities, published in 1601 a philosophical treatise entitled *De la sagesse* (Of wisdom) in which Montaigne's Pyrrhonism was reduced to a system that could be used as a defense for religious belief.[2] Holding the senses to be unreliable and the mind incapable of achieving undisputed truth in metaphysical matters, Charron applied these opinions to develop the ideal of the sage who, guided by his natural lights and experience, would give token acceptance to the laws and customs of his society while jealously guarding his right to dissent in private when his own judgments contradicted popularly held views. For Charron the sage was the epitome of the enlightened person precisely because of his skeptical point of reference.

It goes without saying that Charron's treatise, in its impersonal, ordered, and somewhat dogmatic presentation of theory, showed little or no resemblance to Montaigne's style and method of writing and was in fact alien to the latter's open-ended, discursive method of stating opinion. Yet by his most earnest attempt to reduce the musings of his master to a logical system, Charron gives a clear indication of the very strong influence Montaigne's moral and religious views were exerting on himself and his contemporaries. He further attests to how inaccessible the latter's art form had become even to true believers and admirers.

Other factors causing an eclipse of the personal essay form involved broad and profound changes in literary, political, and religious attitudes in seventeenth-century France, and those changes created an environment inimical to the continuation of Montaigne's project in respect to both style and intent. As regards the literary climate, during the last decade of Henry IV's reign (1600–1610), the freer, more spontaneous, and individualistic mode of expression characterizing French literature of the Renaissance was held up to critical scrutiny. Enjoying a new period of peace and prosperity, the monarchy embarked upon a program to consolidate its power and to banish all remnants of turbulence that had only recently been quelled. There naturally arose a preference for artistic expression that emphasized order, reason, and the perfection of the major literary forms transmitted by the ancients.

François Malherbe was the first great legislator of the new literary norms. He first labored unstintingly to *dégasconner* or degasconize the coarse and free language of Henry's court and French itself by purifying it of Latinisms, Italianisms, and all manner of archaic expression and local or provincial forms that had gained entry and legitimacy in the prose of Renaissance authors. He further taught that proper language usage demanded a more concise and careful attention to precise meaning than that exemplified by the rich but undisciplined prose style of such illustrious poets of the preceding century as Marot, Du Bellay, and Ronsard, and prose writers such as Des Périers, Du Vair, Rabelais, and Montaigne himself. To convey the most intensely felt sentiment in the most restrained and lucid prose became the ideal that he advanced for artistic expression. Himself a poet somewhat lacking in inspiration, he nevertheless considerably advanced the important task of reforming and purifying the French language, and in his role as "professor of grammar," instilled in the minds of poets and prose writers of his day the need for clarity, precision, and patient application of form.

The monarchy allied itself with these attempts to refine taste through literary form in order to bend the arts to the service of the realm. To this end the powerful minister Cardinal Richelieu established in 1634 the Académie Française, which, as Antoine Adam observes: "furnished the cardinal with a number of writers who would, with facility, carry out the tasks allotted to them."[3] And these "tasks" were multiple: theological and political documents supporting the official documents of church and state were to be worked over by the *doctes,* or learned members of the academy; polemicists from the group were to answer attacks on French policy from abroad; and the members were to strive for the greater improvement of the French language, which, in its perfected state, would forward French aspirations for political and cultural hegemony over the rest of Europe. The work of Richelieu's government to create an official climate of urbanity and culture to foster the aims of absolute monarchy was effectively, indeed decisively, advanced by the salon, a social institution that revolutionized modes of conduct and essential attitudes of taste among the aristocracy. So important in fact was the salon as a social and cultural phenomenon that the nineteenth-century critic Hippolyte Taine would characterize the bulk of the great literary masterpieces of the seventeenth century as "salon literature."

Unquestionably the most important of the salons was the earliest, that held in the Hôtel de Rambouillet.[4] Using it as a prototype, we may describe the salon as a weekly gathering at which writers, scientists, artists, and the most fashionable people of the day met in elegant surroundings to discuss topics dealing with sentiment, etiquette, literature, grammar, vocabulary, and whatever else was of current interest. In the "blue room" of her imposing Rambouillet residence, Catherine de Vivonne, the Marquise de Rambouillet (or Arthénice, as she was called in her self-styled anagram), presided from 1608 to 1645. Seeking to banish all vulgarity in conversation, she cultivated an atmosphere of good taste and decorum. In the course of the weekly receptions, the guests enjoyed parlor games, danced, listened to music, and more importantly, engaged in conversations dedicated to elegance and wit in language and refinement in manners. Among her guests she numbered the great noblemen of the period as well as many of its most important literary figures: Malherbe, Racan, Guez de Balzac, Georges and Madeleine Scudéry, Rotrou, and Corneille.

When her salon declined around 1640, that of Mlle de Scudéry gradually gained ascendency and continued to be influential throughout most of the remaining century. An author in her own right of sentimental novels of adventure (*Le Grand Cyrus,* and *Clélie, histoire romaine*), "Sappho," as she chose to be named in the salon, gave to the conversations a more specific direction through an emphasis on topics of gallantry and through a campaign directed not only against vulgarity in language but even common expressions of current usage. In the process she and her guests encouraged affectation and introduced into the language paraphrases or overly fastidious terms (for example, *pomme de terre* for the homely *patate* and *conseiller de grâces* for the functional *miroir*). This parlor exercise, termed *préciosité,* made some inroads in language usage and was roundly condemed by Boileau and especially Molière, who provided a scathing satire of this absurd reduction of language in the play *Les Précieuses ridicules* (1659).

The flowering of the salons corresponded in time to the accession to power of Louis XIV and the early (and brilliant) period of his reign. After 1660 the powerful Sun King assembled about him at the court of Versailles a once proud but now docile nobility, courtiers of varying backgrounds, and leading writers and artists who depended on royal financial support and approbation for their very existence. As a social institution the salon had also formulated an ideal for conduct that both reflected the political reality of an absolute monarchy and that prescribed the ground rules for success in the life of the court—the concept of the *honnête homme*. Prefigured in the Italian Castiglione's *Book of the Courtier* a century before, this ideal of the consummate gentleman had been substantially developed in France in the Rambouillet salon. Here men accustomed to the rude and coarse language of the battlefields were exposed to a radically different atmosphere. Through sustained conversation with intelligent and very sophisticated women, they were induced to acquire a veneer of politeness and gallantry that was soon to become a model for all of Europe. And as the intellectual interests of these fashionable aristocrats was expanded to include literature, philosophy, and science, they also gradually learned to become adept in fine and subtle analysis of sentiment.

This new kind of social being—the polite and cultivated man-about-town—has been very well described by Antoine Adam as follows:

His main virtue—in a sense his only virtue—was urbanity. Whether he belonged to the aristocracy or to the world of letters, he had, above all, to respect the requirement of good manners. He was not allowed to affirm his opinions too insistently, or defend them with blind fury. . . . He was also a man who knew his Cicero and Seneca. He had a sensitive awareness of the requirements of good manners, which caused him to shun extremes and cultivate the middle path. His rule was easy and unconstrained dignity. Honesty he prized to such a degree that he saw no difference between a good man and an *honnête homme*.[5]

In short, the salon refined and bestowed full legitimacy on a new ideal of masculine conduct differing radically from the rough-hewn and independent mores of a Renaissance nobility that had jealously and fiercely defended its prerogatives and power up to the disastrous defeat of the Fronde (a full-scale civil war pitting the old aristocracy against the king). The ideal of the *honnête homme* defined instead the role of the courtier who was conditioned to adapt socially to the demands of absolute monarch and accepted as a matter of course the conventions and cultural interests established in the salon. Gone, then, was the Stoical independence of the Renaissance, the ideal of the skeptical and self-contained sage à la Montaigne, who had strenuously protected his private life and personal attitude from the incursion of the outside world. Now the new man would have difficulties achieving a sense of identity *apart* from his own society.

Writers, as well, underwent a similar transition as regards their art. From its inception, the salon encouraged social intercourse between members of the nobility, the fashionable, and literary personalities who, more often than not, were of bourgeois origins. Though certainly more educated on the average, these writers still were obliged to divest themselves of the kind of academic pedantry or bookishness that it was now felt had characterized the earlier humanist scholars; and in the press of the gatherings, they would have to distinguish themselves with grace and eloquence in the kind of pursuits favored by the other guests. Writers were therefore expected to master and perfect the literary forms fostered by the salon: delicately turned and psychologically astute epigrams dealing with sentiment, conduct, and motive, or finely etched portraits—physical and moral—of famous people. It should here be noted that both of these literary preoccupations were also enjoying a tremendous vogue in the rest of Europe and England at this time because of French influence.

Aside from legislating literary forms, the salon was equally important in shaping the style and point of view of writers. In such an environment, any author wishing to succeed would have to please his audience and conform to the prevailing tastes. Such demands naturally and logically led to a suppression of the self as an author's primary focus. Disposed to social conformity, the group would not be interested or pleased to hear an outpouring of personal feeling or self-revelatory detail. Banned from polite conversation and regarded as indiscreet and in bad taste, such considerations would find no place in literary forms themselves. To capture the topics of polite conversation and artfully render them in written form for general approbation became the role expected of the writer, and from this there evolved the century's strong preference for literature expressing universal statement and devoid of local color or too personal or familiar turns of expression.

The salon therefore constituted the major force in fostering a climate in which the personal essay as Montaigne had written it no longer corresponded to prevailing tastes and consequently fell out of official favor. It is somewhat ironic to note, moreover, that though the major components of the essay—aphorisms, sentences, thoughts, and character sketches—were continued and refined in these *bureaux d'esprit,* or workshops of wit, a new ideal of social deportment stressing conformity in manner and thought turned these literary devices to entirely different ends.

The other force that militated against the continuation of Montaigne's project stemmed from the animosity that even his memory elicited from among the ranks of the *bien pensants,* or committed religious believers of the century. Earlier mention has been made of the renewed spirit of orthodoxy and resulting rigidity in attitudes that characterized the Counter Reformation in France. In ways not so dissimilar from the salon, the Catholic Church was also intent on fostering attitudes of conformity and obedience among its adherents. The individualistic and skeptical approach to religious practice and belief allegedly contained in the *Essais* and kept alive by libertine circles made the work anathema to church officialdom, and Montaigne himself came to be regarded as the mouthpiece of neopagan philosophy through his seeming indifference and nonchalance regarding the commandments of God, the sacraments, death, and final judgment. Such an influential spokesman for orthodoxy as was Bishop Bossuet roundly attacked Montaigne in a sermon (delivered in 1651) in which he identified him as the source of skeptical attitudes regarding the immortality of the soul, attitudes that Bossuet knew to be rampant among free thinkers.[6] About the same time, the eminent spokesman for Jansenism, Antoine Arnauld, delivered a broader attack including both religious and social objections to the *Essais* as a literary project. In the chapter on "Some faulty conclusions people have made regarding public life and ordinary discourse" (part 3, chap. 20), from his very influential work, *La Logique de Port Royal* (1661), he warmly praises Pascal for his contention that the *honnête homme* should avoid naming and exalting the self, or even from using the word "I," since Christian piety has made obligatory the annihilation of the ego. Montaigne, Arnauld goes on to say, had in a social sense displayed one of the most flagrant violations of conduct for the *honnête homme* "by only regaling his readers with his changing humors, moods, inclinations, fantasies, sickness, virtues, and vices. . . . For there can be no more faulty defect in thought than to proceed from such expressions of self-love."[7]

This confluence of political, social, and religious forces and opinions thus created a new climate for literary production and a new role for the writer, both differing radically from that of Montaigne's age. Ultimately, neither personal sincerity nor learning (as it had been understood by the humanists) now counted as much as eloquence in style and conformity in writing on matter supportive of a particular social code. What, then, was the fortune of the essay in this changed cultural ambience? Did an essay tradition continue or was it extinguished under the weight of transformations in tastes and attitudes consistent with strict rules for literary modes of expression, absolutism in government, and strict orthodoxy in religious matters?

The response to this question hinges to a great extent upon the latitude allowed in defining the essay as a genre. In the strictest sense of the word, Montaigne's personal form is consciously forwarded by only one major prose writer of the century, Charles de Saint-Évremond. He indeed presented his reflections and musings in a personal format in which there continues to be exemplified the Renaissance ideal of personal self-cultivation and autonomy of moral and philosophical inquiry. Two other important writers of nonfictional prose also stand out against the century's growing preference for universal expression in their composition of epistolary pieces, many of which seem to include essential traits and features of the essay technique. Guez de Balzac, an eminent man of letters and salon personality of the Rambouillet period, wrote somewhat stylized letters that frequently reflect his personal thought and provide comments and musings on his own life and on events and persons of his period. And Mme de Sévigné, one of literature's greatest letter writers, provided hundreds of pieces rich in personal comment and detail, as well as keen observations and remarkable reportage on the major happenings and on virtually every facet of life in her society.

Whether the other major nonfictional prose writers of the century—La Rochefoucauld, Pascal, and La Bruyère—can legitimately be included for serious consideration in this study has occasioned some debate. Traditionally designated as moralists who, in terms of universal statement, offer extremely astute and penetrating psychological insights on human conduct and motive, they have been denied the title of essayist in the one major critical treatment given to this question in our century. In his article "The Origin of the Essay Compared in French and English," the English scholar H. V. Routh contends that the essay (which he exclusively holds to be Montaigne's model) did not survive in any form in France during the classical period. He claims that

The literature which created the essay and offers so many possibilities for its continuance has failed to produce a successor at all comparable to Montaigne, while another nation [England], apparently less adapted to the cultivation of this art, can claim all the greatest essayists of the world from Bacon to Lamb.[8]

In formulating his thesis, Professor Routh refuses the title to the moralist writers mentioned above, as well as to the first three because, in his opinion, they merely reported upon or formally satirized their society without giving vent to their own most personal thoughts and convictions: "A writer was not expected to reveal his own soul but only to play a part. His works were not required to mirror life but to idealize it, to recreate its artificial conception of sentiment which found favor among the elite of that age."[9]

Though he regards the moralists in particular as having been endowed by nature with every gift requisite to great essayists, he judges them to have fallen short of the mark by providing reflections, maxims, or portraits that only re-create or embellish the mores of court life; and Mme de Sévigné and Balzac he sees as having turned their considerable stylistic skills to a refinement of the oratory and epistolary prose forms, respectively.

Taken in its most literal sense, Professor Routh's assessment has some validity. It is true that, except for Saint-Évremond, Montaigne had no direct continuer in the seventeenth century, no one who closely resembled him or who consciously built on his model. Yet ultimately Routh's thesis must be rejected in any broader consideration for it is too rigid in its insistence that only Montaigne's model constitutes the essay form for all times, and the thesis is too myopic in its apparent assumption that literary genres remain essentially static without naturally adapting to the changing cultural patterns and modes of expression for any given age. Though not essayists of Montaigne's stamp, the great moralist writers are nonetheless very close literary cousins involved in a similar moral preoccupation: the study of man. Keen observers like Montaigne himself, they provide reflections, wise counsels, and precepts culled from their own insights and lived experience. Though, for reasons already advanced, they diverge by their deemphasis of the personal "I" and their reluctance to engage in an exercise of self-analysis conducted as such, they nonetheless manifest their own personal convictions and assuredly provide far more in their writings than a mere idealization of their society. In fact, they are often sharply critical of the mores and foibles of mankind, and of the society and individuals of their own age. In their writings they employ many of the literary components of the *Essais* and in some cases (as with the maxim, portrait, and thought) they raise them to art forms since unsurpassed. They can be regarded, in short, as being in the actual process of adapting the early essay form to their own artistic needs for expression and, in this regard, amply attest to the versatility and flexibility of this most diverse of literary genres. To refuse them entry into the essay tradition because of the moralist cast of their writings would seem, then, to represent unwarranted rigidity and an obsession with the Montaigne model bordering on the belief that literary forms can be likened to Platonic essences. To avoid any rigid method of categorization and for the sake of logic and convenience, I shall conduct the study of the six prose writers mentioned above as follows: The three who consistently use the personal form, the authorial "I," will be examined first in order of chronology as continuers of the personal form. The three moralists, who more often than not show a preference for the universal statement of the classical period, will then be examined as authors who, despite adaptations in taste and form, may legitimately be incuded in the essay tradition.

Jean-Louis Guez de Balzac (1597–1654) was born and spent the better part of his life at his family estate near Angoulême, in the west of France. Leading a tumultuous life as a youth, he was for a time a close friend of the poet Théophile de Viau and became deeply involved in political intrigues. In 1619 he aided Marie de Medicis to escape from house arrest at Blois and was subsequently in the service of the Cardinal de La Valette in Rome. His earliest works were polemical and a political treatise, *The Prince* (1631), an idealized portrait of a Catholic king and in reality a panegyric of Louis XIII, attempted to fix the legitimate limits of the monarch's power along Christian principles. This tract caused him to fall out of favor with Richelieu, and abandoning political ambitions, he definitively retired to his Angoulême retreat (his *désert* on the Charente River) there to compose his polished *Letters* dealing with general, moral, literary, or philosophical matters that he addressed to fellow members of the Académie and to friends at the Hôtel de Rambouillet, where they were read and much appreciated for their elegant style and grace.

Balzac is principally remembered as the *grand épistolier* of the early

part of the century and was largely responsible for the refinement of
artistic prose. His own style, sometimes excessively refined, was not
exempt from terms of *préciosité,* if not bad taste. Yet he imbued his
writings with a musical quality and harmony that would influence
Pascal, Bossuet, Boileau, and other great prose stylists of the later
classical period.

Balzac's major contributions as an essayist are comprised of his *Letters*
(1618–44) and the *Les Entretiens (Conversations),* written from 1651 to
his death and published posthumously in 1657.[10] The earlier *Letters*
reflect personal details of his life, his critical and intellectual interests,
his period of religious crisis and the passage from libertine views to the
devout practice of his faith, his health problems, views on literature,
counsels on virtue, and meditations on the retired life. They are usually
written in a confiding tone as from one friend to another.

It is principally in the *Conversations* that Balzac refined his particular
form of literary and epistolary style and sifted many autobiographical
details of his life through analysis and hindsight to provide a kind of
moral philosophy that both unifies and justifies the life he led. In these
sixty-seven "conversations" he reflected upon his past and gave specific
reference to such matters as his memories of school years at the Collège
de Chambry, his political ambitions and associations with Marie de
Medicis, his definitive renunciation of an active life, various polemical
quarrels in which he had expended much of his artistic energies (the
controversy surrounding the publication of *The Prince* and his religious
tract and profession of faith—*Socrate chrétien* of 1652), his failing health
and nervous stroke. He wove within these principal events and periods
of his life personal reflections on life, death, age, and faith that constitute an inner journal and a kind of apology of his life which to some
extent suggests Montaigne's project and preoccupation.

Yet Balzac as a man of his century gave to the *Conversations* a tone
and structure absent from the *Essais.* Unlike Montaigne, Balzac was
not content to confine his writings to introspective self-analysis but
needed an audience, more precisely a confidant, to whom he could
address his thoughts and with whom he could engage in a dialogue.
Alien to him was the joy of "rolling" in the self or of communicating
alone with the ancients. He writes of his personal feelings on this score
to Dom André, abbot of Saint Mesmin:

In the place where I am, I am reduced to nourishing myself with my own
substance. I only communicate with our friends the ancients. It is true that

they are good company, but they are always the same and only repeat this year what they said a year ago. To give life to my studies I would need a library animated with conversation which I lack here as I would lack leisure and repose in other places.[11]

Some mention must be made, if only in passing, of Balzac's work as a literary critic. At least twenty-five of the pieces from the *Conversations* are concerned with literary appraisals of writers and works drawn from his own day and from the preceding century. Among the most celebrated of these are his studies on Montaigne—"Of Montaigne and His Essays" (18) and "That in Montaigne's Time Our Language Was Still Rude" (19)—and other critical essays, such as "A Comparison of Ronsard and Malherbe" (31), and "Of the Burlesque Style" (38). By and large, Balzac shared Malherbe's view that the language and style of Renaissance writers had wreaked havoc on French letters. He criticized Ronsard's rich profusion of language forms and fondness for latinized borrowings and praised Malherbe's restrained and sober prose.[12] Yet he was measured in his critical assessment of Montaigne, finding him "excusable if he did not always write as many delicate people would wish him to do." And he was able to appreciate much of this author's genius and could understand the prestige that the *Essays* still enjoyed.[13]

Not only, then, did Balzac adopt the personal essay to the tastes of his age, but he also gave impetus to the development of formal literary criticism, which would soon become a major preoccupation of French essayists.

Born of aristocratic parentage (she was the granddaughter of Saint Jeanne de Chantal, founder of the Order of the Visitation), Marie de Rabutin-Chantal, Marquise de Sévigné (1626–96), was no stranger to court circles. She was well known by such social luminaries as the Grande Mademoiselle (the daughter of the king's brother), the queen, Mme de Montespan and Mme de Maintenon, and by the king himself, who had warmly received her into the court. She numbered among her close associates Mme de Lafayette, La Rochefoucauld, and the Duc de Chaulne and was privy to most of the great events of Louis's reign. A most virtuous woman, she was unhappily married to the Baron de Sévigné, a relation of the Cardinal de Retz, and a celebrated rake who was killed in 1651 while engaged in a duel precipitated by one of his many love affairs. Though not in the least a recluse but enjoying country life, she increasingly preferred to be away from court circles and, after her husband's death, she alternated her place of residence between

Paris and the Sévigné estate of Les Rochers, where for all intents and purposes she retired after 1680.

Mme de Sévigné's great passion in life, the object of her care and affection, was her daughter, Françoise-Marguerite, and the lion's share of her more than one thousand extant letters is addressed to this young woman who, after her marriage in 1670 to the elderly Comte de Grignan, lieutenant de Provence, went to live for the next twenty years in the Château de Grignan, near Montélimar. Few if any literary testimonies to maternal solicitude equal that of Mme de Sévigné for her beloved daughter, who became virtually the center of her mother's universe, and in many passages adumbrative of Proust, Mme de Sévigné constantly expressed her obsessive grief at the haunting absence of this loved one. A year after the first separation, during a religious retreat at the Abbey of Livry, where she had spent much time in the past with her daughter, she wrote:

Since my arrival I haven't ceased thinking of you, and not being able to contain my feelings, I began to write to you at the end of this somber little path that you love and where I've so often seen you seated or reclining on this mossy little seat. But, my God, where have I not seen you and in how many different ways have these thoughts not pierced my heart? There is no place, at home, in church, in the countryside or the garden where I haven't seen you or been reminded of something about you; and whatever it may be breaks my heart. (24 March 1671)[14]

Because of this separation Mme de Sévigné found a modicum of consolation in repose and contact with nature at her estate Les Rochers. Though always in touch with the goings-on of the court (gained through correspondence with friends and annual visits to Paris), she was prompted to use her detachment to give vent to personal reflections and feelings. Thus she freely commented upon her inner state, her health, attitudes toward life and death, her religious disposition, and her literary interests (she was an avid reader and especially enjoyed Tasso, Cervantes, Tacitus, Virgil, Montaigne, La Fontaine, Molière, Corneille, Racine, and the great theological writers of her century: Pascal, Nicole, and Bossuet).

Though such reflections constitute a solid core of the matter of the letters, Mme de Sévigné was not naturally given to self-analysis and is as anxious to write on all manner of family matters, including financial advice, suggestions for the education of her grandchildren and peren-

nial worries about her charming but wayward son Charles. A very curious and gregarious woman and a keen observer of her times, she
provides artful and dramatic reportage on such important and memorable happenings of the day as the trial of Foucquet, the death of the
great general Turenne, and Mme de Brinvilliers's trial, confession, and
execution in the scandalous *affaire des poisons*. Court intrigue attracts
much of her attention in lively accounts that she writes on such matters
as the king's refusal to allow the Grande Mademoiselle to marry the
Duc de Launes and this young woman's angry crying fit when she
learns of the king's decision; Mme de Maintenon's gradual ascendency
in the king's affections over her rival, Mme de Montespan; and veiled
criticism of Louis's seeming indifference to the suffering of his subjects
as he avidly pursues his military ambitions. There is also a wealth of
anecdote: Boileau's turning red in the face as he quarrels with a Jesuit
who attacks Pascal's work, *The Provincial Letters;* the suicide of Vatel,
the maître d'hôtel of the Grande Condé, irrevocably disgraced because
two banquet tables lacked the meat course when the king was being
served; and the indecorous conduct of the Archbishop of Reims, who,
when overturned in his speeding carriage by colliding with an uniden-
tified horseman (who flees in terror) wishes, in decidedly nonecclesias-
tical terms, that he could have broken the "scoundrel's" arms and cut
off his ears.

Mme de Sévigné is also the only writer of her century who gives
nature descriptions not idealized or stylized in the then dominant pas-
toral style. From her retreat she writes of the silence of the forests, bird
songs, the play of moonlight, and the beauty of the hills and moun-
tains. A good example is her exquisite commentary on the new color
of buds in springtime:

What do you think the color of the trees has been for the past week? Answer.
You are going to say green. Not at all, but red. There are little buds ready to
open that give off an authentic red; then they all sprout a tiny green leaf and
come out unevenly. This creates an indescribably beautiful mixture of green
and red. (19 April 1690)[15]

With Mme de Sévigné there develops an open style of expression
couched in epistolary form that is much more personal and far less
stylized than that of Balzac. Not a professional writer and not expect-
ing her pieces to be published, she is far more unguarded and spontaneous, not in the least given to precious or self-conscious posing. What

she ultimately creates is a wonderfully crafted combination of personal detail and observed reportage of the very rhythm and movement of life all about her. With an artist's eye for color and a dramatist's sense of presentation, she offers tableaux that are remarkably faithful to the depiction of human beings and their world. Though reticent to make herself the topic and center of her letters, she lends enough of herself to provide a prism through which reality is captured. She, in short, has accommodated the epistolary form to the personal essay and in many ways prefigures the periodical form of the genre to be developed in the next century by Addison and Steele, a form that becomes the means to depict the drama and color of life seen and communicated in a social context.

Charles de Marguetal, de Saint Denis, de Saint-Évremond (1614–1703), is usually briefly described in most manuals of French literature as a writer of libertine leanings and Epicurean tastes, but lacking in depth and conviction, who wrote letters, poems, and essays of a pithy and witty nature. His status as a French exile from 1661 until his death seems to have removed him from the main currents of French literary and cultural life of his time. Moreover, his almost legendary reputation as a bon vivant and gourmet of light-hearted disposition has further diminished serious consideration. He has, in short, been consistently viewed as a kind of practitioner of the late humanist period, a colorful but somewhat unoriginal continuer of the skeptical tradition and of the nonchalant cultivation of the self associated with Montaigne.

This sketchy literary portrait, like most, contains kernals of truth. An Epicurean and a skeptic Saint-Évremond certainly was, but he was hardly a man lacking in courage and conviction; nor can his prose works be summarily described as pithy or superficial.

Of aristocratic Norman parentage, he embarked on a military career as a youth and in 1641 was appointed lieutenant in the Duc d'Enghien's (the Grand Condé's) regiment. He participated in the great battles of Rocroi, Fribourg, and Nordlingen and because of his bravery and intelligence in military strategy was elevated to the rank of *maréchal de camp* about 1651. Known to be a widely read man with deep philosophical interests and of independent thought, he was also notorious for his trenchant and irreverent wit. Because of some unrestrained public utterances, he fell out of a favor with the Grand Condé, who himself was known as a libertine but was far more guarded in his speech.

Chastened by the latter for his verbal excesses, Saint-Évremond next incurred the implacable wrath of Cardinal Mazarin when his pamphlet, *Lettre à Monsieur le Marquis de Créqui sur le traité des Pyrénées*—a work critical of the cardinal's foreign policy for Spain—was found among the disgraced Foucquet's papers in 1661. That very same year he prudently slipped away to Holland, and five years later he arrived in England, where he soon received a royal pension and where he would spend the rest of life attached to a society of English lords, literary figures, and philosophers (he was a good friend of Hobbes), and other French refugees. On intimate terms with the notorious Hortense Mancini, Duchess de Mazarin, he enjoyed the reputation of an urbane and cultivated man not tied to professional or family concerns and with sufficient income and leisure to spend his time writing on whatever struck his fancy. Official circles in France spurned his many attempts to return until he ceased trying in 1689, when he judged the intellectual and cultural climate of his homeland to be too intolerant to allow him the same measure of freedom that he had enjoyed among the English. Lionized in his old age by London society, he had the signal honor of being buried in Westminster Abbey.

The bulk of Saint-Évremond's prose pieces were written in his years of exile. They are diversely entitled "Reflections," "Observations," "Letters," "Characters," "Conversations," or more specifically labeled. Though difficult to catalog, they can be placed in several broad categories: 1) moral-philosophical-religious topics ("On Petronius," "On Epicurus," "Considerations on Religion," "On Pleasures," "On Retirement"); 2) historical-political matters ("Reflections on the Diverse Genius of the Roman People," "Letter on Peace," "On French Historians"); 3) literary criticism ("On the Poems of the Ancients," "On Comedies," "On Tragedies," "On Opera"); and 4) incidental pieces of a humorous or satirical nature ("Letter to a Gallant Woman Who Would Like to Become Devout," "Friendship Without Friendship," "The Character of Madame d'Olonne").[16]

As a writer, Saint-Évremond resembles a Montaigne in his cultural interests, point of view, and method of writing. Like the latter, he consciously nourished his inner life by his readings and meditations on Seneca, Plutarch, Epicurus, and Petronius, whose *eruditus luxus,* or enlightened pleasure principle, he held to be the ideal of the *honnête homme.* His choice of topic for his moral and philosophical pieces invariably seems to stem from his readings and musings on particular authors and texts, and his writings reveal a personal and relaxed style achieved through the authorial "I" and his penchant to reveal his own particular thought patterns as they evolve in the process of composition.

Many of Saint-Évremond's essay topics concern the same matter already treated by Montaigne: moral assessments of famous men of antiquity—Plutarch, Seneca, Alexander and Caesar, Epicurus; or studies on such traditional topics as retirement, pleasure, friendship, extraordinary occurrences and the like. Saint-Évremond also makes frequent allusion, direct and indirect, to the content of the *Essais*. For example, in his essay "On Pleasures" he uses as one of his primary examples of tranquility in the midst of pain and adversity the anecdote of Posidonius's Stoical disregard for gout, which Montaigne had developed at length in the essay "That the Taste of Good" (1:14), and Saint-Évremond goes on in the text to elaborate a concept of moral pleasure reminiscent of Montaigne's strong insistence on the legitimate enjoyment of the senses and a major theme of the later essays:

If I am ever obliged to regret anything, my regrets are more those of tender feelings; if one has to anticipate evil to prevent it, my own anticipation will not lead me to a state of feeling that nothing is troubling me and the further reflection of feeling myself free and master of my own destiny afford me the spiritual pleasure of the good Epicurus. By this I mean that agreeable indolence devoid neither of pain and pleasure but rather inducing a delicate feeling of pure joy and bodily pleasure stemming from good conscience and tranquility of the soul.[17]

Saint-Évremond also possessed a similarly independent spirit and consistently spoke his own mind on matters that were frequently controversial. At a safe distance, it is true, from French theological censorship, he dared to maintain that all attempts of human reason to prove the immortality of the soul—Descartes's recent proofs included—were vain. Commenting on the difficulty of imagining the soul as functioning in an afterlife without the body, he writes:

To penetrate into such hidden matters, I decided to read all that has been written on the immortality of the soul, and bringing to bear on my own reflections the opinions of the ancients and moderns, the best proof that I could find for eternal duration is the similarly eternal curiosity that I shall ever have to be cognizant of it.[18]

He was and remained a Catholic out of preference for what he regarded as the priority given by this credence to good works performed out of love for God, as opposed to the Calvinist stress on legal justification. Yet he was adamant that no form of religious belief, even if it be true, could justify hatred of others or intolerance of any kind because of doctrinal differences: "I could never entertain this indiscreet zeal that causes us to hate others because they don't agree on such matters. Self-love is at the root of such false zeal."[19]

In regard to style, Saint-Évremond resembles Montaigne and other Renaissance writers in his prose, which he refused to adapt to the exigencies of classical rules. He reveled in his somewhat anachronistic style of writing, in which he accumulated striking antitheses, extended comparisons, striking uses of litotes, and archaic expressions and Latinisms, all couched in what could be termed a Latin rotundity of phrase. He contended that the classical purists were responsible for having encouraged a flat, common, and tasteless form of expression in French, and he adamantly asserted an author's right to develop his own most personal style. He also delighted in mixing high and low topics in his works and to register therein abrupt changes in prose form—from scholarly exposition to dramatic and comic narration, and dialogue. Indeed, one of his most striking contributions to the essay tradition is his ability to compose sober, serious moral tracts along with satirical and witty pieces, anecdotes, and portraits.

From his vantage point in England, he attempted to judge his own country's literary works in comparison with those of other modern societies and in the process initiated an approach anticipating a Mme de Staël. Comedy, tragedy, and the works of historians were examined in comparison with British, Italian, and Spanish models, as was the further question of French taste and discernment. One of the most notable observations he made on this score is the judgment that "there is no nation where reason is rarer to be found than in France. But when it is present, there is none purer in the entire universe."[20]

One of the most important French essayists of the seventeenth century, an authentic continuer of the personal form, and a pioneer in the creation of the critical essay, Saint-Évremond is also a precursor of many essential attitudes of the Enlightenment. He provides the bridge over which the essay would pass to assume its many manifestations in France in the centuries to come.

François VI, le Prince de Marsillac, Duc de La Rochefoucauld (1613–80), was born in Paris, of a noble family dating back to feudal times. His early education and training were essentially a preparation for a military career, and at the age of sixteen, he was already a *maître de camp* and had fought in the Italian campaign. For the next twenty years he was intensely involved in the futile struggle of the nobility to defend its prerogatives against the strenuous efforts of Richelieu and then Mazarin to emasculate and subject it to the power of the monarchy. A valiant Frondeur (as these aristocratic rebels were called), he was severely wounded and almost blinded at the battle of La Porte Saint-André in 1652 when Turenne obliterated the troops of the Grand Condé. Barely emerging with his life, he was refused amnesty, was forced into exile, and had his estate in the Loire Valley razed.

Returning to Paris, the now vanquished and embittered feudal lord passed the rest of his life in semiretirement and Stoic resignation while enjoying the solace of associations (both intellectual and sentimental) with some of the century's most remarkable women (Mme de Lafayette, Mme de Longueville, and Mme de Sablé). Virtually an autodidact and celebrated for his erudition and deep grasp of the philosophy of the ancients, he was an influential figure in Mme de Sablé's salon, where he endeared himself by his wit and deep commitment to friendship. In this setting he also refined his celebrated maxims and reflections.

This fierce soldier, transformed by necessity into the epitome of the *honnête homme,* began to compose his trenchant epigrams or maxims as a salon pastime in collaboration with Mme de Sablé and the Jansenist theologian Jacques Esprit. What began for him as a parlor game of composing pithy statements and analyzing sentiment for the benefit of the group eventually engaged his genius in refining epigrams of extraordinary psychological acumen coupled with extreme economy of expression.

He did not initially intend to publish his own maxims but rather circulated them privately among his friends. When a pirated edition of his manuscript fell into the hands of a Dutch printer and was published in 1664, he felt compelled to protect his own reputation and had his first set of maxims printed in 1665.[21] Immediately acclaimed, they were revised and expanded by La Rochefoucauld in four subsequent editions appearing during his life; the last, published in 1678, contained 504 maxims and reflections, compared with the 317 of the first edition.

At first sight, the maxims seem to be lacking in any kind of continuity, indeed even to be devoid of any architectural plan. They consist in the main of finely sketched statements, musings, or probes concerned with conduct, motive, and the many relationships that human beings form with each other for reasons that are obscure and often calculating. They have been compared to individual, finely cut diamonds or prisms, each reflecting in its texture diverse, multifaceted aspects of human behavior. Yet a closer study reveals a direction and a certain motive in development.

La Rochefoucauld in fact composed the maxims in sets or groupings that, like satellites, revolve around many particular moral considerations that are elucidated through systematic probing. Among the topics offered for study are passions and moral states—pride, self-interest, self-love, valor, honesty, envy, hatred, sincerity, folly, jealousy, laziness; bodily humors, youth, age, friendship, love, relations between the sexes, and most other moral topics. Only man's relationship to God and the problem of religious belief are conspicuously absent from this vast project of scrutiny.

Each of the major topics is systematically attacked from many angles through individual maxims, and when these are viewed holistically, it becomes apparent that La Rochefoucauld has in fact composed for each what might be termed a moral treatise. The reader is thus gradually led to a realization of the complex nature of each moral consideration and hence of human conduct and motive as a whole.

For example, the motive of self-love (*amour propre*), which, along with self-interest (*intérêt*), La Rochefoucauld regards as holding absolute sway over all human affairs, is systematically explored in some thirty maxims. At first he emphasizes its hold over every one: "Self-love is the greatest flatterer of all" (2). "Whatever discoveries have been made in the land of self-love, many regions still remain unexplored" (3). "Self-love is subtler than the subtlest man of the world" (4). Gradually the theme is expanded in an attack on the attitudes of stoic philosophers who, though they argue the contrary, are as much addicted to this vice: "The attachment or indifference the philosophers felt to life was but a matter of taste on the part of their self-love, and this can no more be argued about than taste for words or choice of colors" (46). La Rochefoucauld does not even exempt the realm of friendship from the tyranny of this passion: "We cannot love anything except in terms of ourselves, and when we put our friends above ourselves we are only concerned with our own taste and pleasure. Yet it is only through such preference that friendship can be true and perfect" (81). Nor do the motives of magnanimity or generosity, with which we often clothe our actions, provide an escape: "When we work for the benefit of others it would appear that our self-love is tricked by kindness and forgets itself; yet this is the most certain way to achieve our ends, for it is lending at interest while pretending to give, in fact a way of getting everybody on our own side by subtle and delicate means" (236).

Building upon such finely etched nuances and multiplying his bits of evidence, La Rochefoucauld ultimately provides a wholesale depiction of how human beings, whether they choose to admit it or not, are always and ever prey to self-love. The *honnête homme,* caught in this trap of evidence, is thereby ineluctably forced to consider the shattering possibility that what is commonly regarded as acceptable conduct in life's affairs is usually no more than the passion for dominating others in the cool pursuit of self-interest. When one expands this process to include the myriad topics systematically analyzed in the work taken as a whole, it becomes clear that La Rochefoucauld has indeed provided a total moral study of man.

La Rochefoucauld directed this method of moral analysis to elaborate a view of man that had deep ramifications in the major currents of thought in his century—and a view that is in many ways strikingly modern as well. Here man is no longer seen as a creature of God and imbued with grace, but rather as a wholly natural being and a prey to his baser passions and the pressures of his environment. As Antoine Adam describes it, La Rochefoucauld crystallized a concept of man emerging from the works of philosophers like Hobbes that denied "the existence within him of a spiritual 'appetition' that might have led him to a search for universal values, a natural inclination towards the good and disinterested action."[22]

La Rochefoucauld also summed up and mirrored the state of mind of his own society, which saw in the civil disorders, the failure of liberal hopes, and the triumph of absolutism the proof that man was decidedly the product of his passions. And the calculating self-interest of his own class in subjecting itself to the sole end of social success was the spectacle from which he drew his piquant and bitter observations. Like Montaigne, he offered a window into his own society, though he is far more pessimistic in his portrayal of the human comedy because he could not be buoyed up by the solace of retirement and self-cultivation—workable palliatives in the humanist period but ineffective in an age of servile acquiescence to an all-powerful political structure.

Yet despite the dim view that they take to any claim of authentic human virtue, the maxims provide a ray of hope and some kind of therapeutic function. In presenting such a stark and pessimistic portrayal of human nature, La Rochefoucauld intends to force his contemporaries to strip away pretense and view themselves and others with

clear-sighted honesty and freedom from moral blindness and affectation. Insisting on what the true ideal of the *honnête homme* should be
("The true gentleman never claims superiority in anything") (203), he
offers a way out of the moral morass for those enlightened enough to
live with sincerity and openness of heart. In fact, the two are one and
the same: "Sincerity is openness of heart. It is found in a very few, and
what is usually seen is subtle dissimulation designed to draw the confidence of others" (62). The few who refuse to pretend, who refuse to
play the stylized social game, who live in conformity with their truest
feelings, and who are on guard against their baser instincts can, despite
their natural bent, achieve authenticity and sincerity in the personal
realm that can then be extended to their relationship with others—not
a heroic remedy, perhaps, but nevertheless enough to liberate the individual from the infernal circle of blind self-seeking.

Far more than a detached observer, La Rochefoucauld examines the
human subjects that he sees as his own inner reflection, and offers
counsel for a more authentic means to live "à propos." Taken as a
whole, his maxims constitute a full-scale study of man that is both
psychological and social, one that continues and adapts the moral project of Montaigne and the humanists to the social reality of his own
age. All that he lacks as an essayist is a greater emphasis on his own
particular makeup and personal sentiment. Much of what relates to
these aspects can be deduced, however, from his moral view, which
reflects his own bitter disillusionment and yet reveals an anguished
hope that living without illusion can ultimately lead to a greater measure of self-knowledge and virtuous conduct.

Ten years younger than La Rochefoucauld, Blaise Pascal (1623–62)
shared similar views concerning man's condition in the natural state.
Yet the ultimate vision he held of human reality—that of man as a
creature ineluctably linked to God, wretched and unfulfilled until re-
united to Him—could not be more diametrically opposed to the latter's exclusively secular world view.

Of bourgeois background (his father, Etienne, was president of the
cour des aides of Monferrand, near Clermont), Pascal lost his mother
three years after his birth. Shortly thereafter, his father sold his post
and family estate in the Auvergne, and solidly investing his income,
moved with his three children to Paris, where he hoped to live an
untroubled and intellectually stimulating existence. Pascal never went
to school and was essentially educated by his father, whose aim it was
to give the youth not only the customary solid foundation in the hu-

manities but also a strong background in mathematics and science. For that reason Pascal's formation was somewhat unusual in that he did not learn Latin and Greek until he was twelve but was weaned first on mathematics and physics. He was, by all standards a child prodigy in those disciplines. When ten years old he had already deduced on his own the first book of Euclid's principles; a year later he wrote a treatise on sound, and at sixteen, the *Essai pour les coniques*. Three years afterward he invented a machine to perform arithmetic calculations; at age twenty-five, he had successfully concluded experimentation proving that nature does not abhor a vacuum but that physical pressures cause the void to be filled.

When in 1646 his ailing father was cared for by the Deschamps brothers—both recently converted to Jansenism—all of his family was favorably introduced to this austere and uncompromising form of Catholicism. Even though his father converted to the movement, Blaise, though deeply moved, continued his scholarly activities and his immersion in the mundane and fashionable world of Parisian salons, where he had come to know such famous agnostics as Théophile de Viau and Cyrano de Bergerac.

A year after his father's death in 1651, Pascal's sister Jacqueline, long a Jansenist convert, entered religious life and took the veil at the Convent of Port Royal, the spiritual heart of the movement. At first strenuously opposing his sister's intention, he even for a while opposed her desire to use her part of the family inheritance as a dowry for religious life. But he soon underwent a total change of heart through what has become a legendary conversion. On the night of 23 November 1654, a night of "fire," as he always referred to it, he felt himself placed in the very presence of God and filled with indescribable rapture. Emerging from this mystical experience, he became what in modern parlance we might call a born-again Christian. Now totally committed to the practice of religion and the Jansenist cause, he abandoned the comfort of his secure social and financial situation to embrace poverty and extreme asceticism.

Shortly after his conversion, Pascal began to write fragments for the outline of an apology with which he intended to lead to belief the agnostic and religiously indifferent among friends and associates of his worldly period. (Miton and Chevalier Méré are the two he specifically mentions in his notes.) He did not live long enough to bring his project to any kind of definitive completion, and at his death the apology was only skeletal, providing general themes (the grandeur and misery of man, the disproportionate state of man in the universe), broad lines of arguments to be used, and hundreds of fragmentary entries. In 1670, his many notes and jottings were published by the authorities of Port Royal under the title of *Pensées (Thoughts)*, and thereafter by many other editors, who employed various methods of arranging the fragments. In fact, the problem of how Pascal intended the "thoughts" to be ordered and arranged has never been completely resolved. Today there is virtually unanimous agreement that the most authentic version is that edited by Louis Lafuma, which itself is most probably based upon the earliest copy of Pascal's original manuscript.[23]

The approximately seven-hundred "thoughts" or entries that make up the work vary widely in length, form, and content. They range from incomplete phrases (*"Vanity.* the cause and effects of love: Cleopatra"); jottings and epigrams ("Our nature lies in motion; absolute rest in death"); extended reflections ("Imagination" or "Amusement"); occasional dialogues (the celebrated passage on "The Wager") between the author and his intended audience, whom he would wean from disbelief; and long moral tracts or discourses that are essays ("Man's Disproportion").

The author frequently employs the personal "I" in order to reveal the topics and means of approach he envisages for the apology ("I shall here write down my thoughts without arranging them, but not perhaps in deliberate disorder; that is the proper order, and it will convey my intentions by its very want of order"), or to reveal clearly as his own essential arguments ("For, I ask, what is man in Nature? A cypher compared with the Infinite, an All compared with Nothing, a mean between zero and all"). In his dialogues he frequently attributes to the imagined disbeliever remarks of this sort: "I confess and admit it. . . . Yes, but my hands are tied and my lips closed; I am forced to wager, and I am not free."

Yet it is somewhat paradoxical that Pascal, who employed the authorial "I" more frequently than any other of the moralists, thereby revealing his most personal thought patterns, also goes the furthest in denying its validity. He was, in fact, embarked on an essentially antihumanistic venture in this regard and was determined to destroy his contemporaries' confidence both in the self and in the ability of reason alone to arrive at a proper understanding of man's essential nature. In this respect he appears to be almost a disciple of Montaigne, who took the same delight in crushing human presumption and confidence in the rational faculties; and many of Montaigne's most telling

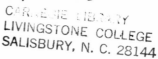

examples on these themes were borrowed wholesale by Pascal and used as powerful ammunition in the *Thoughts*. Yet whereas Montaigne found refuge in the self and proposed to develop a natural kind of wisdom gained through self-knowledge that could be used as a guide, Pascal turned his guns against the very notion that the self had a legitimate existence or reality, even holding that this fictitious concept was inimical to virtue: "The ego is hateful" (p. 79); and he also turned to ridicule the method of self-portraiture that Montaigne had created: "Montaigne's confusion; how he was aware of his want of method, which he tried to avoid by skipping from topic to topic; how he sought to be in fashion. The folly of trying to paint his own portrait" (p. 17).

Pascal nonetheless agreed with Montaigne that the proper study of mankind is man; and he further confessed that he himself had spent too much of his life dealing with "abstract sciences" ("for turning to the study of man I saw that [these] were alien to man" [p. 17]). Yet he would propose a method to conduct this enterprise based not on the findings of self-study or metaphysical theorizing but on a cogent analysis of man's dual reality—a creature in history and a being explained by Christian revelation. With those two considerations in mind, Pascal set out to paint a grim portrait of humanity, by nature mendacious, aggressive, cruel, never in repose, and always seeking diversions to forget its basic anguish while understanding neither its own makeup nor that of the universe. Human society accordingly manifests little reason, virtue, or order. There is no abiding justice on which any political or legal system may repose, no natural law upon which society is founded.

Not at home in the world of his own making, man is equally a misfit in the universe, precariously situated in an intermediary position between the finite and infinite—the micro-macro extremes of all existing matter—hence a prey to his own anguish:

For if a man will look at himself as I suggest, the sight will terrify him; and, seeing himself suspended in the material form given him by Nature, between the two abysses of Infinity and Nothingness, he will tremble beholding these marvels. (21)

Pascal's agnostic-atheist is compelled by these cogent and disturbing observations to divest himself methodically of any hedge allowing him to deny the sorry state of man in the physical universe. Led to this temporary dead end, he is then persuaded to accept the consolation offered by Christianity, which through its prophecies, miracles, and hope of salvation in Jesus Christ alone offers meaning and happiness for man.

The *Thoughts* therefore present a sustained, consequential, and comprehensive study of man. In them Pascal penetrated as deeply into the heart of the human person as Montaigne had done, and for those of strong religious convictions his findings are more profound because he neither diminished nor excluded man's spiritual dimensions by emphasizing only the natural self. Much the same can also be said when he is compared with La Rochefoucauld. Whereas the latter's focus was limited to the portrayal of the individual stifled by self-love in a cruel and artificial society, that of Pascal is cosmic and entails the spectacle of man set adrift, a prey to his own fears and inadequacies, a mere speck in the frightening void of the immeasurable universe. He also proposes a means by which the *honnête homme* may alleviate his angst-ridden condition; yet his antidote transcends La Rochefoucauld's counsel of sincerity of the heart to encompass a higher ideal—a leap to faith induced by the proper use of reason ("All our dignity then consists in thought. . . . Strive we then to think aright: that is the first principle of moral life")(83).

As a scientist writing an apology for Christian belief with the point of view of a moralist, Pascal was and remains an anomaly; and as a writer he virtually created a new prose style by couching emotionally charged, persuasive argumentation in lucid, restrained, and coolly analytic prose. No essayist has since more artfully combined those elements, and French writers from Voltaire on have been obsessed with Pascal's genius in fusing the intuitive ways of knowing (the *esprit de finesse*) with pure ratiocination (the *esprit de géométrie*) in his brilliant moral probings and have consciously striven to do the same. Nor have any essayists revealed more clearly in their writings their deepest convictions and most fundamental patterns of thought. Not only does Pascal belong to the essay tradition, then, but he must also be credited with moulding the genre into an admirable instrument for sustained and extremely persuasive philosophical exposition.

Jean de La Bruyère (1645–96), the third great moralist writer of the century, has traditionally been regarded as a social critic, and his major opus, *Characters,* is the first work of its kind in French literature. Writing during the last decades of Louis XIV's reign—the decadent period

characterized by economic and military decline and much social un-
rest—he had, as Sainte-Beuve has expressed it, "a corner seat in the
first loge to view the grand spectacle and high comedy of his age."

Born in Paris and trained as a lawyer (though he never practiced the
profession), he was appointed in 1684 through the good graces of his
friend Bishop Boussuet as tutor to the young Duc de Bourbon, grandson of the Grand Condé, and after two years in this position was named
a retainer (gentleman of the duke) for life. A spectator in the highest
echelons of society yet barred entry because of birth and economic dependence, La Bruyère was always made to feel an outsider and, resent-
ing his situation, had special incentive to give a sharp and objective
portrait of the ruling social class.

The *Characters,* published in successive editions from 1688 to 1696,
first took form as a somewhat whimsical translation and commentary
of the work of the same title by the Greek author Theophrastus, in
which he had provided irreverent and piquant sketches of his Athenian
counterparts. La Bruyère in fact used Theophrastus as a kind of smoke
screen to mask his own satirical intention. After his introduction, he
abandoned the order of character presentation employed by his Greek
predecessor (who had drawn general, somewhat abstract sketches systematically illustrating by enumeration Aristotle's ethical categories of
vices and virtues). Characterizing his own efforts as "less delicate" and
more concerned with the interior moral dimension of an individual
person, he set out to depict his characters in action—with illustrations
of their habits of speech, movements, facial expression, and the like.
He was not content, moreover, merely to define moral attitudes but
attempted to flesh out his characters by putting them in a specific
social context and by dramatizing their conduct. As finally constituted, the work numbered sixteen topical divisions given to such considerations as "Of Works of the Mind," "Of the Court," "Of the
Sovereigns of the State," "Of Fashion," and "Of Freethinkers." In these
chapters he linked epigrams, essaylike reflections, and an increasing
number of moral portraits to convey his observations and personal
views on man and society in his own period and in a universal sense.[24]

La Bruyère's working method was to introduce a series of thoughts
or themes through epigrams and reflections and to underscore their
veracity and relevance, he would then provide concrete illustrations
drawn from life. For example, in the section "Of Gifts and Fortune,"
he declares that "Nothing makes us better understand what trifling
things Providence thinks it bestows on men in granting them wealth,

money, dignities, and other advantages than the manner in which they are distributed and the kind of men who have the largest share.[25] This thoughtful reflection is followed almost immediately by a "portrait" graphically illustrating one such person on whom Providence had bestowed such gifts and presents, a boy abbott:

This youth, so ruddy, so florid, and so redolent of health, is lord of an abbey and of ten other benefices; they bring in altogether one hundred and twenty thousand *livres* a year, which are paid him in golden coin. Elsewhere there are a hundred and twenty indigent families who have no fire to warm themselves during winter, no clothes to cover themselves, and who are often wanting bread; they are in a wretched and piteous state of poverty. What an inequality. And does this not clearly prove that there must be a future state?[26]

Portraits such as the above immediately created a *succès de scandale* and were largely responsible for the wide popularity that greeted the work (in its many successive editions) since it was generally believed that La Bruyère had composed a roman à clef, using these literary portraits to designate actual contemporaries. Though there is undoubtedly some truth to the charge (given La Bruyère's bitterness and familiarity with important figures of society), he was just as intent on creating universal types rather than realistic facsimilies.[27] In the main, his literary characters consist of finely etched portraits of all manner of humanity—cruel courtiers, pretentious society women, and vulgar but wealthy tradesmen on the rise; then there are the archetypes—the glutton, the rich man, the poor man, the pedant, the hypocrite, and the like. These portraits are universal in their depiction of moral qualities yet concrete in the psychological and physical traits that give life to the individual personas.

As a social critic, La Bruyère provided profound study of his society that clearly designated its class structure and built-in inequities. As he viewed it, at the top there was a vain and arrogant nobility basely adulating a monarch who jealously (and blindly) defended his prerogatives. In the middle there was a venal and base bourgeoisie scrambling for power and recognition with their new-found wealth. At the bottom was the peasantry living in lamentable conditions, saddled with outrageous taxes, decimated by the king's wars, and slowly dying of hunger.

These strata were not defined and presented abstractly but were vividly brought to life through a method of writing that one modern critic

has termed literary impressionism.[28] La Bruyère in fact painted a series
of prose tableaux that taken together, constitutes an enormous fresco
in which are proffered vignettes drawn from life and illustrating the
nature and mechanism of society. One "sees" on this canvas vain and
shallow noblemen—kinds of domesticated animals—whose full-time
occupation is court life, a "serious and sad game requiring application";
wealthy bourgeois who "simply because they have grown wealthy have
the audacity to swallow in one morsel enough food to feed a hundred
families"; unscrupulous lawyers using the law only out of self-interest;
foppish abbés and wealthy priests who make a mockery of religion;
would-be writers and artists whose stock-in-trade are the ideas they
have pillaged from great authors; gilded fashion plates, and the shock-
ing but mute spectacle of the peasants. La Bruyère was, in fact, the
only writer of the century to give any sort of realistic portrayal of the
subhuman conditions of these wretched people. He writes of them:

One sees certain wild animals, male and female, scattered over the country,
black, livid, and burned by the sun, who are chained, as it were, to the land
they are always digging and turning over with an unquenchable stubborness;
they have a sort of articulate voice, and when they stand up, they exhibit
human features: they are men. . . .[29]

The element of social criticism, important as it may be, constitutes
only one part of the contents of *Characters* and should not be allowed
to overshadow the many moral reflections and personal asides therein.
La Bruyère in fact intersperses his work with literally hundreds of comments and thoughts and frequently provides his most personal opinions
on sundry matters such as art, authors, affections, love, women, youth,
age, religious belief, and death.

Despite the seeming logical arrangement suggested by such topics,
the juxtaposition of so many diverse and disconnected reflections gives
to *Characters* a much less formal structure than that of any of the other
works studied here (with the possible exception of Mme de Sévigné's
letters). For this reason, it is virtually impossible to draw up an adequate summation of La Bruyère's essential thought. In fact, close examination of the text reveals there to be no epicenter, no key works
such as La Rochefoucauld's *intérêt,* no central themes or concepts such
as Pascal's grandeur and misery of man, or Saint-Évremond's Epicurean
principles. Aside from the topical groupings, then, the work provides
no discernible continuity, and for this reason, critics have concluded

that by this random method it was La Bruyère's unexpressed intention to convey the many contradictions inherent in human nature and the resulting impossibility to posit any verities for it aside from fluidity of action and ever changing moods.

Because of its lack of structure, *Characters* has been judged to be a landmark work in French letters. Julien Benda claimed that La Bruyère in fact was the first French author to compose a work that was not organized about a central theme or topic, hence not subordinated to an aesthetic whole but rather presenting artistic prose of changing mood and tone for its own sake. In this respect he and other critics regard *Characters* as a pioneering work that sets the pattern for the impressionist prose style and fluid composition refined and advanced by Stendhal, Flaubert, and the Goncourt brothers in the nineteenth century.[30]

La Bruyère's influence on the development of the essay form as such is also significant. There is immediate proof of this in the enormous vogue that his "portrait" enjoyed in the following century as an essential component of the periodical essay. And in a more general sense *Characters* also influenced the techniques employed in that new form of the genre in which the essay ceased to be primarily a recording of the intimate reflections and musings of an author but rather embraced the broader function of serving as a mirror wherein a society could view its manners, moods, and foibles.

Far from perishing in the seventeenth century, the French essay survived, underwent fundamental changes and evolved in forms that would profoundly affect its subsequent development. From its initial model—a humanistic project of self-study—it was gradually transformed to encompass broader dimensions of human reality by no longer concerning itself exclusively with the individual but with human beings as members of a social aggregate, and with special emphasis on the tensions resulting from that problematical relationship.

From this most important shift in emphasis there resulted a flowering of moralist literature, with its penetrating study of conduct and motive applied in a universal sense but still intended to reeducate the *honnête homme* by making him aware of his foibles and of the sterile, artificial conventions of his social order. The seventeenth-century essayists—moralists in every sense—bent their efforts to like ends and provided ethical and social commentary stemming from their respective moral attitudes. Thus the essay's survival and evolution from its earlier manifestations along humanist lines (provided in the main by

Saint-Évremond and, to a lesser extent, by Balzac) was largely the result of its being grafted on to moralist prose forms, which favored
aphoristic expressions or more extended reflections of universal statement in disconnected pieces.

The Though Montaigne's model was thereby transformed through a decisive emphasis on social concerns, the seventeenth century "moralist-
essayists," if we may coin the expression, still substantially possessed
the essential attitudes and point of view associated with writers of the
genre. That is to say, they still had the temperament of the essayist.
Men and women of their times, intensely interested in their social
world, indeed often privy to it in its highest echelons, they nevertheless retained a certain distance from it and nourished an introspective
taste common to them all. They thus subjected their observations to
inner reflection and probings—though never to the degree pursued by
Montaigne—and forwarded their findings in prose works that reveal
their particular thought patterns and strongly held convictions, even
when couched in universal terms.

The essay itself passes from a form exclusively linked to Montaigne's
model to ultimately become an amalgam of forms, levels, and styles of
expression. Clearly in a stage of transition during the seventeenth century, it reveals itself to be a most supple instrument that can be applied
to moral probings, lucid analysis of philosophical themes, literary criticism, colorful portraiture, lively reportage of all manner of human
activity, and of incidental pieces of wit and humor. Finally, the special
predilection of French writers for composing brilliant and perceptive
studies on moral and philosophical problems in lucid and finely analytic prose can be seen already operating and adapting a form of the
essay to this end. Such, then, is the varied and rich legacy bequeathed
by seventeenth-century French essayists to those who will follow.

Chapter Three

The Essay in the
Age of Enlightenment

New Social and Cultural Patterns

The fortunes of the essay in the eighteenth century are inextricably linked to the era's changing political, social, and religious modes of thought and conduct. In the preceding century, the essay had served primarily as a means to educate the *honnête homme,* to make him aware of his role as a social being in a static, hierarchical society. Though small tears had begun to appear in the fabric of general belief in an absolute monarch and church, the major essayists had, in the main, elevated their views on human conduct and motive to a level of detached analysis, for they were fundamentally concerned with the reform of the individual and did not press for changes in social or political spheres. They provided, in sum, an essentially timeless, unchanging view of man's moral interior and of the period's social geography.

Such attitudes would not survive the political vacuum resulting from the death of Louis XIV. Indeed, the last two decades of his reign had constituted in reality only a delay for a society that, inwardly at least, was already in a state of serious decay. In fact, only by dint of his enormous prestige and massive consolidation of power had the Sun King been able in the final years to stem the mounting tide of disaffection and disillusionment that existed on all levels. Thus, when in 1715 the five-year-old Louis XV ascended to the throne, the facade of decency and order that Louis XIV's religiosity had imposed on the court vanished, to be replaced during the regency years by a pursuit of pleasure virtually unparalleled in French history.

The new social and moral climate created by this sudden relaxing of moral restraints is admirably illustrated by the *fêtes galantes,* or court diversions, that Watteau and Fragonard have immortalized in a number of their paintings. In them one sees courtiers in elegantly artificial garb plunged, through sumptuous and frivolous festivities, into a world of make believe—one in which the wretched social conditions of

the less privileged classes were banished from view. Professor Robert
Niklaus describes the function of the *fêtes galantes* as "a universal desire
for escape, for liberation, for freedom. . . . There were endless masked
fancy-dress balls symbolising the same desire to escape, from oneself
and from reality, by assuming another personality, and hiding behind
a mask, firework displays to dazzle eyes that did not wish to see things
as they were."[1]

Such sublime indifference to the realities of the day naturally accel-
erated a full-scale attack from below against the institutions of the
ancien régime because they callously fostered such frivolities at the expense of the poor and ambitious. Yet the moral indignation that this
spectacle of court life generated among the bourgeoisie and lower classes did not create a groundswell for moral reform and a return to the
rigid and puritanical society of the past decades. On the contrary, the
pleasure principle had already become well engrained in the middle
classes (particularly among the new, powerful group of magistrates con-
stituting the *noblesse de robe*), which aspired to their own proper share
of wealth, well being, and the free exchange of goods and ideas currently enjoyed by the reigning aristocracy. Those desires were sharp-
ened, moreover, by a decline in religious influence. Restraints
traditionally applied to worldly pleasures by religious belief and practice were therefore swept away, and the emphasis shifted to a frank and
immediate pursuit of the pleasure principle. It would not, in fact, be
inaccurate to describe the prevailing social climate as thoroughly he-
donistic. For example, in his poem *Le Mondain* ("The Man of the
World"), which he wrote in the first decade of the century, the young
Voltaire heaped scorn on the notion of asceticism of any kind and openly advocated the creation of a heaven-on-earth through the full enjoyment of all that civilization had to offer in physical and aesthetic
pleasures. "*Le Paradis terrestre,*" he states in the poem's conclusion, "*est
où je suis.*" Turned to that end, architecture, music, painting, sculpture, all flourished and reflected, as Professor Niklaus aptly puts it,
"the wit and elegance, the bravura, the aristocratic good taste and so-
phistication, and the growing scepticism of a troubled age, the final
flowering of a civilization about to disappear forever."[2]

In such a climate, social institutions that had formed and influenced
literary and intellectual tastes also changed markedly. The number of
salons did not diminish, but they ceased to idealize court life. In fact,
in the early part of the century there occurred a wholesale retreat by
the "fashionable" from Versailles to salons conducted in various sites in

and around Paris. The court therefore no longer constituted the very heart of social life. Indeed, sunk as it was in the grossest forms of gallantry-now-turned-to-debauchery, the court lost much of its appeal and luster. This is not to say that the salons were themselves untouched by the moral laxity of the period or noticeably opposed to the pleasure principle. (The Society of the Temple and the Salon of Ninon de Lenclos were in fact notorious for their own brand of licentiousness.) Yet eighteenth-century salons of such powerful women as the Duchesse de Maine, the Marquise de Lambert, Mme de Tencin, and Mlle de Lespinasse continued in the spirit and habits of Rambouillet to bring together a cross-section of the most important elements in French society—the fashionable and powerful, leading intellectuals, writers, and artists—thereby providing forums for the dissemination and exchange of ideas. Insisting on high standards of conversation and literary expression, such gatherings continued to be a major means by which writers could become known and circulate their works and ideas.

There was, however, a major difference in what could be discussed at these gatherings. As intellectual forums, these later salons were far more unrestrained, even audacious, in the liberty accorded to the introduction of new and "dangerous" concepts and ideas. In fact in some salons such as that of Mme Geoffrin, which Diderot, Helvétius, and D'Alembert regularly frequented, many of the new attitudes used to spearhead the rational assault of the *philosophes* against the beliefs and institutions of the old order were openly refined. For all that, the salons in general remained tied to aristocratic conventions and hence fixed limits as to how polite conversation might respectably stray from traditional or class-oriented attitudes. They have even been described as being in the long run, somewhat regressive since they remained attached to classical formulas of expression that tended to block the way to innovations of a decisive kind.[3]

It is certainly true that, by offering elegant forums for conversation, the salons greatly influenced the tone that essays written in the century would assume; yet other influences also existed. Another social institution, for example, that contributed more heavily to the form and content that many of the eighteenth-century essays were to take was the coffee house. Coffee had first been introduced as a beverage to Parisians by the Turkish ambassador around 1667. As the drink caught on, there soon grew a new kind of social life centered on "cafés" (coffee houses) or clubs. The most influential of these were located near the Pont Neuf (of which the best known was the Café Procope, established in 1687). Male havens from their inception, fashionably open to all new ideas, and sites of no-holds-barred debates among a motley clientele of fashion plates and intellectual hangers-on, the coffee houses became the new locus in and around which were written and sold a large number of clandestine essays on a diversity of forbidden subjects.

The Essay as Underground Literature

In an important work on French intellectual history of the period, Professor Ira O. Wade has carefully studied the phenomenon of these clandestine essays. At one point in the work, he quotes from a Parisian police dossier of 1729 (investigating a certain Mathieu Morléon), which admirably documents the practice as a whole:

There are in Paris some so-called intellectuals who in cafés and elsewhere talk about religion as if it were a chimera. Among others, M. Boindin has been spotted more than once in the Café Conti at the corner of the rue Dauphiné; and if we don't get them in order, the number of these atheists and deists will increase and many people will create a religion of their own, as in England.[4]

As to Mathieu Morléon's alleged activities, we learn that "he collects and sells copies of several works filled with impious sayings and maxims against the existence of God, the divinity and morality of Jesus Christ. Many people, Abbés and others, pay dearly for copies of these works."[5]

As Professor Wade further describes the phenomenon, clergymen, members of Parliament, connoisseurs and the intellectually curious bought copies of the manuscripts (some of which sold for as high as two-hundred *pistoles*), or had their secretaries reproduce them. The essays were obviously circulated in covert fashion to avoid official censorship; that they were numerous is manifested by the 102 titles alone that Professor Wade discovered in the *Catalogue général des manuscrits des bibliothèques publiques de France* and which deal in an unorthodox fashion with religion, natural theology, problems of morality, and politics. Generally inimical to the established church, these pamphlet-essays proposed sweeping changes along deist or Spinozist lines or, frankly atheistic, sought to liberate the reader from any form of belief in a deity.

Because in many instances the authors were anonymous, only a very few achieved notoriety in their own period. Of these the best known are Jean Meslier, whose *Testament* represents a vigorous attempt to make nature synonymous with matter and hence to create an ethical system based wholly on naturalist tenets; the comte de Boulainvilliers, whose *Essay de métaphysique* constituted a violent Spinozist attack on the historical veracity of the Bible (Voltaire would later give him the place of honor in his dialogue essay *Le dîner de Boulainvilliers*); and Jean de Mirabaud, secretary of the French Academy, whose *Opinions of the Ancients on the Nature of Man* was a pointed denial of the immortality of the soul and the existence of an afterlife.

A few of the other titles unearthed by Wade should be cited in order to indicate the audacious nature of the topics and themes that frequently reoccurred: *The Divinity of Jesus Christ Refuted*; *The Dissertation on the Resurrection of the Flesh, by the Author on the Treatise on Popular Errors*; *Pantheism or the Formula to Celebrate a Socratic Society*; *The Three Imposters* (Moses, Jesus, Mohammed); *An Examination and Censure of the Books of the Old and New Testament*.

Because most of these essays are available only in rare-book libraries and because the few that have been printed interest only specialists, we need linger no longer over their contents. Yet they deserve our brief consideration here. For such underground writings prefigure many of the thoughts and topics that would come into vogue later in the century, subjects that would be addressed in important essays by notable authors.

Early Philosophical Essays: Voltaire and Diderot

Two of the most important early manifestations of the eighteenth-century essay, Voltaire's *Lettres philosophiques* and Diderot's *Pensées philosophiques* reflect the spirit and attitudes of the earlier clandestine pieces. Both men were young when they wrote their works, in which they consciously assumed the role of *philosophe*, which Diderot would himself later glowingly describe as "the *honnête homme* who in all things acts according to reason, and who combines good morals and sociable qualities with a mind disposed toward reflection and precision."[6]

The *Lettres philosophiques* (or *Lettres anglaises*, as the work is sometimes entitled) is a journalistic rendition of the observations and impressions gained by the "tourist" Voltaire during his nearly three years of exile in England (1726–29). He writes the work while still smarting from the indignation and disgrace of having been soundly beaten by the Chevalier de Rohan's lackeys for having purportedly insulted the nobleman's reputation with the quip, "I'm beginning *my* name while you are finishing yours." As a bourgeois, Voltaire was not allowed, however, to defend his honor personally but was forced to submit to the humiliation of a public thrashing. Now on English soil, he obviously took special delight in pointing out to his countrymen the social and political injustices of their country, outrages rendered more odious through a comparison with English institutions, attitudes, and way of life.

On the surface the book seems to be informally, even casually composed by a somewhat ingenuous observer who reports without guile on whatever he observes; the style is neither detached nor scholarly, but rather warm and chatty. Yet the author often barely conceals (if he does so at all) his deep-seated resentment at the lack of "enlightenment" present in his native land when it is contrasted to England.

In the first four chapters, he feigns amazement at the proliferation of religious sects and some of their "outlandish customs" (notably those of the Quakers). Then observing, "This is a country of sects. An Englishman as a free man goes to Heaven by whatever road he pleases,"[7] he makes one of his most telling comparisons. Moreover, he continues, odd as the Quakers may seem to be to the French Catholic, one of their number (William Penn) established in America

a new sort of spectacle: that of a sovereign who everyone familiarly "thees and Thous" and speaks to with one's hat on; a government without priests, a people without weapons, citizens all of them equals—magistrates excepted— and neighbors free from jealousy.[8]

Next Voltaire praises the legal wisdom of the English system and gives a history of that nation's evolution from serfdom, civil war, and dissensions, to the creation of a society of law based on the great English Charter. There he states, no man is above the law; priest and nobility have no special legal privileges; and all are subjected to taxation. He argues that such enlightened principles have created a climate wherein scientific, artistic, and economic development has thrived. English academic institutions have produced the two greatest geniuses of the past hundred years: John Locke and Isaac Newton. Furthermore, the theory of the "Vortex tourbillons" proposed by Descartes to explain the movement of the universe pales in comparison with Newton's system of attraction: "I do not think one can truly compare his [Descartes's] philosophy with Newton's. The first is an experimental sketch, the second, a finished masterpiece."[9]

For a man of Voltaire's business sense and ardent desire to achieve wealth, the favored social position of the successful English merchant is strikingly different from that of his own society, "where the merchant himself often hears his profession spoken of so disdainfully that he is fool enough to blush." Continuing, tongue-in-cheek, he feigns not to know who is more useful,

a well-powdered lord who knows precisely what time the king gets up in the morning, and who gives himself airs of grandeur while playing the role of the slave in a minister's antechamber or a great merchant who enriches his own country . . . and contributes to the well-being of the world.[10]

For the artist, writer, or man of learning England also provides not only recognition but a standard of living not possible in France. In fact, Englishmen of singular talent have made their fortunes and held positions of importance: "Mr. Newton was minister of the mint: Mr. Congreve held an important office . . . Doctor Swift is a Dean in Ireland. In France, however, artists and authors are more likely to die of hunger."[11]

Finally Voltaire uses the *Letters* to attack the French author who seems to him to best personify those religious beliefs that are most antithetical to the progressive systems realized by England—the illustrious Pascal. Taking him to task in a long chapter, "On the Pensées of M. Pascal," Voltaire maintains that the latter's primary intention was "to show mankind in an odious light. . . . And for that he eloquently insults the human race."[12] Carefully selecting certain of Pascal's "thoughts," Voltaire rips off its very foundation Pascal's vision of man in metaphysical anguish. Man, Voltaire posits, is not "double," as Pascal holds, but far more changeable by nature: "He is composed of a countless number of parts"; thus he is not an enigma; his variations are most explainable: "Man appears to be where he belongs in nature, superior to the animals, which he is like, inferior to other beings, which he resembles in thought. He is, like all we see, a mixture of good and evil, of pleasure and pain."[13]

Voltaire ends by declaring that delivered from the mystery of existence, man can thus achieve a full measure of happiness in this life; he is not a stranger to the earth but has it as his home; thus he should bend all his efforts to better the human condition in all respects.

When Diderot surreptitiously had the *Pensées philosophiques* published over a decade later in 1746, he also indicated that he was heavily influenced by the themes of the clandestine essayists. In fact, as the well-known Diderot scholar Professor Arthur Wilson tells us, the work itself was sold "through various bootlegging techniques and was quickly condemned by the Parlement de Paris which observed that 'The *Pensées* presents to restless spirits the venom of the most criminal and absurd opinion that the depravity of human reason is capable of. . . .'"[14]

The title of Diderot's work suggests what is in fact a marked resemblance in content and form to Pascal's apology. Composing his *Pensées* as sixty-two aphorisms, Diderot consciously imitates Pascal's own method. Yet the content could not be more diametrically opposed to the Jansenist views of Pascal and indeed to much of orthodox Christian belief itself. Essentially, the essay provides a forum in which the author can discuss and debate claims and counterclaims of the three positions of skepticism, deism, and atheism as each deals with the truth or falsity of religious belief. In fact, though not individuated through identification with distinct personas, the entries nonetheless give the impression of being parts of a lively conversation/dialogue among three participants.

The most convincing arguments advanced are those of the deist persuasion, all of which appear to be almost as negative to orthodox Christian beliefs as atheism itself. Regarding the traditional image of God, for example, we read:

As to the portrait that is given me of the Supreme Being, on his penchant to become angry, on the rigor of his vengeance, on certain comparisons which enumerate for us the rapport of those whom he allows to perish and those to whom he deigns to help, the most just would be tempted to hope that he indeed does not exist at all. . . .[15]

Diderot goes so far as to say that the greatest threat to belief in God is the point of view of the traditional "superstitious" believer, be he of Jansenist or Jesuit persuasion. For in philosophical debate, "the deist alone can stand up the atheist"; the superstitious person is not effective since "His God is a being existing only in his imagination."[16]

Perhaps the most important theme of the *Pensées* is a strong plea for tolerance and diversity in matters of religious belief: "The question of God is so profoundly complex: 'What is God? a question we give children and one which philosophers have a great deal of trouble answering.'"[17] The deist therefore has particular compassion for skeptics saying, "I pray to God for skeptics since they lack the light."[18]

With these early works, Voltaire and Diderot create a new form of the essay—the philosophical discussion in the form of a letter or discourse—which would become a popular vehicle to disseminate the essential attitudes and teachings of the *philosophes* in their assault on traditional beliefs and institutions. Falling somewhere between Montaigne's familiar model and the serious or formal essay treatise, such a new format (which I designate as "the epistolary essay") allows the writer to advance an argument or point of view clearly presented as his own that he holds deeply, even passionately; and by a convincing use of logic and often brilliant (or dazzling) rhetorical skills, the writer attempts to win over the designated audience as if he had the opportunity to engage it in a conversation. The epistolary essay differs from Montaigne's model in the strong reluctance, even resistence of the eighteenth-century writer to provide self-revelatory detail or to be involved in the process of self-disclosure for its own sake. Whatever personal details may be given are therefore usually secondary to the main goal of convincingly and attractively presenting a thesis that the writer would share with the reader. As such, these conversational exercises are clearly essay forms since they reveal an author's innermost convictions, thought processes, and skills in argumentation and persuasion in a literary context.[19]

The Formal Essay

The eighteenth century also develops a vogue for another kind of essay, less personal, more tightly constructed, often of great length, and with little of the impassioned or conversational tone of the essays just analyzed. With increasing frequency this more formal essay uses the designation *essai,* and its avowed purpose is to present a tentative statement or study on a topic that is not intended to be exhaustive but rather a kind of dry run in thinking out or formulating ideas.

Gustave Lanson has credited the reappearance and relatively common use of this form not to a revival of interest in Montaigne's works, nor to a somewhat overdue hommage to his memory, but rather to the strong influence that such English models as Dryden's *Essay on Lyric Poetry* (1668) or of course John Locke's monumental *Essay on Human Understanding* (1690) had been exerting on French thinkers for a half-century or more. It can be said, then, that transplanted anew in French soil, the term essay had by the beginning of the century lost virtually all of its identity with Montaigne's project and became instead largely synonymous with philosophical/literary/ethical works traditionally identified in French with the terms *traité, histoire, discours, considerérations* (to mention the most frequent), all of which served to cast a writer's ideas in formal, scholarly prose.

Limiting my study here only to those works entitled *essai,* I can only introduce a few landmark essays of the period, which in many respects are the sources of scholarly articles or treatises published in such enormous volume by university or commercial presses in our day. Of major importance as a philosophical treatise was the Abbé Condillac's *Essai sur l'origine des connaissances humaines,* published in 1746. Throughout the work the abbé reveals the strong influence exerted on him by Locke's essay of similar title. Building on the Englishman's philosophy of sensation, Condillac develops the thesis that sensations and ideas were both equally important as primary sources of experience (though he regards thought to be an analytic faculty that had developed after the more primitive operation of understanding). The abbé's major aim in this scholarly exposition is to cast doubt on metaphysical theories purporting to explain the operation of the mind and to replace them with a methodology based on observation and empirical analysis that he wishes to adapt from mathematics and the physical sciences.

Also important in this essay is the theory that Condillac provides to explain the origins of human language. As he develops it, he claims that language evolved through a number of stages—first, that of body movements; second, a period in which gestures gradually evolved to a conscious imitation of the sounds of nature. Then these articulated sounds were made to designate objects or phenomena. Ultimately Condillac regards the development of language as linked to characteristics stemming from race, climate, and forms of human society and government.

Condillac's essay is of major importance in the century because it was the principle vehicle to disseminate the principles of Lockean psychology to the French. It also served as a catalyst to inspire other thinkers of the period (Rousseau in particular) to develop similar theories on language, its origins and its role in civilizing man.

Finally, this essay is an excellent example of the use and meaning that eighteenth-century writers attached to the term *essai* as a literary form. Condillac clearly regarded it as an exercise that permitted him to test his ideas on psychology before he presented them as fact in his definitive *Traité des sensations* (1754). The concept of the *essai* as a dry run or tentative expression of ideas was therefore very much in evidence in formal manifestations of the genre of the period.

Much of the same use of the essay obtains in Rousseau's *Essai sur l'origine des langues* (1761). First conceived as a kind of footnote appended to the *Discours sur l'inégalité*, it gradually developed into a full-scale study. The work represents an amalgam of borrowings from Condillac's *essai*, Rousseau's own private theories on language touched upon but not worked out in the two *Discours*, as well as theories suggested by works on music that he had completed (*Dissertation sur la musique moderne* [1743], and *Lettre sur la musique française* [1753]).

Though he conducts his own theory of language development through the stages that Condillac had established, Rousseau differs sharply with him by refusing to grant his contention that some kind of society as such had already been established when man was at that crucial point of forming signs or words with fixed, permanent meanings. For Rousseau, language itself had established social stratifications. Clearly predating society, language was, moreover, an important cause for the inequalities that natural man was to be subjected to (such as private property and unequal divisions of labor). In fact, he contends that language was that force that both caused man to be cut off from the state of nature and that created the strongest bonds of class slavery.

In the second half of the essay Rousseau then charts the slow but inevitable decadence that he recognized in language forms and usage. After a brief "Golden Age" in which man had struck a satisfying equilibrium in expressing (and satisfying) his physical and sensual needs, he gradually lost the sound of nature's voice speaking in him and emerged from his primitive state. "Tone deaf" to his vital origins, he was no longer governed by natural but by positive laws (conversations, contracts, discourses) that bit by bit enslaved him. His vital earlier language (sounds of nature) was replaced by "la vaine parole," by a form of "bavardage" devoid of all passionate and living content. Language, like man, became worn out and lost command of older, authentic human sounds and accents. It was now primarily used as the means of imposing tyrannical expressions; lacking in any natural eloquence, it was only suited henceforth to demand servile obedience. It was about this time, Rousseau claims, that society had taken on its definitive form. Change would only be effected therafter through exchange of property titles or pieces of money.

Rousseau ends his essay by comparing the speech of modern man with that of his primitive forebears. There is, he stated, a new but similar silence. The savage was aware only of moments passing in fleeting succession. The Parisian of the present also lives in a state of ennui and inaction; hence he is a prisoner of fugitive, fleeting moments. Language has become merely the droning words uttered "on the divans of cultivated society"[20] and man's history ends with a paralyzing repetition of its origins. Language—now debased and having become even an antilanguage—has succeeded in closing the prison door behind which modern man is incarcerated, a stranger to himself and to others. The only remedy that Rousseau suggests to alleviate this tragic and somber fall is the liberating effect that the pure words of music—that relic of man's harmony of expression in a Golden Age—may have in releasing him from the prison that human language has developed.

Jean Le Rond D'Alembert's *Essai sur les éléments de philosophie ou sur les principes des connaissances humaines* (1759) constitutes a valuable document indicating how this celebrated mathematician-philosopher viewed the progress of lights at midcentury. He remarks on the rapid and unprecedented changes and events "which shake us, our mores, our occupations, and even our conversations. . . ." In the midst of this heady intellectual upheaval, he attempts to "define the nature and limits of this revolution whose consequences and advantages our posterity will better understand than we."[21]

D'Alembert saw the retreat of the limits of the Enlightenment as the essential movement of his century. In his *Essai sur les moeurs et l'esprit des nations,* Voltaire takes that notion and applies it to the march of civilization as a whole. Written during the period from 1740–56 for Mme de Châtelet (who had constantly complained of her total lack of interest in historical matters), this massive, land-breaking essay is nothing less than Voltaire's conscious attempt to rival Newton's intellectual accomplishments. For just as Newton had shed "the eternal light of reason" on the physical universe and discovered its laws, so Voltaire aimed to do the same on the history and civilization of mankind. More concretely, Voltaire wished to continue Bossuet's prestigious work, *Discours sur l'histoire universelle,* (which the venerable churchman had ended with the reign of Charlemagne), to the beginning of Louis XIV's monarchy. And in the bargain, he relished the prospect of challenging Bossuet's working thesis that history should be interpreted in terms of the Christian drama: that it was guided and animated by Divine Providence, whose focal point was the history of the Jewish nation. Such an ambition also made necessary a reexamination of other major civilizations (Chinese, Indian, Arab), which, Voltaire felt, Bossuet had slighted. Before he could expand his history up to modern times, he would therefore have to reinterpret and rewrite huge segments of human history.

In his study Voltaire substituted for the principle of Divine Providence the element of chance, which, he believed, constantly dominates human events. In so doing, he not only opposed Bossuet but also contested Montesquieu's celebrated theory of causes. Instead, Voltaire saw man in history as a constant prey of passions and folly, and the history of mankind itself, from early states of barbary to the present, as nothing more than "a mass of crimes, follies, misfortunes, among which we have seen some virtue, some happy periods, just as we happen upon dwellings located, here and there, in savage deserts."[22] Yet he could regard this assortment of horrors without despairing. Certain perceptible signs of progress had been registered, he felt, particularly in his own century. Moreover, he contended that "in the midst of these plunderings and destruction observed in the space of nine-hundred years we have seen a love of order that has secretly animated the human race and which has prevented its total ruin."[23]

Not only remarkable for its scope and philosophy, the essay is also a landmark work in historiography because of its successful attempt to synthesize the general theme—the slow rise of human intelligence—with particular aspects of civilization, local color, and vignettes drawn from the social life of all the periods dealt with. He concentrates, not as earlier historical writers had done by relating the history of wars and great events or exemplary actions of heroes, but rather on the history of peoples, the ideas that distinguished each group, intellectual movements, currents of thought in religion, the state of belles lettres, and conditions of life. Voltaire was also the first historian to extend his considerations to include a study of commerce, industry, and agriculture as indexes of civilization. He also provided anecdotes that have since become proverbial (Newton and the apple, Columbus and the egg). He sought, in sum, to provide a complete portrait of the material and intellectual state of the lives of peoples not only belonging to his own civilization of Europe, but also of Asia and the New World.

Though the staggering amount of matter that he deftly sifts through the work has since been judged remarkably free of factual error, the work is partisan and strongly colored by its author's adverse view of Christianity (for him the living essence of fanaticism and barbarism). Accordingly, he refused to credit it with any major civilizing influence on mankind throughout the course of history. In contrast, he painted the influence of Hinduism, Buddhism, and Islam in highly favorable terms since he felt that these religions, less mired in dogma or theology, were more reasonable and more enlightened. Despite this major flaw, the essay set the mould for works on universal history up to our own day.

If one wished to designate a single formal essay written in the century as quintessential in form and matter, Baron D'Holbach's *Essai sur les préjugés* (1770) would be an appealing choice. Written by a fervently committed atheist freethinker—one whose considerable fortunes were generously expended to advance the philosophical battle against "fanaticism" of all kinds—the essay is an ambitious diagnosis of the nature and evils of prejudice, how it arises, infects human beings, and is transferred from age to age.

The 300-page tome is both sharply polemical in tone and ponderously repetitive in composition. Through it all Baron D'Holbach never relinquishes his dogged intention "to write a reasoned apology for a philosophy which, in all periods, has been denigrated by rascals and fools"; and he strongly maintains that much remains to be done since "apostles of falsehood even now continue to be strongest amongst us."[24]

The essay methodically explores such topics as the source of prejudice, the utility of truth, the advantages of reason, the nature of true philosophy, the necessity for one to abandon speculative goals and to direct his activity to immediate social ends; and the need to make philosophy the watchdog against superstition in literature, art, and all areas of learning.

A major portion of the text is dedicated to deploring the small number of "reasonable" people—those not victims of prejudice—in the author's day. But most people, he laments, continue to be victimized by sundry scoundrels and tyrants. The major villains among the exploiters are predictably designated as "ministers of religion who, having become in every country the principal teachers of the people, have vowed eternal hatred against reason, science, and truth."[25]

Despite this bleak assessment, much enlightenment optimism shines through the essay. Human beings, D'Holbach insists, are only unhappy, close-minded, and contentious because during childhood they have been forced to wear blindfolds fashioned by false teachers. People can be reasonable, he insists, if permitted to be so; and man is perfectible provided he has been inculcated with a proper moral foundation.

D'Holbach pins his hope for improvement on the influence of the true philosopher, the free man, "apostle of reason and truth who does not tremble before these dreaded chimeras." He it is who must animate others with "love of the human race, the desire to serve one's species and to merit its esteem; for these are the matters that should motivate men of good will."[26]

The Periodical Essay

Despite the vogue enjoyed by the formal essay, it would be false to regard it as the predominant form that the genre was to take in the century, or even as representing the best essays written. The most free-wheeling of literary forms, the essay did not remain congealed for long in the scholarly English mould, which was only one of a number of forms to continue. In fact another English model had already been imported into France—the periodical essay. Known chiefly today as novelist and playwright, Pierre Carlet de Chamberlain de Marivaux dedicated fully a quarter of his literary output to composing purely literary essays in the mode of the English *Tatler* and *Spectator*; and in little more than ten years he composed three collections of essays: *Spectateur français* (1722); *Indigent philosophe* (1728); and the *Cabinet du philosophe* (1734).

Initially Marivaux's intention was to provide a continuing series of essays on a wide range of topics like those of his English counterparts, Addison and Steele. The *Spectateur français* never achieved, however, the degree of regularity enjoyed by the popular *Tatler* (three issues a week in folio half-sheet from 1709–11), or still less than that of the immensely successful *Spectator* (which appeared daily from 1711–12, and then eighty times in 1714). The publication of the French periodicals was intermittent at best: twenty-five issues for the *Spectateur français;* seven for the *Indigent philosophe;* and eleven for the *Cabinet du philosophe*, with weeks to months intervening in the last two series.

The English model was primarily the creation of Steele, with Addison providing no more than a quarter of the pieces. Newsworthy, unabashedly informal, and unlike the dry moral sermons of the Puritan period, the *Spectator* and *Tatler* purported "to recommend truth, innocence, honor, and industry as the chief ornaments of life." Intended to be read in the evening (when they in fact appeared), they strived to capture the intimacy and familiarity of conversation around a tea table and were much less introspective, less personal, and certainly less consciously learned than Montaigne's model.

The audience was by-and-large not intellectual but consisted of the growing number of middle-class readers. As to topics, Addison referred to two types of *Spectator* papers: "serious essays" on such perennial topics as love, marriage, death, friendship, education, and religion; and "occasional papers" presenting any number of satirical commentaries on "the folly and extravagence" of the age: women's fashions, dueling, country-vs.-city life, servants, the cries of London hawkers. Of particular importance was the presentation of several character portrayals drawn throughout the series: Mr. Spectator, Sir Roger de Coverley, Sir Andrew Merchant, and Captain Sentry, to mention a few of the most important.

In the *Spectateur français* Marivaux also provided many such La Bruyère-like character sketches, but he considerably broadened their scope by adding moral dimensions that extended beyond social criticism or satire. In fact, the "Spectator" declares himself to be a philosopher who forces his discipline "to emerge from private studies and libraries."[27] Thinking and writing "not as an author but as a man," he prefers to deal with incidents presented to him by chance rather than with those requiring ingenious or applied research. More the moralist than the philosopher, he holds that observations seized immediately from life are more expressive of human nature and conduct than abstract reflection. Not a judge, then, but "the most human of men," not wealthy but on the same level with the good people of Paris (who pass with instantaneous necessity from good to evil actions), he saunters through the city, recording what he sees.[28]

Many of the *feuilles* (issues) are simply accounts of his ambulatory strolls. In one, while leaving the Comédie Française and ruminating on the "sublime" tragedy *Romulus* by LaMotte, which he has just seen, he suddenly becomes aware of the stark, threatening aspect of the many human faces he meets. Most seem engaged in a fight to impose the view that they have of themselves on others: The women, whether ugly or fair, demand to be recognized as beautiful; young men demand that others affirm their arrogance and strength. In this vision, Marivaux finds sharply defined social battles and concludes that society does function along these lines: we form varying relationships of domination and servitude even in such superficial areas as demeanor, bearing, and attractiveness.

In another "outing" he describes the ceremonious entry of the three-year-old Infanta of Spain into the city. In the midst of all that splendor, the Spectator enters the shop of a poor cobbler who, despite the spectacle blithely continues to mend shoes. When asked to comment on the event, this "basic Socrates" declares himself to be untouched by such a magnificent display of wealth; from this the Spectator declares that it is the wisdom of the cobbler to be content with his lot.

The Spectator's direct narration of chance meetings, experiences, and reflections on what he sees makes up only about half of the twenty-five issues. The rest are written in the form of letters that the Spectator claims to have solicited (as did Addison) through a letter bureau: in one, a young girl writes to describe the dangerous effects of a rigid and austere religious upbringing that her "devout" mother has imposed upon her; in another, a pregnant and abandoned young woman writes to repent of her imprudence in succumbing to the blandishments of her heartless lover; in another, a man writes to describe the avarice of his wife in terms worthy of a Balzac and asks for counsel and help to prevent him from murdering her. There are also memoirs of various personages (a Spanish traveler in Paris, the confessions of an aging coquette, the autobiography of "an unknown man"). The remainder of the material consists of articles or direct commentaries supplied by the editor of such sundry matters as the malevolence of critics, the shallowness of leading wits, the fickleness of men and women in love, and the like.

The last two volumes of Marivaux's essay trilogy are just as eclectic in content and as filled with moral reflections. Yet the author creates for each an entirely different persona to relate and present the topics. In the *Beggar Philosopher* the Spectator has been replaced by a vagabond no longer living in Paris but who has "passed five hundred leagues beyond." Originally the scion of a wealthy family, he has squandered his inheritance and now lives from hand to mouth. Not the least oppressed by his poverty, he has become a genial "Diogenes of the streets" who exuberantly proclaims the joy of life. A disciple of Montaigne, he strongly proclaims that "nature is an excellent mother. When fortune abandons its children *she* will not desert them."[29]

Throughout the seven issues, the beggar weaves a narrative of his picaresque existence and the many escapades that have led him from poverty to the role of leading actor in a wandering troupe. The saga of his personal adventures is constantly interrupted by a torrent of moral asides (really free associations) flowing from a penetrating but unrestrained or undisciplined intelligence. Totally opposed to Stoical control

or the false front that others use to project untrue images of the self,
he is ever the natural man whose portrait is his mirror: "There is not
the slightest bit of prudence in this face . . . I will give my reader a
portrait without cares."[30]

The Philosopher's Study was written at one sitting in the summer of
1733. To establish the persona of this narrative, Marivaux uses the
conventional device of a recently found chest of documents. Their author, a man well known and respected for his great intelligence and
wisdom, had recently died without having published any of his writings, and the eleven chapters of the work thus represent the fruits of
his random reflections and literary diversions.

Of the three essay series, the Philosopher's Study is by far the most
rambling and disconnected. It contains neither the artful orchestration
of themes in the Spectateur, nor the autobiographical filament of the
Beggar Philosopher to give it structure. A pot pourri of literary forms
then in vogue, it contains fairy tales, allegorical exercises ("The Road
to Fortune" and "The Country of I Know Not"), an imaginary voyage
("Journey to the Real World"), dialogues, personal memoirs, and reflections ("serious, gay, moral, and Christian").

Despite its tremendously eclectic contents and purposely disjointed
format, the last series contains some of Marivaux's most serious, personal comments on a broad range of moral topics. Assuming the identity of a mature, wise, and detached philosopher well experienced in
life, he goes beyond his previous attacks against the injustices of the
social order to ponder the mystery of human existence, the paradoxes
of human nature and conduct, the instability of love, the battle of the
sexes, and the perplexing nature of religious belief, to mention a few.
No longer as flippant and ready to engage in "badinage," the philos-
opher-turned-sage is now far more detached and reflective, often
couching his observations in moralist maxims.

The Essay and Art Criticism

To Diderot belongs the distinction of adapting the essay form to art
criticism. Before he wrote the Salons, several formal essays on aesthetics
and art theory had been published and enjoyed wide circulation. In his
Réflexions critiques sur la poésie et la peinture (1719), Abbé J. B. Dubos
broke away from the classical concept of fixed and immutable forms of
beauty; linking art to social ends, he also developed what has been
called the earliest sociology of art. Père André, in the Essai sur le beau

(1741), took an opposing view and sought to return to the concept that there existed eternal underlying criteria for beauty. In his *Essai sur le goût*, Montesquieu argued convincingly for a humanistic, man-oriented system of aesthetics. Holding that taste depended upon analogies or relationships established between the senses and exterior objects, he went on to postulate that the source of beauty resided not in the object itself but as it was perceived in the mind and heart of the viewer.

Diderot's essay title "Salons" refers to special showings of painting and sculpture held every two years in the Grand Salon of the Louvre. Baron Grimm, a close friend and well-known critic, asked Diderot to cover the Salon showings for the *Correspondance littéraire* (a private newsletter on cultural activities in the Paris area which was circulated throughout Europe in manuscript form) which Grimm was editing. Diderot agreed to take on the assignment and wrote articles on various Salon exhibitions during the years 1759–81. Ironically, as was the case with many of his other major essays, none of these Salon articles were published until well after his death, when the *Correspondance littéraire* was finally printed in 1812.

Before Diderot wrote his art essays, artistic journalism of this kind had not existed in France, or for that matter, in Europe. In fact, very little communication then existed between artists and professional writers. Art literature that was extant consisted mainly of official minutes of Royal Academy meetings (presumably of interest only to specialists) or of the kind of treatises mentioned above, which were predominantly theoretical in content. In his reportage, Diderot adopted an ambulatory, impressionistic approach. He would pass before the works of art, halting before those that particularly struck his fancy or elicited his disapproval. He showed himself selective in his tastes and gave the most of his commentary during the period to a handful of painters: J.-B. Van Loo, Jean-Baptiste Chardin, François Boucher, Philippe Lutherbourg, Jean-Baptiste Greuze, Joseph Vernet, and Maurice Latour.

The most striking feature of his articles is the exhaustive and minute pictorial description he provides for his reader when any work of art captures his interest. This close description is very understandable when one remembers that, before the invention of the camera, most of his readers could never hope to travel to see these works and thus expected such complete treatment. The other dominant feature is Diderot's strong penchant to provide, when at all applicable, a moral analysis of the characters and themes presented pictorially.

As a result, the *Salons* contain long and often emotionally charged passages describing in intimate terms such subjects as "The Bride's Toilet" (Baudoin, 1767), which depicts the timid preparations of a young woman to meet her husband at the nuptial bed;[31] or Greuze's "The Ungrateful Son" (1765), in which a rake returns arrogant and unrepentant to the bedside of his dying father and is alone unperturbed by the sad spectacle.[32]

Diderot's tendency to moralize throughout the *Salons* on such maudlin subjects often severely limits his appeal to modern readers; it also somewhat restricts his critical range of vision. A painting is worthy of praise, he believes, only if it elicits exemplary moral sentiments on the part of the viewer. In one instance he goes as far as to say: "Artists, if you are jealous or care for the lasting fame of your work, I advise you to limit yourselves to upright moral topics. Anything that induces corruption is doomed to destruction."[33]

In spite of his moralistic preoccupation, Diderot nonetheless is often a good and reliable critic. For example, he highly regards Chardin even though that artist's subjects were often devoted to still-life motifs and not to sentimentalized topics; and in reviewing these canvases Diderot is keenly perceptive of the magic in Chardin's artistry—his superb technical skills and expert use of color. Referring to some still-life models that Chardin had reproduced—biscuits, vases, olives, wine in a glass—Diderot was moved to declare: "O Chardin, it is not white, red, or black that you crush on your palette, but the very substance of objects; it is the air of light that you bring to the point of your brush and that you attach to the canvas."[34]

The Dialogue Essay

As a literary form, the dialogue provides an essayist with an admirable means by which to reveal and dramatize his most essential patterns of thought; and through the dyamics of conversation he has, moreover, an unsurpassed opportunity to refine and explore nuances of the idea presented. Finally, the dialogue allows for a more spontaneous, less abstract means through which to direct philosophical or intellectual disquisition by the use of real or fictional agents who embody and forward arguments and discussions through personal oral reaction and commentary.

The first French models of any consequence were developed by such seventeenth-century writers as Fontenelle and Fénelon. In *Entretiens sur la pluralité des mondes* (1686), Fontenelle simulates a conversation that takes place one starry evening in a magnificent garden between himself and an attractive marquise. He uses the occasion to instruct the intelligent but untrained lady on basic elements of astronomy: the existence and location of celestial bodies, the Copernican system, and the speaker's theories of possible habitation of the moon and other planets by superterrestrials. What ensues is an elegant exchange wherein expressions of gallantry are pleasantly intermingled with scientific exposition of fact. Fénelon wrote *Les Dialogues des morts* (1712) as a pedagogical tool to instill virtue and a sense of public duty in his young pupil the Duke of Burgundy, grandson of Louis XIV. The dialogues are conversational exchanges between illustrious ancients (Confucius, Socrates, Plato) and moderns (Mazarin, Henry IV, Richelieu, and others). All draw from their personal experiences to discuss such matters as patriotism and the need for virtue in politics and valor in battle.

In the eighteenth century the dialogue essay was most frequently used by Voltaire and Diderot and most brilliantly developed by the latter. Most of Voltaire's dialogues are minor or incidental pieces; as such, they express his major ideas and themes in a more direct (often even simplistic) fashion than in his longer treatises in prose or poetry. They therefore provide an excellent mirror to reflect the major themes that he continued to advance, and even to belabor. Among the best examples are pieces contained in the *Dictionnaire philosophique* (1764). Under this title he grouped, without any order other than by alphabetical arrangement, brief essays on a broad number of philosophical-religious topics.[35] The articles vary considerably in length and tone (some serious, others indignant, acerbic, or mocking); they are invariably spiced with touches of malice and irony suitable to the polemical attack in progress. A veritable hodgepodge, the pieces of the *Dictionnaire* are illustrative of what Faguet earlier described as "The clear chaos of ideas" which, he claimed, characterize Voltaire's philosophical writings.

In these essays Voltaire's frequent use of dialogue form can in most cases be reduced to two basic patterns: the simple person (distinguished not by formal education but good common sense) is engaged in conversation by a learned pedant (the mouthpiece for the dogmas of institutions Voltaire wished to attack). The naive interlocutor, of course, consistently confounds the learned voice by a process of right thinking based on natural lights.

In the article "God," for example, the theologian Logomachos (lit-

erally, windy word maker) pompously asks the sheep farmer Dondinac
whether or not matter is eternal. The shepherd responds:

What does it matter if it exists or not. I certainly don't exist from all eternity.
God is still master; he has given me the notion of what justice is, and I want
to follow it. I've no desire to be a philosopher but am content with being a
man.[36]

Almost as frequently, Voltaire's mouthpiece is an educated and virtuous ethical person (a disciple of Confucius or a good Brahmin) whose
nondoctrinary views put to shame a host of cynical or misguided "doc-
tors" or learned specialists of morality (fakirs, mandarins, bonzes, Jes-
uits, Papists, or any close-minded ideologue). By and large Voltaire's
dialogue patterns seem wooden and rigged and the interlocutors anemic or one-dimensional. One senses, in fact, that they have been conceived merely to mouth their author's key ideas and, for that reason,
are lacking in psychological depth and physical realism.

With Diderot we are put in the presence of one of literature's greatest writers of the dialogue, one who rehabilitates it in his century and
gives it a scope and amplitude it had rarely possessed in any period.
Like Plato, he accommodates the dialogue to his own age, peoples it
with personal friends or contemporaries with whom he is acquainted,
and thus makes it reflect the modes of thought and manner of life of
his day. As a vehicle for his thought, the dialogue records the exhila-
rating pyrotechnical display of what Diderot himself called his "mental
debauches." Throughout the conversations he systematically reveals the
complex layers of his mind, spins theories, and lays bear the very process of his thinking. Indeed, any sustained contact with Diderot's dialogues leaves the reader gasping at the speed and locomotivelike
intensity of the author's thought process, the profundity of his intelligence and boldness of his ideas—all of which distinguish him as perhaps the most challenging and original French thinker of the century.
Diderot's principal dialogue essays are *Entretien d'un père avec ses enfants
ou du danger de se mettre au-dessous des lois* (*Conversation of a Father with
His Children; or, The Danger of Submitting Oneself to Laws*), 1771; *Sup-
plément au voyage de Bougainville* (*Supplement to Bougainville's Voyage*),
written about 1772 and not published until 1796; *Entretien d'un philosophe avec la Maréchale de * * **, 1774; and *Le Rêve de D'Alembert*, written about 1769 but published in 1830.

Conversation of a Father re-creates a discussion held in the intimate atmosphere of Diderot's father's house (among the father, daughter, and two sons) on the eternal disparities existing between legal and natural concepts of justice. The father introduces a striking example to indicate how unfair life is and how the law only magnifies this injustice (the situation of a virtuous and most needy person disinherited through the terms of an outdated will that gives the inheritance to an arrogant and cruel bounder who has wealth to spare). The tale of injustice then elicits a heated debate, chiefly between Diderot and his more conservative brother, on whether one is ever justified in taking justice into one's own hands or whether one can ever play the role of Providence by direct action (all of which anticipates Raskolnikov's anguished interrogation in *Crime and Punishment*). Diderot leaves the issue unresolved.

The *Supplement* is a fictional journal that Diderot pretends had been written by Bougainville, the celebrated explorer and discoverer of Tahiti, presumably to accompany his travel account, *Voyage autour du monde,* published in 1771. In the first part of the journal, a venerable Tahitian patriarch, Orou, delivers an impassioned harangue against the evil influences that the French (already ashore) have imported into his island paradise, and he urges his compatriots to expel the Europeans before it is too late. The second part of the text presents a dialogue between the chaplain of the French expeditionary forces and a Tahitian under whose roof he has spent the night and whose hospitable offer of his youngest daughter the priest, with hesitation, has accepted. This morning-after conversation contrasts the free and innocent sexual practices of the natives with the corrupt and seemingly highly inconsistent (as far as natural reason is concerned) customs and laws of Europe. In the final analysis the dialogue constitutes a cogent attack on the bourgeois concept of marriage and family.

Conversation with a Christian Lady (as the dialogue with the Maréchale has come to be translated) portrays a spirited and graceful dialogue between an attractive, virtuous, even devout woman (Mme de Broglie) and Tomasso Crudeli, an Italian freethinker and poet. The discussion revolves about what today are uninteresting subjects but what were burning issues of that time: whether the atheist can also be a virtuous person (a question resolved in the affirmative to Mme de Broglie's mild discomfort), or whether God will save even the nonbeliever who lives honestly and in conformity with his moral beliefs. The dialogue is a masterpiece of Gallic charm and grace both by the ele-

of its conversational patterns and the gentleness of its power of persuasion.

The most lengthy and challenging of dialogues, "D'Alembert's Dream," is written in three parts, which Professor Otis Fellows has described as three acts of an intellectual drama.[37] The first, the "Conversation" between D'Alembert and Diderot, involves a forceful attack by the latter against the strong profession of deistic faith championed by D'Alembert. Diderot gradually forces him to concede that at the root of his desire to regard the universe as the work of an intelligent being is, in reality, the desperate need on his part to mask the chaos that he fears may very well exist there instead. Gradually Diderot forcefully silences his opponent's arguments to the contrary and eloquently postulates his theory of evolutionary materialism. He then proceeds to posit the process of spontaneous generation of matter as the cause for the coming into being of all matter; and he goes so far as to deny that there are distinct elements that individuate mineral, vegetable, and animal entities. Instead, he suggests "there is only one substance in the universe; one for man, and for animal." All beings, he concludes, should be viewed as living in a swirling ocean of ever changing matter.[38]

Confounded, silenced, but still unconvinced, D'Alembert (like Montaigne in the essay on Sebond) takes refuge in the consolation of universal skepticism. To Diderot's observation that he, like Montaigne, will "dream on his pillow about this conversation" and perhaps even come to acknowledge, if not the truth, then at least the probability of some of his friend's claims, D'Alembert retorts: "You're wrong; a sceptic I'll be when I go to bed and a sceptic when I get up."[39] Diderot responds by denying that skepticism can ever constitute a reasonable attitude toward such problems, since there is a pro and con for every question and "the scale is therefore never equal."[40] On this note they part amicably, Diderot to untroubled repose and D'Alembert to spend a night of fitful sleep, broken by a series of what appear to be violent nightmares.

The second and lengthiest part of the dialogue ("D'Alembert's Dream") relates a serious-comical sequence of events. D'Alembert's mistress (Mlle de Lespinasse), alarmed by his physical disturbance and seated at his bedside, records his troubled utterances. As his condition seems to worsen, she calls in the famous physician Théophile de Bordeu. The remainder of the dialogue consists of a discussion between the doctor and the woman in which he draws her out in a series of questions on ethical, scientific, and psychological issues or theories. Intermittently D'Alembert joins their discussion as he treads the border between sleep and consciousness. A kind of "delirious babbler," he mouths bits and pieces of theories and ideas that he had earlier contested in his encounter with Diderot and often becomes an unwitting foil in the conversation of the other two.

The gist of the conversation turns on too many topics to be adequately discussed here: There is introduced a theory of evolution through mutation of organs. The formation of organs is described as a reversible process: organs create needs and needs create organs. In the most striking passage, the nervous system of the human body is compared to that of a spider and its web: the web is taken as the nervous system situated at the outer limits of the body and the spider as the nerve center located in the brain.[41] The psychological importance of dreams and the "natural" causes involved in the creation of freaks and monsters are among other matters also discussed. Pressed by the need to attend to other patients, the doctor takes his leave but with the promise to return for lunch and a more private tête-à-tête with the lady.

In the third part—the "Following Conversation"—the discussion turns to a moral application of the theories advanced the preceding night. Now in the more relaxed and intimate atmosphere, over coffee and malaga, the doctor both entertains and shocks the young woman with his frank pronouncements in favor of sexual freedom. Viewing man as a product of evolving matter, Bordeu regards considerations like sin, virtue, and merit as totally irrelevant in determining the morality of any human act. There are consequently, no acts "against nature." Chastity and continence are discarded forthwith ("What profit or pleasure can chastity and continence render either to the individual or to society?") Sexual desires, he declares, will not be denied, and if silenced, sickness and nervous disorders are the predictable results ("Nature abides nothing that is unused").[42] All gratifications of the senses are thus legitimate, and even the practice of eugenics may be lawful.

In the press of thee bold arguments, the doctor is even himself disconcerted by the rapid pace and audacity of his theorizing. He then quickly takes leave of the lady, who, in retrospect, is herself more than a little abashed by the keen interest she demonstrated and complicity she shared in the discussion of such dubiously "moral" topics. "That's something which you shouldn't teach children," she soberly concludes.

Intimations of Montaigne's Project:
Rousseau's *Rêveries d'un promeneur solitaire*

Written from 1776–78, the *Rêveries* are a collection of ten lyrical
essays, each one designated by Rousseau as a "promenade." In them he
records his meditations during ten separate walks through the countryside surrounding Paris. In using the literary vehicle of the promenade, Rousseau suggests that the physical exertion of walking was the
means he needed to trigger his mind to muse over vital matters lying
just below the surface of active consciousness; for important as these
matters were, he did not seem able to contemplate them except
through the stimulus provided by hiking in a natural environment.

Not completed until the last few months of his life, the *Rêveries* are
a precious document recording Rousseau's final attempts to find peace
and justification for himself in the forum of his innermost conscience.
Now absolutely convinced that he was the victim of a deliberate and
vicious campaign of character assassination by Voltaire, his former
friend Diderot, and other *philosophes,* he ceased to appeal to his public,
submitted himself to Providence, and strived in his pages to regain the
harmony and balance he felt he had once enjoyed as a being in com-
munion with God and nature. The *Rêveries*, then, are the musings of a
man irrevocably turned away from society, of one who bends all his
efforts to "see" himself through his inner eye, and who attempts to
understand and to come to terms with the apparent inconsistencies of
his "I."

Rousseau possesses by his own admission striking affinities with,
and differences from, Montaigne's project and method. In the first
"promenade" he describes the form his essays will assume as "no more
than an unfinished journal of my reveries. In them I will be much
concerned with myself, since a solitary person who reflects is necessarily much taken with the self."[43] And like Montaigne, he will record
reflections that come upon him at random; from these will result "a
new understanding of my makeup and temperament through the feelings and thoughts that each day my mind will graze on in the strange
state that I am in."

Though he would like to proceed, like Montaigne, with order and
method, he professes himself to be incapable of such; and in a striking
analogy he compares his aims (being aware of the "modifications" of
his soul) to the tests that physicists make to determine the daily composition of air: "I shall apply the barometer to my soul and these oft
repeated operations should furnish results as certain as the latter."[44]

In a later passage Rousseau then specifically compares (and contrasts) his efforts with those of Montaigne: "I am performing the same enterprise but with a goal completely contrary to his own; he wrote his essay chiefly for others, and I only write my reveries for myself."[45] By that statement Rousseau apparently means that while Montaigne probed the singularity of his own "forme maîtresse" or individual makeup, he was as intent on elevating and exalting the common pattern that we all more or less resemble. Rousseau, on the other hand, strives to emphasize what is uniquely different about his own being, the personal "I" so dear to romantic introspection.

A close study of the *Rêveries* reveals as the unifying element Rousseau's systematic attempt to peel away the surface of the superficial self in order to reveal the natural yet exceptional caste of an individual who claims to have lived according to his own norms and to have been misunderstood and badly treated by others. Several dominant themes also emerge from an analysis of the work. One of the most urgent themes is that of the perscecution suffered by Rousseau, a loving, caring person, at the hands of Voltaire and his cohorts. This concern soon takes on the dimensions of a veritable obsession and colors the relating and interpreting of many events that surface in the meditations. For example, the accident that Rousseau endured at Ménilmontant (when he was run over by a huge white Great Dane running in the retinue of a nobleman's carriage) is at first introspectively dealt with in much the same way Montaigne relates his fall from a horse (2:5). Both authors analyze their inner dispositions and study their varying states of consciousness and unconsciousness during their respective ordeals. Yet Rousseau soon turns from this psychological study of his unconscious state to bring up real (or imagined) examples of malicious conduct that the accident elicited among his enemies. He accuses Voltaire, for example, of having deliberately circulated the rumor that he had been killed. Nevertheless, he will bear with his persecutors without murmuring because "God is just, he wants me to suffer, he knows that I am innocent, and this is the motive for my confidence."[46]

This fear of persecution (certainly not all imagined) then prompts Rousseau to examine for the reader the question "What or who am I?" In the process, he deals with such themes as his constant goal of personal integrity, his strong preference for solitude, and the real difficulties he has always had in dealing with others in society.

As regards the truth and his adherence to it, Rousseau presents a vigorous apology for his own fundamental (and much contested) integrity. He constructs his defense on his personal motto borrowed from

Juvenal: *Vitam impendere vero* ("To him who consecrates his life to the truth"). Though he admits to a penchant for inventing details and then dealing with them as if they are facts, he would, as it were, yield to no man when a question arises of sacrificing basic interests, security, and well being in the service of truth.[47] After some personal and extremely sensitive probings, he posits as the causes of his paradoxical state and personal makeup: extreme shyness, an inability to express himself artfully in society, and the overweening desire to please and be pleasant to others. (He tells them what they want to hear.) Yet he holds emphatically that such difficulties and dichotomies in conduct are not only his own but everyone's and stem from the moral dilemma we all have in determining what we owe ourselves and others.

The response arrived at by Rousseau to this vexing question involves a stance far more radical than that of Montaigne. Rather than balancing responsibilities owed to the self and the social realm (as Montaigne had done) Rousseau makes a definitive retreat inward and virtually denies any form of reality that does not originate with, and end in, the self.

Once this apology and profession of faith in his own intregrity have been established, Rousseau proceeds through reveries induced in solitude by the movement and sounds of nature to construct a concept of happiness that places him beyond time and space. In a passage recalling supreme moments of rapture on the Island of St. Pierre, he expresses his ideal as "a sufficient happiness, perfect and full, which leaves in the soul no void that it feels the need to fill." This is not, he says, like the imperfect happiness one finds among the joys or pleasures of life, but rather such as he found "in solitary reveries, either stretched out in a boat that I had let drift at will, or seated on the banks of a wind-tossed lake, or near a stream murmuring over its gravel bed."[48]

Not only an apology for the self but a philosophy of life, the *Rêveries* forward moral concepts that will have great repercussion and lasting effect in literature, from the Romantic period to the present. Through Rousseau's poignant example, other French writers will have the courage to pursue similar artistic forms of the *culte du moi* and to express the uniqueness the individual self in their works. Certainly Baudelaire, Gide, Rimbaud, Barrès, Proust, Montherlant, Camus, and many other authors who adopted this lyrical form of the essay in diverse ways are deeply indebted to Rousseau's project.

As regards its literary form, the work constitutes a milestone in artistic expression. In the lyrical prose of his essays, Rousseau creates a musicality before unknown and still unsurpassed in French literature (and certainly equal to the best of Chateaubriand): a soft, fluid harmony that simulates in prose the mental state of musing. Ultimately it becomes a means by which Rousseau composes a poetry of the self, one that fixes the very modifications of the changing heart and soul of man, the *intermittences du coeur* that Proust would also capture in his great analytic novel.

The evolution and growth of the essay in eighteenth-century France can virtually be said to imitate the intellectual evolution and growth in French society itself. A prose instrument ranging in content and form from sturdy, clandestine essays to the artfully rendered pieces of Voltaire, Rousseau, and Diderot, the essay served admirably to disseminate the great ideas and issues of the Enlightenment. More particularly as regards its literary form as a genre, it can best be described as Protean, hence changing from scholarly, well-knit treatises entitled "essays" to imaginative prose pieces that were often personal, sometimes even confessional, in tone and intention.

If one quality may be designated as especially characteristic of the essay's cast in this century, it would doubtless be the persuasive and conversational tone that a number of great writers achieved in their pieces. Intent on opening the hearts and minds of their readers to the great enlightenment enterprise, these authors evolved a mixture of stylistic tones and nuances. Often intimate and vibrant, frequently irreverent, ironic, even indignant, the essay was ever compelling and challenging. As it expanded its scope and greatly varied its forms, the essay also constituted a major force in altering the role of eighteenth-century writers themselves. In the recent work, *The Literary Enterprise in Eighteenth-Century France,* Professor Rémy Saisselin has observed of the literary scene in general that the "literary space" of authors (to use Blanchot's expression) had changed to become political and social rather than merely scholarly. As a result, no longer confined to his humanistic library, the writer emerged to come into contact with the beau monde itself as a professional in his own right.[49]

The prose vehicle par excellence in exploring the expanded areas of communication available to the writer (as we have seen in this study), the eighteenth-century essay must be regarded as of paramount importance in the coming of age of the committed professional writer of modern times. Yet, ironically, the essay still did not gain admission as a genre in French literature. Such a designation would have to wait until the following century.

Chapter Four

The Essay in the Nineteenth Century

The Essay in the Aftermath of the Revolution

Basically the kind of essay written during the first two decades of the nineteenth century did not vary significantly from the serious, formal model introduced a century before. And unquestionably, the major factor determining the matter for the major pieces written in this period was the French Revolution. This great cataclysm which, in Hegel's words, "had set humanity on its head," not surprisingly dominated the mainstream of French thought and intellectual endeavor and flowed naturally into fictional and nonfictional prose works of the most important writers of the period. Three in particular wrote landmark formal essays whose catalyst is this gigantic social upheaval and in which the respective writers assess its nature and impact or strive to influence the form that French society should take in its wake.

In his *Essai sur les révolutions,* Chateaubriand investigates the concept of revolution as a political phenomenon and compares its recurring manifestations from the earlier historical periods to the French experiment. In several political essays, Joseph de Maistre mounts a bitter attack on what, from his vantage point as an extremely conservative and devout Catholic, he regards as the "godless," even satanic nature of the event, and Hughes Lamennais, a proponent of the republican principles fostered by the revolutionary movement, writes on the then burning issue of the adaptations that Catholicism would have to make in the new democratic society. Taken as a whole, these early essays constitute important documents on initial philosophical, political, and social reactions of the French to the course of events that, having forever severed their nation from its venerable monarchical traditions, had plunged it almost immediately into a climate of moral and social malaise that would endure for generations to come.

By far the most impassioned of these essays is Chateaubriand's enormous *Essay on Revolutions*. The work was written from 1794 to 1796, during the period that Chateaubriand as a young émigré recently escaped from France spent in moral isolation and extreme poverty in England. In it he records his loss of faith in Enlightenment ideals—in particular his belief in the natural goodness and perfectibility of man, which the horrible reality of the revolution had, he believed, forever discredited. Divested of his former optimism but not yet able to extirpate his deep-set prejudices against even the notion of religious belief, this future apologist of Christianity gropes for something in which to place his faith. In the process he first expresses here his and an entire generation's sense of failure in having lost faith in one ideology—Enlightenment rationalism—and yet having nothing with which to replace it. This state, the celebrated *mal du siècle* ("century sickness"), Chateaubriand would more graphically illustrate through the personage of René in the novella of the same title that would appear a few years later.

Topically the huge, two-volume work of over 400 pages offers a history and analysis of revolution as a permanent state that had existed in one form or another from ancient Greece to France of 1789. From this concept the essay deduces as a philosophy the theory of the ever recurring, cyclical nature of human history viewed as a whole:

Men emerge from nothing and return; death is a great lake hallowed out of the midst of nature; human lives like so many streams are borne along to be immolated in it; and from this lake other generations are spread over the earth, to be returned after a more or less brief period to their common source.[1]

The essay is less interesting for its often facile creation of historical parallels (seventeenth-century France with Solon's Athens, or Carthage as an earlier model of the British monarchy, to mention only two) than for its thesis that Christianity, now "obsolete" since it had failed to satisfy mankind's persistent need to believe in some spiritual principle, would eventually be replaced by another form of religious faith still to be determined. In Chateaubriand's opinion, the "purest" religion—for him a kind of natural deism—had little chance to replace Christianity since "though the sage can adhere to it, it is still too elevated for the masses." Yet he realizes that a form of religion is necessary "if society is not to perish," and he is led by this certitude to wonder if the frightening decline that Christianity has everywhere experienced is not, in fact, a harbinger to a greater European revolution for which that of France is only a beginning.

Politically, Chateaubriand posits the principle that freedom and a democratic form of government are both naturally desired by all people and constitute ideals. He laments, however, that neither has ever been appreciably realized for any length of time. Indeed, the work ends with the pessimistic observation that man (free in "the state of nature") is enslaved the moment he submits to any form of government. He asks, "What difference is there if it be a law or a king which drags me to the guillotine. . . . The greatest misfortune of man is to love laws and government."[2] "Or," he states in another passage, "if it is our lot to be slaves, let us drag our chains uncomplaining; let us learn to beat them into rings for the fingers of kings or tribunes as the age or customs may dictate."[3]

To render this sad conclusion more concrete, Chateaubriand appends to it an exquisite tableau evoking and depicting the freedom that man might indeed once have enjoyed in the state of nature but which has now forever closed to the civilized European. In the episode "Night with the Savages of America," he recounts from his travel experience in North America an encounter with a family of Hurons (two women, three warriors, and two infants) in the Niagara Falls area. Using sign language and the aid of a Dutch trader as interpreter, he makes contact with these exemplars of pure liberty who symbolize for him that innocence that the avarice of his fellow Europeans will soon destroy; and he eulogizes them in these terms:

These same savages whom we have pursued with sword and flame, to whom our avarice would leave not even a handful of earth to cover their corpses, in this vast patrimony once their own; these same savages, who receive their enemies in friendly huts and share with them their wretched meals, their unsullied bed, illustrate virtues that are as elevated beyond our conventional virtues as the soul of man in nature to that of man in society.[4]

Deeply moved by these meditations, Chateaubriand the political theorist retreats from view to be replaced by Chateaubriand the poet as he ecstatically describes the ravishing landscape where, under the changing patterns of the full moon, a stream resembling "a ribbon of watered silk and azur" flows through a vast natural prairie.

As shaken as was Chateaubriand at the spectacle of revoluton, Joseph de Maistre (1754–1821) held radically different views as regards its meaning. To the former's cyclical view of history and concept of ever recurring revolution, he in fact opposed a staunch religious belief in human history as absolutely willed and ordained by a Divine Being. A Savoyard of noble birth whose language was French, de Maistre is the author of four major essays: *Considérations sur la France, Essai sur le principe générateur (Essay on the Generative Principle), Du Pape (The Pope),* and the ten dialogue essays, called *Soirées de Saint-Petersbourg.* In this brief treatment of de Maistre as esayist, my primary focus will be the political essay *Considerations on France,* which faithfully reflects the major currents of his thought.

To understand the importance of this essay, we must recognize it to be a conscious attempt on its author's part to write the continental version of Edmund Burke's *Reflections on the Revolution in France* (1790). Burke, the father of British conservatism, set out in his essay to refute the liberal claim that the English people had the right to "choose . . . [their] own governors, to cashier them for misconduct, and to provide a government for themselves."[5] Burke contested this notion on the grounds that every English citizen had received rights and duties under a constitution as an inheritance derived from his forefathers and that the same had thus to be transmitted to posterity. The recent events in France were, moreover, eloquent examples of the damage that ensues once a people exchanges an inheritance historically set (in this instance the monarchy) for any sort of metaphysical abstraction ("the rights of man," for example).

Following Burke's thesis in the *Considerations,* de Maistre advances as his central point the concept that no people can ever grant itself a constitution or rights by popular fiat. Rather, all rights come from on high and cannot be abrogated by man. In the opening sentence of the essay he therefore both echoes and contests Rousseau's preliminary statement of the *Social Contract* ("Man is born to be free and is everywhere in chains") with the statement, "We are attracted to the throne of the Supreme Being by a supple chain which holds us without enslaving us."[6] The forces of irreligion and human pride have, however, led man to the state of revolution. By thus shattering the gentle ties that link him to legitimate authority, man "is carried along by an unknown force, rebels against authority and bites the hand that upholds him [Divine Providence]." De Maistre then goes on to develop the thesis that will reoccur as an idée fixe in all his subsequent works: The horror of the Jacobin period viewed as a blood bath wrought by

Divine wrath against a corrupt, venal French church and state. As de
Maistre interprets it, the Jacobin leaders (and in particular the "infernal
Robespierre") were really only instruments of the will of God "in
strengthening the soul of the French by soaking it in blood."[7] Only in
that way could France survive the Terror and its aftermath: a Europe
militarily and politically united against it; only the return of the Bourbons could, he claims, rehabilitate through atonement the sins of the
revolution. Finally, only a reinstated and legitimate monarch could
exorcise the satanic effects of the revolution and bring political stability
back to a sinful France. Through such concepts de Maistre quickly
gained the reputation as being the nineteenth century's most ardent
apostle for religious and political absolutism and foremost apologist for
the supremacy of Catholicism as an institution necessary for the main-
tenance of legitimate government and authority. His essays have, up
to our own times, become the bible of monarchists, legitimists, and
conservatives of all stripes.

In his four-volume *Essai sur l'indifférence* (1817), Hughes Félicité de
Lamennais (1782–1854) takes a diametrically opposite stance to de
Maistre's indictment of democratic principles of any kind; his essay
represents, in fact, nothing less than an ambitious attempt to render
genuine religious faith and practice compatible with modern democratic forms of government.

Along with Renan (forty years his junior) Lamennais was nineteenth-
century France's most eminent apostate. How this ardent defender of
the faith, who never ceased to declare his adherence to the truths of
the Catholic faith, was ultimately repudiated by the French Catholic
hierarchy and subsequently excommunicated by Pope Gregory XVI is
a fascinating topic that cannot be dealt with here. The evolution of his
religious convictions—from his initial point of view of royalist-exile to
champion of popular democracy—may, however, be viewed in microcosm as prefiguring the essential tensions in the French Catholic
Church's anguished struggle to reenter the mainstream of French political and social life after its disastrous alliance with the institutions
of the ancien régime.

Published in 1817, two years after its author's ordination to the
priesthood, the *Essay on Indifference* made Lamennais a celebrated figure
over night; and Catholics soon came to regard him as "a young Bossuet" worthy to be admitted into the august company of de Bonald,
Chateaubriand, and de Maistre (the leading Catholic intellectuals who
had labored to bring the practice of religion back into favor in the early

century). The contents of the essay can be broken down into four topic headings: 1) definition and refutation of various forms of religious indifference; 2) the importance of religion in the social and political forum; 3) the means or "signs" given to man to discern the true religion; 4) a defense of Christianity as the only religion revealed by God and Catholicism as its only true form.

As the central thesis of the work Lamennais holds that the nineteenth century was indeed gravely afflicted with a sickness. He diagnosed it as not so much caused by erroneous philosophies (as Chateaubriand claimed in his essay) but essentially by an attitude of indifference. This state he describes as "the extinction of all feelings of love or hatred in the human heart because of the absence of any judgment or belief in the mind."[8] He holds that such an unnatural and inhuman state "morality, good works, obligations and the most sacred as well as the most noble principles and sentiments become only kinds of dreams—brilliant and light fantasies—that are played out in the depths of the mind." Yet, he argues, such matters can never be isolated from, or held to be "indifferent" as regards their relationship to, society. Such a situation is clearly inimical to man as a social being and destructive of society itself; and in an obvious reference to his own contemporary period he concludes: "Once a people has arrived at such a state then its end may probably be very near at hand."

After this diagnosis of what ails his society, he conducts a vigorous assault on the forms of indifference that are especially threatening; these are variously identified as atheism, natural religion or deism à la Voltaire, and Protestantism. In dealing with these three "heresies" Lamennais, rather than emphasizing their differences, lumps them together on two essential points. What they share in common, he says, is their adherence to two principles against which doctrinal certitude or clarity of any kind cannot endure: these are: 1) the use of free examination of conscience, and 2) the concept of tolerance for all opinions. Through the first, he holds, man is ever encouraged to prefer his private judgment over that which is universally true and taught as such; through the second he is inclined to water down essential truths or moral principles and to extend credibility even to atheistic points of view. Thus in the long run, universal tolerance is merely another term for "absolute indifference" and leads, like the former, to the destruction of all religions.

The remainder of the essay contains a conventional but cogent apology for Catholicism as the universally true form of Christianity (observable through the traditional "signs") and as that most likely to promote order, justice, and peace in society. What is especially significant here (and somewhat surprising given his opposition to free examination of conscience) is his belief that the Catholic Church should not be the state-supported religion, and indeed, that there should be de facto separation of the two. The ultimate truth or reasonableness of Catholicism he bases upon the principle of universal consent arrived at through natural reason: "The more the Christian is reasonable the more he perceives the truth of the general beliefs of the church. In a word, because we are human, this principle resides in our very nature."[9]

Two Psychological Studies: Love and the Dandy

Despite the dominance of longer, serious essays like the above, a more personal form of the genre was kept alive by two significant psychological studies: One on the passion of love and the other on a special kind of social deportment. In the essay *De l'amour*, (1822), Stendhal prepares an anatomy of this passion ("the highest form of human activity") and records its manifestations in his own age. With *Du dandysme et de Georges Brummell, un dandy avant les dandys* (1845), Barbey d'Aurevilly presents the moral anatomy of the dandy, as embodied in the most celebrated paragon of this singular species, Beau Brummell.

Written eight years before the novel *The Red and the Black,* Stendhal's essay *Love* gives in its introduction the intention of being a dispassionate treatise using for its methodology the theories of the sensualist philosophers of the eighteenth century (Condillac and Condorcet) or of the nineteenth-century *idéologues* (Cabanis and DeStutt de Tracy). By this Stendhal meant a rationalist and positivist study of the passions relying on such determinants as temperament and environmental factors which were thought to have very heavy influence on an individual's response to outside stimuli. Despite the scientific trappings initially presented (the reduction of love into four basic states and a methodical analysis of the psychological development of love—the famous process of "cristillisation"), it soon becomes clear, however, that the essay is, in truth, one man's passionate attempt to record his own observations and experiences as regards "this fever which comes and goes quite independent of the will." Stendhal wrote it, in fact, at the end of a long and unsuccessful pursuit of a young woman Mathilde (or Métilde as he called her) Viscontini Dembowski, who spurned all his advances and refused even to see him after he had given up his quest. This twenty-eight-year-old Milanese beauty (one of many femmes fatales to whom Stendhal would devote passionate attention) neither liked nor understood her plain and somewhat clumsy suitor; yet she is responsible for his having put to pen the difficult, somewhat masochistic, but extremely intense feelings that he experienced while courting her. As such, they describe the very special kind of love that Stendhal held for a beautiful, cold, and difficult woman; yet they also capture the nature of passionate love, elevate it to a general state, and investigate its special manifestations on the contemporary scene.

In his introductory analysis, Stendhal posits four kinds of love: passionate, mannered, physical, and vanity love. He makes it clear, however, that he regards only one of these, passionate love, as totally desirable and humanly fulfilling. For Stendhal, this state—devoid of vanity or the stylized decadent tastes of the salon or boudoir—represents the élan vital of the passions, the highest form of energy, and the supreme source of happiness. He follows this delineation with an analysis of the stages extending from the birth of love to its full recognition and enjoyment by the lovers. This process ("cristallisation") is based on the theory that a person in love actively uses his power of imagination to transform and embellish the image of the beloved in his own mind until he has created a new being, a unique reality. He describes this process of transformation in almost chemical terms in his celebrated analogy of the Salzburg branch:

Leave a lover with his thoughts for twenty-four hours and this is what will happen: At the mines of Salzburg, they throw a leafless wintry bough into one of the abandoned workings. Two or three months later they haul it out covered with a shining deposit of crystals. . . . What I have called *cristallisation* is a mental process which draws from everything that happens new proofs of the perfection of the loved one. [10]

The remainder of the first book contains copious examples of "cristallisation" drawn from his own observations, comments in the moralist mode on society, with such insights as "The ideal breeding ground for love is the boredom of solitude with the long-awaited ball; wise mothers of daughters are guided accordingly";[11] and Stendhal gives personal, sometimes self-revelatory observations as, "I am trying extremely hard to be dry. My heart thinks it has so much to say, but I keep it quiet."[12] There are amusing, minute descriptions of phenomena such as the *coup de foudre* ("thunder bolt," or love at first sight) and analyses on human types most likely to be struck with such passion. He also provides extracts from the fictional diary of a certain Viscio Salvati [Stendhal's shadow], who records his similar frustrations in the pursuit of a haughty belle.

The second part of the essay broadens its focus to include a compilation of sociological/psychological details on love as it manifests itself in various present-day societies. Much of the matter is appealingly presented in the form of travel journals kept by an urbane and experienced observer of life. In an examination of love in Europe, Italy unsurprisingly bears the palm. Italians surrender to inspiration of the moment, and "since passion is not infrequent, it is not ridiculous."[13] France (and especially Paris) is captive to vanity: "To find love in France you must go down among the classes where the absence of education and vanity . . . have allowed more energy to survive."[14] In England a puritan society uses its "nervous fluids" in exercise and excessive drinking rather than in love making; and in the United States, "a government which does its citizens no harm but rather gives them security and tranquility" nonetheless creates a serious lacking in its people and dries up "the springs of sensitiveness."[15] Intertwined with these entertaining comparisons are several chapters concerning the social condition of women that reveal Stendhal to be (as Simone de Beauvoir has claimed) a feminist well before his time. He lashes out at the cruel and arrogant subordination in marriage (a kind of slavery) to which women have been subjected through the refusal by men to allow them to have a proper education ("With the present system of education for girls, any genius who happens to be born a woman can make no contribution to public happiness").[16] And he goes on to opt for easy divorce, forms of free love, and equal opportunities.

In his brilliant essay *Dandyism and George Brummell* Barbey d'Aureyvilly sketches out not only a compact biography of the first English dandy but provides a treatise on the theoretical aspects of dandyism. In the process he probes the psychological motivations prompting the dandy's scorn of conventional patterns of behavior and uses his findings to justify his own deep dislike for modernity. His study, like Stendhal's *Love*, is therefore semiautobiographical in that it represents a faithful evocation of the author's frustrated aspirations in a society in which he did not fit.

For indeed Barbey, as he wished to be called, was a man thoroughly at odds with his century. A Norman aristocrat from a ruined family (his grandfather had been guillotined), he grew up in the backwaters of the provinces (the Cotentin peninsula) as the sole companion of his idle and embittered father. Unwilling to accept any social change, this man spent his days filling his son's head with stories of their Viking ancestors and other Norman legends. Barbey developed into a proud, retiring young man with great aristocratic bearing but with decidedly exotic tastes in speech, dress, and conduct. An ardent convert to Catholicism, celebrated for such singular literary works as his *Les Diaboliques* (a selection of strange but brilliant short stories combining mysticism, sex, violence, and death), and an outspoken and often keenly perceptive critic (he was one of Baudelaire's first strong defenders), he became notorious for his antidemocratic views and his bitter disdain for what he regarded as the triumph in France of an extremely vulgar and venal society.

In the essay Barbey first makes much of the fact that Beau Brummell was born (in 1778) to a family that was neither noble nor of great wealth. (He did, however, attend Eton and afterwards became a Hussar and a favorite of the Prince of Wales in the latter's Tenth Regiment.) Not of superior intelligence and not even a man of strong passion, Brummell, Barbey claims, "was the gainer for this indigence, for being reduced to the simple force of what distinguished him, he raised himself to the rank of a thing: he became Dandyism itself."[17]

What Brummell the dandy better embodied than anyone else was, for Barbey, a state of being "composed entirely of fine shades (as usually happens in a very ancient and hypercivilized societies in which breeding rarely triumphs over ennui)." And England, caught up as it was in "the endless struggle between a code of manners and boredom" was, for Barbey, just such a society.[18] Far from being, then, merely a term synonymous with exquisite fashion (as Carlyle had used it in *Sartor Resartus*), dandyism had for its purpose the goal of "producing the unexpected" for a society mired in deadening routine. And in a larger sense it represented "the revolt of the individual against the established Order."[19] Such resistance, he claimed, is not merely a political stance but a personal calling, really a form of "grace" to which one responds. And in possessing it to the fullest, Brummell was a fated man destined to fall before society's fury for the cold and indolent contempt that he meted out to it. Brummell was also symbolic of a new rise of Puritanism; and after his persecution and demise, "immortal, imperturbable Cant," in Barbey's view, "again triumphed over England."[20] For that nation which also had banished the "atheist" Shelley as well as Lord Byron, was once again revealed to be "the white sepulchre of stiff pharisaism." Brummell represented finally for Barbey not only a magnificent prototype of human resistance to repression but also an important part of the "Divine Handwork." Individuals like him ("Androgynes of History, of an indecisive intellectual sex") are eternally needed "because they afford intelligent beings the pleasure that is their right."[21]

The Father of the French Critical Essay, Sainte-Beuve

Charles Auguste Sainte-Beuve (1804–69) was both the most prolific essayist of the nineteenth century and an illustrious pioneer in the development of the genre. Writing at the very beginning of modern journalism in France, he fashioned his critical writings on literary subjects in the form of newspaper and magazine articles of exceptionally high quality. In the process he created a new form, the critical essay, which would be of monumental importance in the history of the genre and its dominant manifestation up to our own day. As Professor Chadbourne has astutely described the posterity of Saint-Beuve's model:

The majority of nineteenth-century French essays, following the Sainte Beuvian archetype, were critical rather than confessional in nature (though not always on literature), centered about a book or books to be judged, and reached their destination between hard covers by way of great periodicals.[22]

Initially Sainte-Beuve was intent on pursuing a career as poet. Three years younger than Victor Hugo, he was admitted into the latter's inner circle of admirers (the *Cénacle*) after he had written favorable but frank reviews of the poetic collection *Odes et ballades* for the *Globe* (1827). Then there commenced a tempestuous friendship with Hugo and an intermittent affair with the latter's wife Adèle (with whom Sainte-Beuve would be amorously involved for almost a decade). It was during this period that he wrote his celebrated novel *Volupté*—a classic study of love and the ravages caused by a sensibility that lacked moral force or discrimination.

Sainte-Beuve spent the last three decades of his life in back-breaking labor as literary critic and writer of nonprofessional scholarly works and churned out week after week his literary articles, first for the periodical *Moniteur,* and then for the *Constitutionnel.* By any measure his production of critical essays is staggering: He left behind five volumes of "Portraits contemporains"; two volumes of "Portraits littéraires"; fifteen volumes of "Causeries du lundi" (Monday Chats); and thirteen volumes of "Nouveaux lundis" (New Mondays). The essay form that he made famous—the literary "portrait" or miniature—reached its perfection in the pages of the Monday Chats. In what was primarily a newspaper article consisting on the average of approximatley five thousand words, the Chat would essentially investigate a given author's claim to genius and lasting fame. The method pursued would stress not so much the explication of an author's primary works but more a study of his life, with emphasis given to salient details on personal habits indeed often idiocyncracies that Sainte-Beuve judged to be psychologically illuminating. What first impresses a reader of the Chats is their extraordinary diversity of topic. Sainte-Beuve in fact dedicated only a portion of these essays to literature of his century—nearly eighty of the articles deal with seventeenth-century figures, just under one hundred for the eighteenth, and many articles are dedicated to classical literature (Pliny, Cicero, Virgil); the Middle Ages (Joinville, Froissard, Commynes, Villon); the Renaissance (Ronsard, Amyot, Montaigne, Rabelais); to general literary topics ("What Is a Classic?" "Dramatic Art and Morality," "Tradition of Literature," and "The Condition of Writers in the Nineteenth Century"), to mention a few.

Nor did Sainte-Beuve confine himself only to great authors and works, but he continually manifested a lively interest in secondary sources: correspondence, theretofore unpublished chronicles, memoirs of slightly known writers (Senancour, Mme Roland, Mme des Houlières, for example). Outside the field of literature, he was attracted by statesmen and military figures (Maréchal Marmont, Bonneval Pasha, Thiers, Hamilton, Guizot, Talleyrand, and Napoleon). Infrequently he would dedicate articles to foreign writers (Lord Chesterfield, William Cowper, Gibbon, and Franklin). He would also make numerous references to foreign authors whom he very much admired (Shakespeare, Pope, Wordsworth, Goethe, the Brothers Grimm, and Matthew Arnold).

The average Chat can first be described as a beautifully written appraisal of an author, the article most often inspired because the author had received recent attention in a critical work of note or because there had recently been published a new edition or his or her works. The pieces begin with some general reflection, aphorism, statement, or judgment by Sainte-Beuve upon which the article revolves. For example, the essay on Geoffry de Villehardouin (a medieval chronicler) opens with the maxim "One must not pass through this world without making something of one's life on earth."[23] After citing that, Sainte-

Beuve then lauds Villehardouin's "joie d'homme de coeur" (joy of a courageous man), which he finds clearly manifested in the latter's accounts of the great events of the Crusades. For Molière, he constructs his review on the "rare gift of universality" that the great dramatist possesses with a very few exceptional writers of genius, "(five or six even among the greatest)."[24] For Benjamin Franklin it is not "the flower of religion, of honor, or of chivalry" that Sainte-Beuve will use as a measure for greatness, but rather the element of "what is useful."[25]

After that kind of introduction, Sainte-Beuve generally uses a certain portion of the article to weave biographical details to explain the character and elucidate the promise of the author in question. The approach often involves some treatment of family influence, environment, and historical period. Montaigne, as an example, is first described as "a simple, natural, common soul, and one most evenly tempered." The reason for his balanced temperament, Sainte-Beuve suggests, is the fact that "he was born of a father who, though of mediocre education, had initiated his son in the new learning and had corrected the too heady enthusiasm of the Renaissance with great finesse and correctness of judgment."[26] In the case of Pascal, we read that "He possessed a great mind and heart, not always the situation among the best or greatest intellectuals." We also are informed that Pascal was, by nature, "very often the prey to passionate and stormy outbursts," yet his moody temperament had been moderated through the pious education given him by his father, "an outstanding man who also taught him to direct his acute sensitivity toward good and against evil."[27]

With such painstakingly minute character sketches provided, Sainte-Beuve then attempts to trace the evolution of an author's genius to that moment when he had fully realized the artistic achievement for which he had been "called." In the case of Rousseau, it was "that day on which he both discovered himself for himself" and could offer to his century language expressing "a feeling for nature . . . and the sensibility for domestic life."[28] For Pascal it was the time when "his singular, nervous sickness" (caused by excessive intellectual labors) began to be fed by the "religious nourishment offered to his moral life through contact with the Gentlemen of Port Royal."[29]

The "moment" given, Sainte-Beuve then, in the final pages of the essay elaborates an assessment of the special contribution the author had made, not only to letters, but to society as a whole. Pascal, as an example, had made it impossible to blaspheme or make fun of religion, even if one were a nonbeliever; and thus "did he vanquish in this respect the spirit of the eighteenth century and Voltaire."[30] Montaigne, the spirit of moderation and temperance in a mad world, becomes both the voice of "natural man" and the "French Horace." As Sainte-Beuve puts it: "His book is a treasure of moral observations; no matter to what page we turn nor in what state of mind we are in, we are assured to find there some wise thought expressed in a lively and lasting manner."[31]

Sainte-Beuve would ultimately regard his critical writings as a form of education and himself as a professor whose task would be to inculcate in his readers the sense of a tradition for all that is worthy in the garden of literature. In what is certainly one of his best known pieces, "What Is a Classic?" (invariably reproduced in every world anthology of great essays), he defines a "classical" author as one

who has enriched the human mind, who has actually added to its treasures and carried it a step forward, one who has discovered some unmistakable moral truth or recaptured some eternal passion in the human heart where everything seemed known and explored . . . one who speaks to all in a style of his own, which happens also to be that of common speech, a style new but without neologisms, new and old at the same time, and easily acceptable to any epoch.[32]

His critical method ("psychological impressionism" as it has come to be called) has been discredited first by Proust and, in our own day, by French "New Novel" critics and writers largely because of its premise that the best avenue of approach to any given work lies through a study of its author. His myopia in failing to recognize such geniuses among his own contemporaries as Stendhal, Balzac, and Baudelaire has further dimmed his reputation. Yet his personal contribution to the essay in France can neither be underrated nor denied. In his essay writings he in fact bends the spirit and intention of Montaigne's liberal cultivation of the self and others to a critical analysis of literature; and he habitually employs in the process the same spirit of skeptical tolerance and openness of view as his cultural predecessor.

The Second Generation of Major Nineteenth-Century Essayists: Baudelaire, Renan, and Taine

The most innovative literary critic of the century, Charles Baudelaire (1821–67), was also among its greatest essayists. Unlike Sainte-Beuve, he did not employ (nor did he favor) a historical/biographical approach to criticism, with its customary stress on personal data and extraneous details, as his primary means to evaluate an author or artist's work in any given period. Rather, his writings possess a striking unity of theme and consistency in theory; they can therefore be best examined as an organic whole from which can be extricated the major concepts and topics that determine their basic structure.

Baudelaire composed all of his critical essays between 1845 and 1862, when his creative powers were at their height. This was the period during which he wrote the major part of the *Fleurs du mal,* and it was also one of intense moral suffering for him. For in 1857 his first publication of these poems by the narrowest of margins escaped prosecution and was withdrawn from circulation on the charge of being an offense to public morals. Deeply hurt but unyielding to public opinion, he doggedly held to his artistic principles, now fully matured, and applied them to essays on painting, sculpture, literature, and music of the period.

The definitive modern edition of the essays (the Pléiade Edition) divides them into two categories: art and literary criticism. The major pieces dedicated to art are the "Salon" essays (1845, 1846, the "Universal Exposition of 1859," and 1859); other major titles are "The Essence of Laughter," "Philosophical Art," "The Painter of Modern Life" (an article dedicated to Constantin Guys, a water-colorist of the period), "The Works and Life of Delacroix," and "Richard Wagner and Tannhäuser in Paris." The principal literary essays consist of several reviews on individual works: Flaubert's *Madame Bovary,* Hugo's *Les Misérables,* and Charles Asselineau's collection of novellas entitled *La Double Vie.* There are two long articles dedicated to contemporary poets: Théophile Gautier and Pierre Dupont (a now somewhat forgotten realist poet of the day) and a series of ten articles on poets grouped under the rubric "Reflections on Several of My Contemporaries" (including Victor Hugo, Leconte de Lisle, Gautier, Petrus Borel, and others virtually unremembered today). There is finally the very important essay *New Note on Edgar Poe* that Baudelaire composed as preface for the second volume of his translation of the American's poetry, an article in which perhaps more succinctly than in any of his other essays he expresses his aesthetic and poetic principles.

Of the two groupings, there seems to be little question that those dedicated to art criticism are the more successful and significant. As Professor Enid Starkie has observed, Baudelaire himself felt more assured in his criticism of paintings, for which he had been trained since childhood.[33] This is not to deny his perceptive work as a literary critic. On the contrary, he early recognized the genius of Balzac, Stendhal, Flaubert, Banville, Gautier, and of course, Poe. His essays on art, however, naturally achieve a unity not possible in the literary pieces, which are somewhat disparate and fragmented because most were written incidentally. Moreover, since they are inspired by, and continue, Diderot's earlier enterprise, Baudelaire's art pieces (and in particular the "Salon" essays) seem especially appropriate matter for our study of the essay.

When we compare the "Salon of 1845" with the three others of that title that follow, it is obvious that Baudelaire had to experiment with this form of art criticism before hitting his stride and certainly before using it as an adequate expression for his essential aesthetic/artistic views. This first attempt represents little more than a systematic, very literary appraisal of the paintings of the year grouped into genres or "tableaus." "Our method of writing," Baudelaire says, "will simply consist of dividing our work into tableaus of history and portraits, of landscape, sculpture, engravings, and sketches, and to group the artists according to the order and rank that public esteem has accorded them."[34] The prose descriptions that follow are somewhat dry and prosaic. There are few colorful asides, and little theory or instruction is provided for the reader during a business-like and straightforward "promenade" through the Louvre. The author's artistic tastes are briefly stated without further comment or explanation and in very absolute terms (for instance, Delacroix is described as being "the most original painter of modern and ancient times,"[35] while Boulanger's canvases are summarily dispatched as representing "the very last ruins of old-style romanticism . . ."[36]).

The "Salon" of the following year (1846) gives undeniable proof that Baudelaire had come of age as an art critic. Almost twice as long, this essay takes a far broader view of its role of evaluating artists and their works; moreover, it subordinates descriptions of paintings and the other art forms to lively digressions or discourses on such topics as "What Good Is Criticism?" "What is Romanticism?" "Why Sculpture Is Boring," "On the Heroism of Modern Life," and "On Color." It is as if Baudelaire has renounced the role of a tour guide in favor of that of a teacher/expert whose aim it is to inculcate his reader with concepts of theory and practice so that deeper appreciation of the works of art may be obtained. To this end he gives early on a tentative definition of the role of criticism, defining it as amusing and poetic, and not a cold mathematical appraisal . . . but since a beautiful picture is nature reflected by an artist, the best criticism will be the reflection of that picture by an intelligent and sensitive mind. The best criticism of a picture thus well may be a sonnet or an elegy.[37]

Insisting that criticism should be both creative and poetic, Baudelaire holds that art must also serve a dual role: it should create lasting works of beauty while at the same time drawing subjects from modern times. This theme—the one most persistently repeated throughout the art essays—prompts Baudelaire to offer his famous definition (and revision) of romanticism as a creative theory. A second generation "romantic" who, like Sainte-Beuve, recoiled at what he considered to be the pretentious claims and false expressions of some of the early romantic writers, he believed that the term signified not so much a movement or literary school but more a state of mind or artistic spirit: Romanticism lied, he declared,

neither in the choice or subject nor in exact truth, but in the manner of feeling. . . . For me romanticism is the most recent, the most contemporary, expression of the beautiful. . . . To speak of romanticism is to speak of modern art—that is, of intimacy, spirituality, color, and the aspiration to the infinite expressed by all the means that art has available to it.[38]

The essay entitled "The Universal Exposition of 1855" is very important both in the development of Baudelaire's aesthetic ideas and his use of the essay form. As the title suggests, the work makes a very strong defense for the cosmopolitan nature and spirit that should imbue art. It is here, in fact, that Baudelaire in the strongest terms declares his independence from any school or preconceived set of criteria and asserts that the concept of beauty will always elude any fixed definition:

The beautiful is always strange. I do not mean that it is deliberately, coldly strange, for in that case it would be a monster that has jumped the rails of life. I mean that it always contains a little strangeness, an artless, unpremeditated, unconscious strangeness. . . . [39]

The Exposition essay also emphasizes another dominant theme of Baudelaire's writings—his indignant rebuttal of the erroneous hope in progress that permeated his age:

This grotesque idea, which has flowered on the rotten soul of modern folly, has released each man from his duty, freed each soul from its responsibility; and has liberated the will from all bonds imposed on it by love of the beautiful."[40]

The last and longest "Salon" essay—that of 1859—is the most artfully composed and indicates that its author had now thoroughly mastered and was supremely at home with this form of the essay. Published in four installments, it is the most rambling, disjointed, and humorous (containing far more witty, ironic, acerbic asides than all the others combined). It also meshes much more gracefully the theoretical critical commentary with pure journalistic reportage, hence illustrating to the highest degree Baudelaire's special brand of eloquence as an essayist. In the two chapters dedicated to the artist-poet's sublime function ("The Queen of Faculties" and "The Role of Imagination"), he gives mature expression (one might even say his definitive view) on this essential question. He asserts the truism that no artist can be worthy of the name if he does not possess a poetic sense of the universe. All human beings have, he states, "a dictionary of Nature" that allows them to express the basic elements of life (the problems of the human condition) in commonplace terms. However, only poetic souls—those imbued with divine imagination—can avoid merely "copying the dictionary" and hence can escape the fault of banality in realizing works of authentic, enduring beauty.[41]

The "Salon of 1859" also represents Baudelaire's most ambitious assessment of the current state of the arts of painting (presented under the topical categories of religion, history, fantasy, landscape, portraiture, and sculpture); and the reader is often accorded many lessons in art appreciation. On the subject of what to look for in a "good portrait," for example, we read: "Whatever the means most obviously used by the artist, whether he be Holbein, David, Valesquez, or Lawrence, a good portrait always appears to me to be like dramatized biography, or more like the natural drama inherent in the life of every human being."[42] And as an example of his many humorous, often acerbic asides, there is the following commentary on Millet's "pretentious peasants," as he calls them: "His peasants are pedants who have too high an opinion of themselves. They display a kind of brutishness that makes me want to hate them. Whether they harvest, sow, milk cows, or shear their animals, they always seem to be saying: 'Poor disinherited people of this world we may be, but we're nevertheless the ones who make it fertile.'"[43]

The essay was also immeasurably enriched through the form and direction given it by France's foremost scholar and outstanding intellect of the period, Ernest Renan (1823–92). This fascinating and most challenging thinker occupied in his century a role analogous to Voltaire's in the previous one in that, like him, Renan crystallized the dominant currents of thoughts and intellectual tensions of his period in an encyclopedic range of works. A scholar whose specialization was Semitic languages and literatures, Renan is chiefly remembered today for his monumental seven-volume treatise *L'Histoire des origines du christianisme* ("The History of Origins of Christianity"), in which he traced the history of the Hebraic peoples to the end of the Roman period. In the course of his many scholarly works he also systematically introduced French intellectual circles to the new and controversial biblical scholarship of the German rationalists (David Strauss, Johann Eichborn, and Frederich Greuzer, among the most important).

Renan was also undoubtedly the most controversial intellectual figure of his age. A former seminarian who had lost the faith of his pious Breton forebears in the course of theological study, he afterward dedicated the rest of his life of scholarship to the very intellectual and academic areas (philology and biblical exegesis) that had first provoked his youthful crisis of belief. Appointed professor of the Hebraic, Chaldean, and Syrian languages at the Collège de France in 1862, he soon became engulfed in a cause célèbre prompted by the publication in 1861 of his most controversial work, the *Vie de Jésus*. Written in much the same rationalist spirit as David Strauss's *Das Leben Jesu* (1835), Renan's *Life,* while extremely sympathetic toward and laudatory of Jesus as a supremely good, attractive, human being—"a gentle dreamer," as he is described—denied his divinity and attempted to explain away many of the miraculous events described in Scripture as having been invented or caused by natural phenomena: The resurrection of Lazarus, for example, was a pious fraud engineered by Christ's followers, and Saint Paul's vision on the road to Damascus was produced by an attack of sunstroke. Because of the tremendous controversy that the work engendered, Renan lost his professorship in 1864 (only to be reinstated in 1871). From this period to his death, Renan was the most forceful and eloquent spokesman for what could be called the primacy of the historical-positivist method for explaining human reality. History alone, he claimed, was the science that some day would provide the *oeuvre de synthèse* (definitive synthesis) and ultimate statement unlocking the mysteries of the human condition, of man's presence in the universe, and of his ultimate destiny.

Renan's essay production consists of five major collections: *Etudes d'histoire religieuse* (1857); *Essais de morale et de critique* (1859); *Questions contemporaines* (1859); *La Réforme intellectuelle et morale* (1871); and *Feuilles détachées (Separate Pages)*, 1872. These collections were made up of articles and reviews previously published individually in scholarly periodicals (*Journal des débats, Liberté de penser,* and *Revue des deux mondes,* to name the most important), as well as from public lectures and speeches given throughout his long and extremely productive life as a scholar.

Relatively early in his career Renan understood the growing importance of the critical essay of the Sainte-Beuvian model for presenting ideas to the educated reading public, and he adopted it as his favorite vehicle for writing. He seems also to have been one of the first to publicly promote and defend Sainte-Beuve's practice of gathering articles for publication in durable volumes, provided they were not merely light extracts or reviews of books, but critical pieces of enduring substance. Renan in fact claimed that these selected article-essays ("which often required more research and reflection than the original book") constituted "a new genre of literature, one most essentially belonging to our period, and the one in which we have demonstrated the most success."[44]

Renan also wrote two long essay-treatises: *Averroès et l'averroïsme, essai historique,* his doctoral thesis, which he published in 1861; *L'Avenir de la science, (The Future of Science),* written from 1848–49 at the height of his religious crisis but published only two years before his death in 1890; and three *Dialogues philosophiques* (1876) written in the style and tradition of Diderot's conversational essays and entitled *Certitudes, Probabilités,* and *Rêves.* In them Renan pursues his quest for answers on such questions as the nature of God and man's destiny; and there are also fascinating predictions of what man and human existence would be like in the world of the future.

The first collection of critical essays, *Etudes d'histoire religieuse,* appeared in the period during which the spirit of positivism was at its height. Renan's avowed goal in bringing together these essays recently published in the *Revue des deux mondes* was to bear testimony to the enduring presence of the "sentiment religieux" as the deepest human instinct. The scope of the collection is vast. As Renan describes it in his preface, "the pieces that compose the present volume all relate to the history of religions and in them are reflected (without prepossession) the principal forms that the religious principle or feeling has embodied from antiquity, to the Middle Ages, and to modern times."[45] Using the philological method suggested in *The Future of Science,* Renan explores this consideration in ten essays of which the most important are: "The Religions of Antiquity," "The History of the People of Israel," "Critical Historians of Jesus," "Mohammed and the Origins of Islam," "Life of the Saints," "John Calvin," and "Channing and the Unitarian Movement in the United States."

In these essays Renan employs for his scholarly method a motif favored by romantic scholarship, that is, the explanation of origins and innate preference for what are seen to be the most "spontaneous ages" of antiquity.[46] As a result, ancient religious forms are viewed as more poetic and less burdened with the growing materialism of later periods of history. The most glowing testimonies of the inextinguishable presence of the divine instinct propelling man to "inexpressible truth" are therefore found in the first three essays, particularly in the pieces on Greek religion and the monotheistic strivings of the Hebrew people (see titles above). There then follows the inevitable moment of decadence when the religions of antiquity are systematized into a state religion (during the reign of the Emperor Julian), and at this point, religious sentiment finally loses the *naïveté merveilleuse* ("the marvelous naïveté") of the Hellenic period.

The next collection, *Essais de morale et de critique,* is clearly the masterpiece of Renan's essay writings. Here he shifts his focus from the *sentiment religieux* to *sentiment moral,* or that "moral sense" that all human beings share. In his preface he in fact states that the existence of a "moral instinct" in the human heart is the one principle that no skeptical system can deny; and that in the midst of all other uncertainties, "good remains good, and evil evil."[47] This "tradition of what is good," he claims, further attests to a certain goal for every human life. Hence man cannot be fulfilled merely by cultivating personal happiness but must, in a Kantian sense, direct his actions to some form of moral obligation.

The thirteen essays that follow apply this principle of a self-evident moral instinct to topics designed to stimulate critical reflection on the moral, political, and social climate of France during the Second Empire. Written in the first and most repressive decade of Louis Napoléon's regime, they are intended to raise the level of consciousness of their presumably liberal-minded readers to the immediate dangers that the rot of materialism and untrammeled egoism of the period pose to the nation's very soul. Renan achieves his end by a very artful choice and arrangement of topics in the essays. Four of the first pieces explore the evolution of the liberal spirit (transmitted by the French Revolution) in the lives of four prominent Frenchmen of the generation before Renan: "M. de Sacy et l'école libérale," "M. Cousin," "M. Augustin Thierry," and "M. de Lamennais."

Editor of the prestigious *Journal des débats,* eloquent spokesman for the liberal school, and a most devout Catholic (Renan calls him a Jansenist), Silvestre de Sacy exemplified an unshakeable moral integrity. Victor Cousin was the "official philosopher" of the romantic period (espousing the new Kantian-Rousseauist tradition that stressed the very moral instinct that Renan was dealing with here). A distinguished historian of the Merovingian period who, after having lost his sight, heroically continued his research, Augustin Thierry is described in saintly terms as the very incarnation of a scholarly vocation pursued in the highest degree of disinterestedness. And Lamennais is presented as a fiery critic of the "old church" who, because he attempted to link democratic principles to Catholic dogma, was branded an apostate.

Though in every case Renan praises the lofty, serious moral aims manifested in the lives and works of these four men, they were he concludes, tainted in varying degrees by a similar flaw or failing, that is, a lack of rigor in their critical thinking. Then Renan goes on to suggest to his contemporaries that scholarship, eloquence, loyalty to existing governments or political traditions are in themselves not sufficient. Rather, efforts should be made to develop a new critical sense impervious to the excesses of romantic eloquence and rhetoric, one capable of clear-sighted commitment to the political and social realms.

Renan's severest critique of the modern age and the antidote he would offer to transform it are eloquently conveyed in the two closing essays of the series: "The Poetry of the Exposition," and the very celebrated piece "The Poetry of the Celtic Races." The first employs the Universal Exposition of 1855 as a means to assess the moral condition of French society at mid-century. Unlike Baudelaire, Renan seems to have little hope in, or fascination for, modernity, its potential "heroism" as Baudelaire viewed it, or its hidden charms. Instead he makes a disparaging comparison of the modern industrial exposition in Paris to the fair of Ocadh—a commercial and literary congress of the Arab world dating back centuries before Mohammed. This ancient fair, he claims, "valued poetry and regarded works of poets as major contributions"; the modern exposition, however, closed "without communicating with the imagination or providing a single stanza worthy of memory." This omission merely emphasized the most striking characteristic of the modern age: "general lack of grandeur and, consequently, of poetry."[48] Not denying that his century possessed "possibly more brilliant minds" than any previously, that it had come perhaps closer "to the truth in every respect," that it had perfected mechanical arts to a degree hitherto unknown, Renan nevertheless concludes that it had lost itself in sacrificing its best efforts to foster "the useful" in industry and technology.[49]

Having exposed the false values of the exposition, Renan, in his visionary piece on the "Poetry of the Celtic Races," posits his own ideal for human achievement. In it he juxtaposes the pragmatism of the modern age to the mystique of the Celtic peoples—that extended family of the Welsh, the Irish, the Bretons, and the Scots whom he regarded as sharing many similar traits. He characterizes the Celts as "an essentially feminine race"—one imbued with "power of imagination, love of adventure, and limitless vision." ("This race desires the infinite, thirsts after it, pursues it beyond the tomb.")[50] He devotes a large portion of the essay to a study of the Celtic imagination, as illustrated in primitive works dating from the sixth century (in particular, the Welsh epic *Mabinogion,* which incorporates Arthurian legend with combats of Breton heroes). From these accounts of idealist strivings against obstacles of all kind, Renan suggests that the "Celtic imagination" offers an appropriate model or vehicle for the "voyage" of human self-realization in the modern age. Like Brendan and Patrick ("dreamers and poets of old"), modern man must also have the courage to go beyond the known limits to develop his particular genius and philosophy. Hence in a period mired in materialism (the new "age of tin"), the Celtic spirit could well provide new spiritual impetus to effect the fusion of the poetic and critical spirit for the society to come.[51]

From the vantage point of a moralist concerned with the spiritual crisis of his age, in his two other major collections of essays Renan turns to comment directly upon the political situation of France during a period of unmitigated disaster. In the series *Questions contemporaines* (1869), he outlines what he views to be the dominant problems obstructing the development of a balanced and just society; and the fifteen essays in the collection examine such issues as the burning question of the relation of church and state: "Du libéralisme clerical"; the disarray in university education, "L'instruction supérieure en France"; a plea for academic freedom and the secularization of academic institutions in France (occasioned by his dismissal from the Collège de France), "La Chaire de Sancrit au Collège de France"; future trends in religion, "L'avenir religeux des sociétés modernes" ("The Future of Religion in Modern Societies"); and concrete proposals for the reform of the French university and secondary school system using the German institutions as models, "Les études savantes en Allemagne" ("Scholarly Studies in Germany").

The collection *Réforme intellectuelle et morale* represents an even more urgent appeal for wholesale reform and offers specific prescriptions to heal a society now viewed in an advanced state of moral and political turmoil and decay. Written during and just after the *débâcle* of 1871, these essays reflect the anguished state of Renan's mind, his frustrations and exasperation at the French failure to meet the Prussian challenge. They are also among the most provocative pieces that he wrote and have been responsible to a large extent for the persistent charge of his critics that, under the benign facade of liberalism, Renan harbored latent antidemocratic, if not fascist leanings.

The other major essayist of the second half-century was Hippolyte Taine (1828–93). Also a brilliant scholar with deep interests in philosophy, psychology, and history, he, along with Renan, was the most influential French thinker of the period. Appointed professor of aesthetics and art history at the Ecole des Beaux-Arts (Paris) in 1864, he received a doctorate from Oxford University (1871) for his works on English history and literature. A prolific writer, he published works that were encyclopedic in scope: five volumes on art history and theory; a massive twelve volume history of France, upon which he labored during the last twenty years of his life (*Les Origines de la France contemporaine*); very influential treatises on modern philosophy and psychology: *Les Philosophes classiques du XIXe siècle en France,* and *De l'intelligence;* and a very influential study on English letters still much read today: *Histoire de la littérature anglaise.* His essay writings consist of three volumes of collected articles on literary and historical topics entitled *Essais de critique et d'histoire; Nouveaux essais de critique et d'histoire* and two long essay-treatises: *Essai sur les fables de La Fontaine* (his doctoral thesis, published in 1853), and *Essai sur Tite-Live* (1856).

As much an advocate of science as Renan, Taine was far more taken, however, with the positivist spirit of the new sciences and, in particular, with the experimental method of investigation introduced by Claude Bernard in the fields of medicine and human psychology. Bernard's method was primarily one of gathering and classifying for the purpose of establishing necessary relationships. Once this was done, the scientist could then formulate a hypothesis on the basis of the cases observed—and even possibly discover general axioms or rules governing the phenomena in question. Taine's particular contribution, and certainly an epoch-making one in his day, was to apply this positivist methodology to the study of moral considerations and, more precisely, to those disciplines offering the richest possibilities for investigating the operations of the human mind: art and literature. Much influenced initially by the critical approach of Sainte-Beuve, Taine considered him "an inventor" because he had imported the methods of natural history to the area of moral considerations. Taine particularly admired Sainte-Beuve's emphasis on the study of "successive" milieus forming an individual—the forces of "race and the tradition of blood" found by studying family background. All of this he designated as "a kind of botanical analysis practiced on human individuals," which, in his opinion, was "the sole means of bringing together moral and positive science."[52]

Innovative as he was, Sainte-Beuve had not, in Taine's opinion, gone far enough. What remained to be done to bring the method to fruition was, he claimed, "to apply it to peoples, epochs, and races." And it was to this end that Taine would strive to write a history of the human mind using physiological and psychological methodology combined. Ultimately he viewed his role as that of a "psychological historian" who sought to unearth psychological and physiological factors shaping and even influencing peoples and events. What Taine proposed to study once he had established his method were three interrelated (and interlocking) considerations: 1) the analysis of the *faculté maîtresse* (master faculty) of great authors and artists; that is, the factor that gives the particular cast to their creative works and which distinguishes them from all others; 2) the reigning model (ideal man) whose spirit and genius characterizes a given century or age; 3) the history of an entire race or nation and the formulation of its national character by employing Taine's famous categories of *race, milieu,* and *moment* (heredity, environment, and historical period).

The essays are the dominant means that Taine used to conduct these experimental studies. The formal essay on Titus Livy represents, in fact, his first attempt to investigate what was the "master faculty" of this great political figure and chronicler of Cicero's period. In the preface, Taine first quotes Spinoza's dictum that "Man does not reside in nature as one empire in another but rather as a part of a whole . . . and the movements of that spiritual model which is our being are as controlled as those of the material world of which he is also part."[53] After an exhaustive biographical study of the man and a probing stylistic analysis of his works, Taine arrives at the conclusion that Livy's particular genius is contained in the formula "an orator turned historian."[54] By this he means that the orator Livy who combined the virtues of "a religious patrician and decent man" was turned by the force of events of his time (the fall of Rome and establishment of the Empire) from the role of statesman to that of historian. Hence the special eloquence in is own works and those of his contemporaries could thus be explicated and understood as a conjunction of these forces and events.

Taine's most sustained (and successful) attempt to define the spirit of his epoch is contained in his *Essai sur les fables de La Fontaine*. Using La Fontaine as the reigning model of the age of Classicism, Taine minutely explores the physical and moral environment in which he was formed—an approach he defends as valid since, he claims, "we can consider man as an animal of higher species who produces philosophies and poems a bit like silk worms build their cocoons and bees their hives."[55] The reader is thereupon invited to imagine himself before one of the "hives" created by human genius—the fables of this celebrated poet—as Taine proceeds to situate and delineate the factors responsible for these works. In his *oeuvre de synthèse* he describes La Fontaine as the product of the province of Champagne (fifty leagues southeast of Paris), where, he contends, "beauty is lacking but intelligence blazes forth."[56] By intelligence Taine says that he does not mean "the petulant verve and worldly gaiety of the Southerner, but that base wit, carefully calculated, malicious, inclined to irony, which finds its pleasure in the misfortunes of others." In short, Taine states, he is describing the geographical region of the *esprit gaulois,* that mordant, mocking spirit so brilliantly reflected in La Fontaine's works. "Just so," Taine concludes the chapter on "L'esprit gaulois," "does the mind reproduce nature. And because there has been a France, there has been, it seems to me, a La Fontaine and a French people."[57]

Turn-of-the-Century Critical Essayists:
Ferdinand Brunetière, Jules Lemaître, Paul Bourget,
Anatole France, and Rémy de Gourmont

Five major writers close the century with significant, even brilliant
contributions to the essay. All of the generation born between 1850
and 1860, they are well known for their literary criticism, and four of
them are literary authors in their own right: Bourget and France are
important novelists; Lemaître a popular playwright in his day; and de
Gourmont, a poet and novelist. Brunetière, the reigning critic of the
1880s and 1890s, alone confined his writings to literary studies. All
five also follow in the tradition set by Sainte-Beuve and Renan in that,
like them, they also first published their critical essays in various periodicals and then collected them in volume or series form.

As critics, the five acknowledged a debt of influence to the *grands
maîtres* writing earlier in the century. Brunetière and Bourget considered themselves disciples of Taine; Lemaître and France declared their
strong intellectual affinity and allegiance to Sainte-Beuve and Renan;
de Gourmont, as much an encyclopedist in his own right as Renan and
Taine, continued their project of disseminating new theories of science,
linguistics, and psychology in his prolific writings. And during the
last two decades of the century, all five became engaged in one of those
perennial literary skirmishes so cherished by French intellectuals on the
topic of whether literary criticism should best be conducted along sci-
entific/objective lines of investigation or whether it was by nature a
subjective, "impressionistic" function.

In the eloquent polemics that ensued, the five seemed, in fact, to
be playing out the tensions latent in the philosophies of their great
critical predecessors mentioned above. The skeptical temperament, reliance on intuition, and distrust of rigid classification of authors which
had come to be identified as features of Sainte-Beuve's approach were
elevated by Lamaître and France to a method they called impressionism. Sharing Taine's preference for scientific methodology, Brunetière
and Bourget advocated more formal and exact standards for interpretation: the first with his study of genre evolution and the second
through the psychological analysis of works conducted along sociological lines. Distrusting both rigid dogmatic rules or a totally subjective
appraisal in criticism, de Gourmont opted to educate the reader to
understand an author's particular sensitivity; hence he attempted to

educate the reading public to the aesthetic and psychological concepts contained in new forms of literature, such as symbolism or naturalism.

For over two decades the *maître de conférence* at the Ecole Normale Supérieure and the more or less official French critic of this period, Ferdinand Brunetière (1849–1906) adapted Taine's study of centuries or "ages" in literature to the historical evolution of literary genres, and some of the best written essays of the last (and present) century were composed by this intensely intellectual critic. His essay production consists of the series *Essais sur la littérature contemporaine* and the *Nouveaux essais*. There are also nine "series" volumes entitled *Etudes critiques sur l'histoire de la littérature française* (written between 1894 and 1906), which principally deal with earlier authors and periods. In his writings Brunetière developed a great facility for vast syntheses, and universal themes (for example, such topics as "Le caractère essential de la littérature française," "L'influence des femmes sur la littérature française," or "Le classique et le romantique"). Written in polished, measured prose, and free of affectation or idiosyncratic traits (except possibly the author's inordinate penchant for precise classification), these pieces develop what might be called the *style normalien* (academic style of writing), which a host of future French critics would adopt and continue. A convert to Catholicism and very conservative in his politics, Brunetière's was the voice in literary criticism advocating order, authority, and tradition against what he viewed as the greatest evil then abroad— rampant individualism and the various forms of the "cult of the self."

If Brunetière represented the critical views dominant in academic circles, Jules Lemaître (1853–1914) was, during the same period, the mostly widely read and popular critic. Born in Touraine of parents who were both *lycée* teachers, he first pursued a career in teaching as university professor, but after his writings became well known, he devoted himself full time to literary pursuits (writing plays and critical articles) and to editing the prestigious periodical *Journal des débats*. Lemaître's wrenching religious experiences—his early education in a minor seminary, loss of faith and conversion to positivist views at the Ecole Normale Supérieure, yet his enduring attraction to his childhood faith— made him emblematic for many of his own generation who had experienced a similar religious crisis. Like Renan, whom he greatly revered, he maintained throughout most of his life a "Christian piety without faith," but unlike the "Breton magician," as he once called him, he finally returned to the practice of his religion.

In the eight-volume series *Les Contemporains* (published between 1888 and 1918), Lemaître provides some of the most lucid and perceptive essays on literary criticism of the day. The more than one hundred pieces therein (collected from articles published in *La Revue bleue* and *Journal des débats*) offer substantial commentary on virtually all the significant writers (novelists, poets, playwrights, and critics) of the period, as well as on the literary movements and dominant issues. Attention is given to the Parnassian poets Leconte de Lisle and José-Maria Heredia; the realist-naturalist debate (amply covered by articles on Flaubert, Zola, Maupassant, Huysmans, and Bourget); and the symbolist movement (Baudelaire, Verlaine, and Mallarmé), for which Lemaître manifestly had little sympathy or enthusiasm, is nevertheless given serious attention. There are also a number of essays on major political figures such as General Boulanger, Kaiser Wilhelm II, and Barrès. The series *Contemporains* can thus be regarded as a valuable chronicle that records some thirty years of French intellectual, political, and artistic life.

Lemaître's critical approach was rooted in the traditional education in the classics—Greek, Roman, and French—that he had received during his formative years. Relying on judicious judgment formed by this system and on a philosophy of life inherited from these classical-moralist authors, he recorded and emphasized in his writings the personal "impressions" that he received in reading and reflecting over works. He dealt often with many of the same considerations—historical details, movements, genre study, and comparison of authors—as did Brunetière; yet he differed markedly from the latter in his conviction that his work was only the transmission of impressions admittedly personal and subjective. There is also a distinctly different style, one that uses the authorial "I" and is free of the professorial manner of lecturing, less aloof and rarely, if ever, moralizing or censorious.

Paul Bourget (1852–1935) was, after Zola and along with France and Loti, one of the period's leading novelists. In fact his work *The Disciple* (1889) caused a furor by its calling into question the morality of scientific positivism and the determinist theories of naturalist writers. During a long and productive literary career he tried his hand at poetry, drama, social commentary, travel commentaries, and major works of literary criticism. His considerable essay production consists of the two-volume series *Essais de psychologie contemporaine* and *Nouveaux essais de psychologie contemporaine,* published between 1883 and 1901; the *Etudes et portraits* (3 vols., 1898–1906); *Pages de critique et de doctrine* (2 vols., 1912); *Nouvelles pages de critique et de doctrine* (2 vols., 1912); and *Quelques témoignages (Several Testimonies,* 2 vols., 1928 and 1934).

Bourget's deserved reputation as major essayist and important literary critic rests primarily on the *Essais de psychologie.* In them he applies his astute psychological and sociological analysis of principal French writers of the generation of 1850. The subsequent essay collections, consistent in method and thought with those above, are applied to a broader spectrum of considerations: writers of the contemporary period (Barrès, Loti, Zola, Maupassant); art criticism; essays on political, social, and religious topics that reflect Bourget's increasing anxiety with the times, his personal crisis in religious belief and gradual espousal of political conservatism as remedy for what he views as France's deeply rooted social ills and moral malaise.

Also born into an academic milieu (his father was a teacher of mathematics in a *lycée*), Bourget was early attracted to the positivist thinking of the time and became a disciple of Taine, who was first his teacher and then close personal friend. Imbued with the Spinozist and Tainian belief in the heavy weight that the intellectual environment exerts on the individual, he developed the concept that literature (an essential if not dominant indicator of this climate) itself constituted "a living psychology." It therefore followed that through the psychological analysis of the greatest literary influence of a given period, a history of society's collective psyche, state of mind, and moral health could be established. Once he was convinced of the validity of this approach, he decided to compose a study along these lines for his own generation.

What motivated Bourget to involve himself in this inquiry was that state of moral depression and suffering (a veritable new *mal du siècle*) that he believed was afflicting himself and his generation. He describes it as "a kind of literary intoxication preventing me from living my life for myself."[58] This malady he saw as stemming from the fact that he and his peers "had asked books to educate their respective sensibilities." For as microcosms of the intellectual climate, books corresponded to the needs, problems, and thoughts of his particular group. Bourget therefore resolved to select those authors living between 1850 and 1880 whose influence on the young of the period had been decisive. These he would take to an "anatomy table," as it were, to determine of what particular nature and quality their sensibilities were composed.

The first volume of essays contains studies of the five major authors with whom, as historian of the "vice moral" of the period, Bourget

chose principally to deal: Baudelaire, Renan, Flaubert, Taine, and
Stendhal in that order. The superbly written and most insightful analyses given these authors revolves about finding the chink in each's intellectual and psychological armor, or more precisely, Bourget's
assessment of the respective flaw or flaws by which each had misused
or perverted his genius.

As he judged the matter, the principal "negative" states of mind or
morally damaging attitudes developed by these authors and transmitted as moral contagion to the French themselves could be reduced to
the following: dilettantism (Renan); cosmopolitanism (Stendhal); decadence (Baudelaire); excessive analysis (Taine); and a failure of will and
loss of energy to act (Flaubert).

The second volume of the essays does not add to the number of basic
ills introduced in the first but only testifies to the their continued
"presence" and influence on a new set of literary figures: Alexandre
Dumas *fils* is linked to Baudelaire through the "perversion of love" that
his theater depicts;[59] Leconte de Lisle reaffirms in the form of poetry
Flaubert's impassivity through a moral vision starkly circumscribed by
minute and exact attention to physical detail; as such he becomes (with
Flaubert) a leading exemplar of "moral nihilism" for the next generation.[60] Through their impressionist prose style the Goncourt brothers
illustrate in its final stages what Bourget describes as "that nervous
illness that is the sickness of this century," and so forth.[61]

Anatole France (1844–1924) early established his reputation as a
leading writer of the period through poems composed in the Parnassian
tradition (*Poèmes dorés,* 1873) and brilliant, short fictional works such
as *Le Crime de Sylvestre Bonnard* (1881), and *Le Livre de mon ami* (1885).
It was not until about 1886 that he began to write critical essays for
the review *Le Temps* which were subsequently printed from 1888 to
1892 in the four-volume series *La Vie littéraire.*

In the first volume of the *Vie,* France credits as his most immediate
influences Sainte-Beuve, "from whom we [critics] all descend," Renan
"our master," and Lamaître, whom he admired "for his sense of the
relative and for his anxiety at the eternal illusion which surrounds
us."[62] Yet it is Montaigne, particularly the skeptic of the *Apologie de
Sebond,* whose "presence" resounds most powerfully throughout the entire essay collection.

As a critic France believed there was no such thing as objective criticism or even objectivity in art as a whole; consequently, all "who boast
of putting anything more than themselves in their works are," he says,

"victims of the most fallacious illusion." Denying in the same passage that we can ever get to know objective reality ("the truth is that we never get out of ourselves. . . .") he goes on to describe criticism as "a kind of novel for the use of clear-sighted and curious minds, and every novel is, in the long run, an autobiography." A good critic for France, then, is "one who recounts the adventures of his soul through masterpieces."[63]

To this disclaimer of objective criticism France also added other comments linking him to Montaigne's personal traits and style of writing. Gratified by the warm reception accorded the first volume of the *Vie* he suggests that this has been the case because of his "natural, spontaneous style" and the "only skill" of which he is capable, that of "not hiding from my faults." He admits that he often had contradicted himself but, he says, "poor human beings, we must ever concede that each of us has two or three philosophies at once."[64] And as to the charge that the articles are loosely constructed, he states as his only concern that "the road be filled with blossoms, no matter where it may lead."

France also offers in terms unmistakably reminiscent of Montaigne his own strong defense of self-revelatory details as a valuable and authentic literary component. Granting that the "superior man" needs only to talk about himself by using those important events in which he has been involved, he holds that "ordinary men" (those of Montaigne's "common herd") are better suited to talk about and paint themselves:

Their portrait is that of everyone and everyone recognizes in their adventures and mental states his or her moral and philosophical problems. . . . Their examination of conscience is as profitable to us as to them, and their disclosures form a manual of confession for the entire community.[65]

Any sustained reading of the more than three hundred essays of the series reveals that France has admirably put into practice the stylistic and philosophical concepts enunciated above. In fact, his articles are far more appealing in their presentation of personal view and attitudes by a very wise, sensitive, and cultured human being than as works of a professional critic. This is not to say that they are lacking in literary perception or acuity, but only that France consistently gives greater weight to the expression of the personal musings and convictions that his readings elicit than to definitive judgments or statements. Taken as a whole, the essays present the observations of a moralist who consistently reveals a most sympathetic, even indulgent attitude toward the spectacle of man, ever the victim of frailty and illusion in a universe that remains essentially impenetrable and mysterious. In a review on the work *La Vertu en France,* by Maxime Du Camp, for example, he writes:

> In the midst of the eternal illusion that envelops us, one thing alone is certain, and that is suffering. It is on this corner-stone that humanity, is founded as if on an unshakeable rock. . . . It is the unique witness to a reality that escapes us. We know that we suffer and we do not know anything else. It is on this burning granite of sorrow that man has solidly established love, courage, heroism, and pity.[66]

And in his efforts to make tangible to his readers the beauty and value of great masterpieces of literature, he consistently strives to apply the themes and "truth" of the work to the common realm of lived experience. Reviewing a performance of *Hamlet* at the Comédie Française, for example, he addresses the prince in these words: "You are of all times and countries. You have not aged one hour in three centuries. Your soul is the age of each of ours. We live together, Prince Hamlet, and you are what we are, a man in the midst of universal evil."[67]

France's other major essay work, *Le Jardin d'Epicure*—a compendium of "thoughts and reflections" composed in the moralist format—was published in 1892. This "manual of skepticism," as "The Garden" has been called, is made up of snippets and more extended passages drawn from articles also published in *Le Temps* but not included in the serial volumes. A product of France's earlier, nonpolitical period (before his conversion to socialism and then to communism), these selections reveal him again to be an arm-chair philosopher much in the tradition of Montaigne as he discourses on such topics as the apparent (but often illusory) conflicts between science and morality ("La morale et la science"), the vain attempts of metaphysics to explain truth and morality (the charming dialogue "Ariste et Polyphile ou le language métaphysique"), and on what he believed to be the arrogant claims of Brunetière (whom he does not name) to have established rules for a "universal consensus" for critical taste ("Château des cartes").

The most original critic of the group (to whom T. S. Eliot referred as "the critical conscience of his generation"), Rémy de Gourmont (1858–1915), was also an encyclopedist in the tradition of Renan and Taine. Like them, he synthesized in his writings major new currents of thought in psychology, philology, philosophy, and—his area of particular interest—zoology and physiology. His extant works, numbering forty bound volumes, have been praised by Ezra Pound as providing "the best portrait available, the best record there is of the civilized mind from 1885–1915."

After completing legal studies at Caen, de Gourmont left his native Normandy to assume the post of assistant librarian at the Bibliothèque Nationale in Paris; he was there only a brief period, however, before personal tragedy entered his life. When twenty-five, he was afflicted by lupus, which so greatly discolored and distorted his face that he felt forced to retire. From that point on he had to curb his strong appetite for social life, to renounce his habitual philandering, and to give himself over instead to the solitude of study and writing. The remainder of his intellectual career was tied to his relationship with the avantgarde periodical *Mercure de France* (which he helped to found in 1890) and to his "conversion" to symbolism through the influence of Mallarmé. At first hostile to the new movement and to Mallarmé himself, he experienced what he called "an esthetic tremor" upon reading the latter's *La Vie vague,* which forever affected (and altered) his poetic tastes. As one of the editors of the *Mercure* (along with Charles Morice and Henri Regnier), he continued to promote the symbolist poets and new currents in literature, and to contest the critical approaches to both Brunetière and the impressionist critics.

De Gourmont's essay production consists of several long treatises, the most important of which are *La Symbolique au moyen âge; Le Problème du style; La Physique de l'amour, instinct sexuel;* and two volumes of biographical sketches of symbolist writers, *Livre des masques, portraits symbolistes.* In addition, there are the major collections of essays that had first appeared in the *Mercure: La Culture des idées; Promenades littéraires;* and *Promenades philosophiques.*

The collection *Culture des idées* (1900) may be regarded as a seminal work that presents the major themes that de Gourmont pursues throughout his life: 1) his theory of "disassociation of ideas" (in the essay of that title); 2) his preoccupation with the physiological/psychological elements as they affect the process of artistic creation ("La création artistique"); 3) the problem of style in literature ("Du style ou de l'écriture"); 4) the study of decadence and its true meaning ("Stéphane Mallarmé"); 5) paganism as an enduring ethical and cultural ideal for life ("Le paganisme éternel"); 6) and a strong defense of free love ("La morale de l'amour").

The collection *Promenades littéraires* presents the broadest spectrum of literary topics: modern French authors (Huysmans, La Forgue, Villiers de L'Isle-Adam, Jules Romains, Barrès, Maeterlinck); writers of earlier periods (Marie de France, Héloïse and Abélard, Casanova). What is particularly striking is the large number of articles dedicated to foreign literature and authors (for example, such diverse figures as George Meredith, Gongora, Bret Harte, Shakespeare). There is, in fact, an extensive section entitled "Etudes de littérature américaine (vol. 6), which includes articles on William Cullen Bryant and Ralph Waldo Emerson ("deux poètes de la nature," as they are called) and a very perceptive study "L'Humour et les Humoristes," in which de Gourmont analyzes various aspects of English and American humor: in particular, psychological, sociological, and economic factors affecting the nonreflective, more virulent, freer, and more spontaneous brand of humor of the American—"the result of a nation devoid of cultural heritage and in which citizens are prey to a more primitive environment."[68] The evaluation he gives here of Washington Irving, Twain, and Emerson as humorists is solid by any standard and his analysis of the levels of dialects ("patois") used by Twain in *Huckleberry Finn* demonstrates an astonishing grasp of the racial, demographic, and regional makeup of the United States at that time.[69]

The most versatile essayist of this generational group (and certainly among the most versatile of any in the French tradition), de Gourmont also composed a series of meditative essays, personal in tone, that surely rank among the most moving written during any period. In the three-volume collection *Promenades philosophiques* he is eager to apply the fruits of study and reflection to the problem of how to live "à propos." Written in the form of friendly conversations, many of the more than ninety pieces of the series convey a cosmopolitan spirit and wisdom gained through living both reminiscent and worthy of a Montaigne (for example, the essays "Colors of Life," "Praise of Pleasure," "Rivers of France," "Essay on Envy," "Young Girls," and "Fall of Days"). Other pieces present his scientific-psychological beliefs and theories in a genial, nonpolemical tone that is far less intense and urgent than that of his more formal essays (the titles, "Psychology of Taste," "Place of Man in Nature," "Berthelot the Chemist," "The Insurrection of the Vertebrates," and "The Question of Free Will").

The essay's rise in the nineteenth century to the status of an authentic, widely used, but still undeclared literary genre is intimately bound up with the rapid growth of journalism in France. For it was with the plethora of new periodicals, journals, and reviews introduced during the century that what would become the dominant form of the genre received its initial impetus and evolved. Descending from the political essay (the "letter" and "discourse") of the Enlightenment and remodeled by Sainte-Beuve, any nineteenth-century critical essay worthy of the title was a published, scholarly, even brilliant article that often survived its brief existence in a periodical by being preserved in a bound volume.

Whether out of personal reticence or more probably as a reaction to some of the effusive outpourings of romantic authors of the early part of the century, French essayists by and large seem to agree basically with Renan's judgment that "to speak of oneself is always bad, for this supposes that we have a high opinion of ourselves."[70] In observing this dictum, they develop a tone that is neither familiar nor impersonal, one that I believe to be unique to, or at least best developed by, French essayists. In the writings by such authors as Sainte-Beuve, Renan, Lemaître, and de Gourmont, for example, the use of the personal "I" does not become the source for confessional revelation but rather provides a heightened degree of intensity and conviction by which an author presents his essential views, identified as such.

As regards its function, the nineteenth century essay can best be described as a vehicle for "vulgarisation"—a term that in French conveys the honored process of making a work available to a wide-reading public, in the most talented and appealing way, the new scholarship, thought, and technical knowledge brought forward by the leading minds of any given period, and all of that as it relates to vital issues of the day. Again I am indebted to Professor Chadbourne, this time for having led me to the following apt passage by Matthew Arnold describing this difficult art. Though Professor Chadbourne applies the quotation to Renan's brilliant achievements as an essayist, I believe that it can legitimately be applied as well to the work of French nineteenth-century essayists as a whole, and certainly to the major writers studied in this chapter:

The great men of culture are those who have had a passion for diffusing, for making prevail, for carrying from one end of society to the other, the best knowledge, the best ideas of their time; who have labored to divest knowledge of all that was harsh, uncouth, difficult, abstract, professional, exclusive; to humanise it, to make it efficient outside the clique of the cultivated and the learned, yet still remaining the best knowledge and thought of the time, and a true source, therefore of sweetness and light.[71]

Chapter Five

The Essay in the Twentieth Century

Characteristics and Function
of the Modern French Essay

In the beginning of the twentieth century, the essay finally achieves the status of a major literary genre. This belated recognition of the essay by French critics occurs during a period in which there is also a marked shift in taste for more personal forms of literary expression. In fact Florian-Parmentier, who was a well known critic at the turn of the century, regarded the essay's rise to prominence as somehow symptomatic of this general change in preference. As he saw it, most important French authors of the period (no matter in what literary genre they were writing and whether aware of it or not) were composing works that, in form and content, closely approximated essays.[1] He apparently meant by this that the distinctions traditionally separating the major literary genres (and the novel in particular) were becoming increasingly blurred; hence, French authors were now giving much greater emphasis in their works to self-revelatory matter (thinly veiled in fictional form) or, at the very least, were deliberately and self-consciously fleshing out their works with their most personal thoughts and opinions on a host of topics. And certainly, the introspective forms given to the novel of this period by authors such as Proust, Gide, and Alain-Fournier, to name only a few, bear out Florian-Paramentier's claim of a strong vogue in literature for personal self-expression.

In such a climate it might seem logical to expect the essay to reflect this trend and, given its great flowering in the modern period, to predict that the familiar form of the genre would perhaps emerge as the dominant one. In short, one might think that previous reticence on the part of French writers to adapt Montaigne's model (or something like it) would finally be overcome. Such, however, is decidedly not the case; as any serious examination of the modern French essay will demonstrate, in its major manifestations the genre continues to hew to the critical form handed down by Sainte-Beuve, Renan, Taine, et al. And though the modern essay has broadened its scope to embrace a multitude of topics other than those dealing with literary criticism, it has by and large remained impervious to self-portraiture or disclosure pursued for their own sake. Hence, with few exceptions (chiefly in the case of a few lyrical essayists),[2] the modern form eschews the use of the autobiographical-confessional format. Rather, it strives to transmit, with the use of varying kinds and degrees of critical/scholarly ballast, the convictions, theories, opinions, and speculations of an author on any given topic.

This situation at first may seem quite paradoxical. Why, we may ask, should one of the most freewheeling and personal of literary genres resist the general drift to self-expression and analysis so characteristic of literature of the modern period? One reason for this seeming anomaly must certainly be the enormous vogue also enjoyed by the more clearly (and predictably) personal literary form of the autobiography. A significant and frequently used literary form in France since the appearance of Rousseau's *Confessions,* the autobiography unquestionably rivals the essay in the twentieth century as the most prominent and popular kind of nonfictional writing. Indeed, there are few major modern essayists who have not tried their hand, at least once, at some form of this genre, be it memoirs, souvenirs of childhood, or the *journal intime* recounting stages of a life.[3]

Surprisingly little scholarly study has theretofore been dedicated to elucidating the essential differences that distinguish the essay from the autobiography; and though it is both an interesting and important consideration, it can only be touched upon briefly here. Professor Philippe Lejeune gives one of the most helpful and lucid commentaries on the matter in his excellent introductory work, *L'Autobiographie en France.* In it he describes this literary form as differing from the essay (which he identifies with Montaigne's model) because it is a narrative that, in a definite chronological time sequence, relates the personal history of the individual in his or her words. He sees as the essay's primary function, on the other hand, that of synthesizing "points of view, styles of personal expression, and modes of analysis of thought" on a given subject that the writer presents as his own.[4]

Though the essay and autobiography naturally share elective affinities as personal forms of expression, Lejeune's general distinction between the two is most definitely borne out in any examination of twentieth-century manifestations of the two genres. It is true, more-over, that modern French essayists have tended to use journals, mem-oirs, or other related forms for any sustained project of self-portraiture. Thus, as was the case in the nineteenth century, the modern essay in France continues to operate in a literary space virtually equidistant between autobiographical modes of writing and pure fiction.

Because of this continuing inhibition to use confessional or autobio-graphical forms for its primary focus, the twentieth-century essay re-mains in most instances a serious and quite formal vehicle for expression. Professor Henri Peyre has, in fact, described it as generally "overburdened with serious speculations . . . and [with] philosophy almost as pedantic as that of academic treatises, though not as rigor-ous."[5] Though, in my opinion, he considerably overstates the case in so far as his charge of pedantry is concerned, I would certainly concur with the remainder of his above comments.

Professor Robert Taylor has perhaps more generally (and felicitously) captured the spirit and function of the modern French essay by likening its function to "a spring board for speculations."[6] Using it to this end, an essayist can thus conduct systematic investigations, spin theories, or simply speculate upon a myriad of topics and issues (philosophical, moral, economic, political, social, and other) which, to varying de-grees, reflect the many problems attached to living in the modern world. I believe that Professor Taylor's description admirably char-acterizes the form and function of the modern French essay and have used it in this chapter as a working definition for my study of the genre.

It is impossible within the limits of this compact study to provide anything more than a basic outline for the prolific output of essay writings in the twentieth century. My aim is therefore to provide an overview for roughly the first half of the century in which I provide: 1) a description of the major manifestations of the genre: 2) brief sketches of some of the most important essayists; and 3) short analyses of certain landmark essays that are indispensable for a proper under-standing of and appreciation for the function and place of the essay in the cultural and intellectual life of modern France. As a means of ap-proach (and for the sake of clear and logical development), I have grouped essayists and essays in clusters; the authors and works included within each have been placed there because they seem to share definite affinities (similar views, like concerns, and common topics), or because they have utilized and developed similar forms of the genre.

Essayists Who Continue the
Moralist Modes of Writing

Traditional moralist prose forms (aphorisms, thoughts, extended reflections, and portraiture) find continuation in the twentieth century in the writings of a number of prominent writers. In fact, some of the major essayists I shall consider (André Gide, Paul Valéry, Simone Weil, and Albert Camus) have produced as vital parts of their "complete works" journal-notebooks in which they give free flow to their reflections (often registered on a daily basis) and refine their patterns of thought by the use of aphoristic jottings.

Yet four important writer-essayists in particular demonstrate striking affinities with moralist writers of the past of their intellectual interests, habitual choice of topic, and general predilection for moralist forms in their writings. Alain, André Suarès, Jean Rostand, and François Mauriac have all dedicated much of their literary output to the moralist probing of conduct and motive; moreover, they share a similar preference for universal statement, couch their findings in the traditional moralist literary forms mentioned above, and in their essays are reluctant to engage in confessional disclosure or specific analysis of the self to any great extent. Rather, they apply their observations on the human condition to the needs and problems of human beings as a whole.

The first of these, Emile Chartier (1868–1951), or Alain in his self-styled pseudonym, is one of the most influential intellectual figures of the century. The son of a veterinarian who practiced in rural France (Mortagne, in Orne), Alain had deep roots in peasant life. He never lost, in fact, his familiarity with nature and understanding of country life, which he gained accompanying his father on his daily rounds. Early recognized for his brilliance, he quickly rose through the educational system and completed studies in philosophy and literature at the Ecole Normale Supérieure. Beginning his career as a lycée teacher of philosophy (Alain never wished to teach on the university level), he brilliantly filled several assignments in the provinces before being called to Paris to the prestigious Lycée Henri IV in Paris. There he held the chair of philosophy and prepared students for entry into his alma mater, the Ecole Normale. (He also taught one class each year to the girls at the nearby Collège de Sévigné.) By the time of his retirement in 1933, Alain had attained an extraordinary reputation for being a masterful teacher—creative, demanding, but venerated by generations of students. Unquestionably, he played a major role in shaping some of France's most eminent minds: André Maurois, Jean Prévost, Henri Massis, Pierre Bost, Simone Weil, and Maurice Schumann all emerged from his classes, as did a large number of future teachers who transmitted his method of inquiry and love of truth throughout their own academic careers.

Despite the pressures of teaching, Alain became a prolific writer and authored many long, formal treatises on philosophy, morality, aesthetics, and literary criticism. A few of his most important works are *Système des beaux arts, Mars ou la guerre jugée, Les dieux, Idées, En lisant Dickens,* and *Stendhal.* Yet his enduring reputation as a writer and thinker reposes on the thousands of brief essays composed during his lifetime. As early as 1906 he invented his own essay form, the *propos* ("proposition"). This short aphoristic piece generalizes from a concrete fact, observation, or set of circumstances and usually suggests or conveys ideas for action in the moral, political, or social spheres. Alain never varied the length or manner that he used for writing these brief pieces. (Never exceeding two hand-written pages, they were always composed in one sitting and without recourse to erasure or revision of any kind.) Extraordinarily varied in topic and written in deceptively simple prose, in a genial and familiar tone, the *propos* provide wise and incisive comments on all manner of topics. In them Alain combines the most homely and humble matters—the grooming of horses, the act of yawning, bird songs, animal fables, gymnastics, the phenomenon of laughter—with the most abstruse philosophical concepts or theories drawn from Plato, Kant, Descartes, and Hegel. Through them all he advances his central moral/philosophical ideals and gives generously of his counsels for "the art of living."

One of his most attractive collections of essays, *Propos sur le bonheur* (1925), is, in fact, nothing less than a manual of prescriptions for confronting all of life's problems with courage, discipline, and a good sense of humor. Among the ninety-three entries we find, for example, such titles as: "The Art of Yawning," "Mental Hygiene," "The Art of Looking Well," and "The Obligation of Being Happy." These contain many simple but striking aphorisms and counsels well seasoned by wisdom and experience as, for example, the following comments on happiness (from "Victories"):

As soon as a person looks for happiness, he is condemned not to find it; but there is no mystery about this. Happiness is not like some article in a showcase window that one can pay for and take away. . . . Happiness is only happiness if you possess it. If you look for it outside of yourself, in the world, nothing will ever resemble it.[7]

Numbering over 6,000, the *propos* achieved a tremendous vogue during their author's lifetime. First published in provincial newspapers, they were systematically gathered after World War I into special topical groupings like those above on happiness: *Propos sur la religion, Propos de politique, Propos d'économie, Propos sur la littérature,* to mention a few. Rich in historical relevance and most valuable as reflectors of the French political and social climate in the first half of the century, the *propos* combine the moralist enterprise of observing man and his world in general with concrete suggestions for bettering the state of things observed. Like Montaigne, whom he closely resembles in the emphasis he gives to a man-centered philosophy and the celebration of life as an art, Alain prescribed a nondogmatic method of finding happiness through proper judgment and understanding. Yet as a man of his century he refused to find repose in Montaigne's personal cultivation of the self or to come to terms with the world through the consolation of religion or anything other than an active commitment to transform the social and political order. His ardent espousal of republican principles, his deep-rooted pacifism and hatred of war, and his personal philosophy stressing the power of the will to initiate decisive action, all became powerful modes of thought strongly influencing and motivating French intellectuals during the first half-century.

André Suarès (1868–1948), poet, critic, and essayist, can best be described as a kind of magnificent failure who lived on the margins of the French literary-intellectual establishment during most of his life. A brilliant student at the Ecole Normale Supérieure and a friend of Romain Rolland, Paul Claudel, and André Gide, Suarès, like Léon Bloy, seems to have had a kind of genius in offending friends and well wishers and in creating difficult (if not wretched) living situations for himself. Throughout most of his life an outsider by his own volition, he incarnated Baudelaire's vision of the artist-pariah as tortured soul and passionate seeker of the beautiful. Like Baudelaire, he also expressed utmost contempt for conventional views in art, literature, and music; a self-declared enemy of all such "cant," he viewed himself as a member of an elite (the "happy few") whose role it was to contest the prevailing standards in taste and criticism—the vapid *idées reçues* of the bourgeois world. From his constant vantage point as itinerant scholar and esthete, he proclaimed his belief that his age had hopelessly bastardized all forms of art and culture; and turning his back on his period, he followed his own star with utmost contempt for what others thought of him. Critics responded in kind to his disdain with what amounted to an almost total conspiracy of silence as regards his own writings.

Though Suarès's literary output was considerable, little today remains in print. Works still in circulation include the three volumes of aphoristic "thoughts" entitled *Voici l'homme*, in which the author examines with frank and mordant commentaries basic contradictions in human nature: *Le Livre d'émeraude*, a series of prose paintings of the Breton countryside; *Voyage de condottiere*, lyrically controlled and lucid travel essays on the Italian cities of Florence, Pisa, and Venice; *Bouclier du Zodiaque*, a collection of thirty-four prose poems using astrological signs and Parnassian precision of detail; and several collections of minute and psychologically penetrating portraits of artists, authors, musicians, and other well-known figures chiefly drawn from the nineteenth and twentieth centuries: *Présences* including Musset, Mallarmé, Dostoyevski, Mussolini, Casanova, and Napoléon; *Musiciens:* Beethoven, Liszt, Wagner, Chopin, and Mozart; and *Trois grands vivants: Cervantes, Tolstoï, Baudelaire*.

Voici l'homme (1906) is perhaps the work that best illustrates Suarès's use as essayist of moralist forms. In this collection of "thoughts" that he considered dangerous because of its "free expression of ideas, sharply held opinions . . . [and] its absolute nihilism," he offers both abstract/ timeless views on human nature as well as mordant commentaries on political and social problems of his own period. Writing from the isolation of his sea-side retreat in Brittany, he explores the topic of "power," which he calls "the absolute reality of the human condition," how it can be defined, and the manner in which it has been absolutely incarnated in archetypical human roles (that of Caesar, the saint, and the artist).[8] Other topical divisions introduced are order, force, passion, idols, love, and religion. Suarès's aphoristic statements are provocative and often arresting. We read for example: "To overcome obstacles, more often than not, is to cease to believe in them. One only loves or hates absolutely the religion in which one has been born." or: "We are all pagans by instinct and Christians by instinct—more or less one or the other according to circumstance."[9]

And there are many lyrical dithyrambs to celebrate, in sea imagery, Nietzche's concept of the "eternal return" and the voluptuous linking of natural man to the ephemeral beauty of the earth ("Mother spouse, lover who feeds, mass of pleasure and corruption, eternal sweetness, eternal cruelty").[10]

As a political observer Suarès also presents in violent terms his absolute dislike for modern German civilization ("Brutal Germany is Europe's death . . . born yesterday, European for only a day, this barbarous power has no soul in its power").[11] And he lashes out against the "Yankees who . . . are the brutal boundary, the pyramid of vanity, and light that neither illuminates nor gives warmth."[12] Likening the United States to a kind of Egypt of the modern times, Suarès regards America as "the inhuman power of matter without soul," and calls upon a crusade led by Mediterranean Europe to reunite against this foreign threat.

Jean Rostand (1894–1977) used the moralist format of the essay to pursue his meditations on the substance of man from the angle of vision of the scientist. The second son of the playwright and poet Edmond Rostand, he was an eminent biologist and pioneer in parthenogenesis (that area of biology that investigates reproduction by means of an unfertilized egg). Research that he pursued in this field led, in fact, to the splitting of chromosomes through the process of congealing; and in recent years his work has had vital application to research conducted in genetics engineering. By the time of his death, Rostand had published over fifty volumes of writings. Much of it deals with his scientific research on the life cycle of animals. He also published his autobiography (*Journal d'un caractère*) and a collection of essays dealing with the biological "history" of a human being from first life in the embryo to death (*Aventure humaine*). His best known works and those in which he indulges the free play of his mind are the essay volumes *Pensées d'un biologiste* (1939) and *Carnet d'un biologiste* (1959). In these he muses on the impact that biological discoveries have had in changing commonly held views on what man is and how he as a scientist applies the fruit of scientific investigation to philosophical and ethical concerns.

A man of tremendous erudition and with deep interest in philosophy, literature, psychology, and art, he was well able to relate the results of his biological research to the traditional teachings of philosophers and moralists. Especially challenged as a scientist by Pascal's views, as a believer, of man's place in the universe, he frequently recast celebrated Pascalian "thoughts," contrasting or paralleling them with facts or data drawn from biology and genetics. By his apt references to science, he thereby gave new and striking dimensions to these and other traditional views forwarded by moralists and philosophers. An atheist and fervent humanist, he thus provided his own very personal vision of man, seen as a biological and genetic being. Unfortunately only a few examples can be given here of the remarkably cogent thought and beautifully chisled prose style of this important essayist, who was both a renowned scientist and avowed humanist. On Pascal's view of man as midpoint of the two infinities, Rostand remarks:

> The two infinities that Blaise Pascal trembled to think of are today the familiar ground of science. The infinite of bigness is the province of the astronomers; that of smallness falls to the physicists. The biologist stands midway between; yet it is he who, without ever quitting the realm of living matter, comes in touch with the prodigious. Man has no need to plunge into the Pascalian abysses in order to be appalled by what he is: let him merely scrutinize his own substance.[13]

And on the composition of our human substance—our communality and our individuality—he writes:

> All human diversity results from the virtually infinite combinations of genes. All of us are formed of the same chromosomal dust; none of us has a single grain of it that he can claim as exclusively his own. It is our ensemble that belongs to us and makes our separate identities: we are an original mosaic of banal elements. . . . Through his hereditary make-up each individual may lay claim to a basic originality.[14]

François Mauriac (1885–1970), one of France's greatest modern novelists, had also achieved, at the time of his death, universal recognition as the most prominent Catholic writer and novelist of the age. Like so many of his fellow authors, Mauriac tried his hand at several literary genres: autobiography (*Mémoires intérieurs* and *Nouveaux mémoires intérieurs*), drama (*Asmodée* and *Les Mal Aimés*), and above all, the essay. In fact his essay writings make up a substantial part of his literary output. These fall roughly into two categories: 1) long formal essays on biography and other shorter pieces on literary criticism and apologetics; 2) his journalistic essays, the *Bloc-Notes*.

As regards the first category, it is an author of psychoanalytic essay-biographies that Mauriac seems to have achieved lasting renown. The most important of these are *Vie de Jésus, Blaise Pascal et sa soeur Jacqueline, La Vie de Jean Racine,* and *Dieu et Mammon.* His life of Jesus presents Christ viewed through the New Testament not as an artifical or self-controlled person but rather as "the most quivering of the great figures of history and, contrary to all the characters proposed by it, the least logical because the most living." In a critical study of his life and works, Jean Racine receives passionate attention seemingly because Mauriac views him as a veritable counterpart of himself: that is, a Catholic writer who has been raised in a Jansenist environment of "high tension." Furthermore, like Mauriac, Racine in his own day had had to work out his destiny as a vulnerable man torn between the tug of the flesh and the call of the Divine. Pascal is also presented as a man of passion who knew full well, at the pinnacle of success, that he would have to overcome his pride in knowledge and pleasure in society ("the delicious and criminal use of this world," as Mauriac puts it). These themes converge in the autocritical essay *Dieu et Mammon,* in which Mauriac describes the "split personality" of the believing and practicing Catholic author who, committed to the Christian message, cannot for that falsify reality in his literature. He therefore must present sin in all its natural appeal even though this may trouble and unsettle the consciences of "good Catholics."

Mauriac's most universally appealing (and readable) essay pieces are his short journalistic articles. Like Alain, he in fact created his own personal essay form, the column *Bloc-Notes* that for over thirty years appeared on a weekly basis in such periodicals as *Echo de Paris, Le Figaro, Le Figaro littéraire,* and *L'Express.* Not mere reportage but in his own words a kind of *"journal intime* for the use of the reading public," these weekly essays imparted Mauriac's moralist reflections, musings, and judgments ranging from insignificant details, topics that interested him personally, to reactions on important political events and social issues of the times. The following subjects, culled from the published volumes of *Bloc-Notes,* give some idea of their diversity of topic: Mozart; a visit of Greta Garbo to Paris; reflections on his country house in Malagar; Don Juan; love of Russian novels; denunciation of the Soviet work camps; polemics with Camus, with Sartre, and with leading Catholic clergymen; condemnation of political reprisals after the Occupation; criticism of American economic "imperialism"; the visit of Eisenhower to Paris; portraits of John Foster Dulles, Adenauer, Danny the Red; and the chronicle of "the events of May, 1968."

Collected in six published volumes (five *Bloc-Notes* from 1952–69 and the volume *Le Bâillon dénoué* [*The Loosened Gag*] written during the period of the Liberation), the articles reveal a fiercely independent spirit and one that refuses to be aligned with any particular political party. And though Mauriac concedes that he is of the "Right," he condemns pharisaism, political expediency, and sordid self-interest whenever he encounters them. In the columns he also indicates, long before Sartre and the existentialists launched the enterprise of political commitment, an equal willingness to put his column in the service of his Christian faith and ideals; and far from being an arm chair philosopher or a detached moral observer, he applies these values to the turbulent events of the century in articles remarkable for their frankness, polemical verve, and spirited defense of deeply held convictions.

For example, during the first months of the Liberation he became appalled at what he considered the excessive sentences meted out to persons charged for uncertain or minor charges of collaboration with the enemy (especially if the defendants were intellectuals). Refusing in this instance to confound "justice and vengeance," as he put it, Mauriac thus became embroiled in a celebrated polemic with Albert Camus, then on the editorial staff of the publication *Combat*. Camus had, in fact, suggested shortly before this that Mauriac's expressed charity and solicitation for war collaborators was out of place and itself a kind of scandal considering the horrendous nature of crimes committed and the need to restore confidence in justice after the dark years of the Occupation. Mauriac responded by using an argument to which Camus would have recourse a few years later when he himself would denounce the willingness of all political parties in postwar Europe to use murder to forward their aims:

Charity and love, two words to indicate what Pascal is writing about here: "All minds and bodies taken together are not equivalent to one act of charity. . . ." But this is decidedly of a more elevated order. Charity now has been retired from both camps and this absence creates an unsettling sameness between enemies who believed themselves to be irreconcilable. Certainly we are not any less aware than is Mr. Camus of how our enemies would handle the question of reprisal if they again came to power. But more perplexing is the fact that they would find their penetential system just about intact. We haven't let any rust grow on the machine we inherited from them.[15]

The Essay in the Service of the Past: The Assault on Modernity and the Cult of France

Many manifestations of the formal essay written during roughly the first two decades of the century share remarkable consistency in topic and concern. In general terms these can be described as embodying two major themes: the first involved a distrust, or discontent with, and even revulsion from modernity in most, if not all, of its moral, political, and social implications; the second consisted of a poignant and spirited defense of the traditional values of "old France" that were now regarded as having been placed in jeopardy by the spirit and doctrines of the modern age. These general topics (which I name "the assault on modernity" and "cult of France") were promoted by a distinguished number of authors and essayists. Prominent among them were the leading writers of the Catholic Renascence of the early century (Léon Bloy, Charles Péguy, and Henri Massis), who demanded that Christian values be lived absolutely and with conviction. They therefore castigated the political and spiritual condition of French bourgeois society (in particular, its anemic moral condition, rampant secularization, and deflated spiritual values). Three other authors (Maurice Barrès, Charles Maurras, and Julien Benda), though not believers (or even Catholic in Benda's case) shared many common concerns and a similar repugnance for various aspects of modern thought and life. And all of the above (whether committed Catholics or not) adhered strongly to Péguy's celebrated dictum that *le monde moderne avilit* (the modern world degrades).

Léon Bloy (1846–1917) belonged to the nineteenth century in his formation and beliefs but possessed what has been described as a keen visionary sense of political and social problems prevalent in the twentieth century. Throughout his life he led what can best be described as a lonely, wretched, even lamentable existence. Of an extremely violent, polemical nature, Bloy constantly turned on his would-be friends and allies and became a kind of "thankless mendicant," hurling invectives at friend and foe alike during his constant wanderings. He was, on the other hand, a man of apocalyptic vision and with absolute faith in Christian revelation which he interpreted in an uncompromising form of Catholicism. Assuming the role of a Jeremiah (some have said a latter-day Torquemada), he condemned the modern world for having turned away from Christian values and the spirit of poverty, and toward the odious evils of business and profit motivtion, with the resulting manipulation of the poor. He also constantly denounced the new Pharisaism of the bourgeois who, he claimed, legalistically interpreted scripture and doctrine to justify their own slavish attachment to material gain. The visionary part of his witnessing consisted in the unshakeable conviction, often expressed, that God continued to manifest His power and presence in the world even though human beings were too sunk in corruption to recognize His presence; furthermore, He would come again, Bloy proclaimed, in some cataclysmic occurence that would make Christians recognize anew "the predestination of their baptism."

In the work *Le Sang au pauvre* (1893), Bloy constructs a series of moral essay pieces advancing the theme that the poor, closest to Christ and exemplum of the way anyone practices Christian virtues, were being systematically devastated by the greed of the rich in the modern world. He identifies the "blood of the poor" as money and likens it to the "flagrant and sweating symbol of Christ the Savior." The "blood of the rich" he describes as "a fetid puss exacerbated by the ulcers of Cain."[16]

Embroidering on the theme of the systematic exploitation of the poor, he writes extraordinary passages filled with indignation, passages in which he violently condemns all "respectable" and "powerful" elements of society. For example, in the section entitled "Worldly Priests," he deplores the moral calibre of the contemporary ministers of Christ. Counting them in dozens of ten ("'We need ten to make a dozen,' say pig merchants") Bloy contends that "A total of fifty worldly priests would not even make up one single Judas, a Judas who returns the silver and hangs himself out of despair."[17] And in an extraordinary revision he makes of the silk factory scene in the medieval verse romance *Yvain ou le chevalier au lion* (in which young girls are made to work in cruel working conditions), Bloy inveighs against the modern world's similar exploitation of child labor: "And here is the horror of horrors: the work of children, the misery of the very young exploited in industry conducted for the rich. And this occurs in every country. Jesus had said: "Let them come to me." The rich say, "Let them go to the factory, to the workshop, in the darkest and most lethal of our hells."[18]

Charles Péguy (1873–1914) resembles Bloy in his condemnation of many aspects of the modern world; yet more measured in tone, Péguy held out hope for reform through committed action. Moreover, as a faithful student of the philosopher Henri Bergson, he would devote his life to incorporating socialist ideals to the latter's concept of *durée* (time or duration)—which implies man's duty to conquer time and space in a humanistic project.

During his rather brief life, Péguy was an encyclopedic essayist and publicist. In 1900 he founded the periodical *Cahiers de la Quinzaine* and filled its issues through the next fifteen years with book-length essays covering a vast range of social problems, political issues, and personal crusades of one sort or another. The essays also intermittently provide (depending upon the topic) many biographical details and a kind of continuous narration describing the adventures of a soul through many phases of thought and commitment: from being an ardent socialist, Péguy became disenchanted with left-wing political ideologies, returned to Catholicism in thought and spirit, if not in membership, and then became the theoretician of a new political mystique. This mystique he would later describe as the "harmonious city"—a kind of marriage of the City of God with social concepts of justice advanced by republican-socialist principles.

Now almost a legend in France, Péguy is extremely difficult to describe. He is not simply one of many intellectuals to found and publish a review dedicated to literary, political, and social issues (and one that failed as a business venture). Rather, he has been described as "the expression of a sensibility, of a conscience, of a will or, as he would have said, of a 'charity.'"[19] What he incarnated was a strong national aspiration to reform and renewal analogous in his own age to the efforts of Joan of Arc centuries past. Péguy was to attempt, in fact, to restore for France the purity of the republican ideal, which, as he saw it, had become calcified and debased by submersion in the political arena and official adoption by the Socialist party. And, in a celebrated passage from one of his essays, he laments the passing of the socialist ideal from a "mystique" to a political doctrine now manipulated for selfish ends by Jean Jaurès and other prominent left-wing politicians.[20]

Though much of his prophetic, mystical vision for France is developed in his collections of poetry (*La Tapisserie de sainte-Geneviève et de Jeanne d'Arc* and *Le Mystére de la charité de Jeanne d'Arc,* in particular), the essays of the *Quinzaine* gives a better idea of his day-to-day concerns and battles as a committed journalist. Foremost among the themes he relentlessly pursued are his sharp attacks against the moral and religious dispositions of the modern world. In the essay "Zangwill" (1904), Péguy singles out the two "evil geniuses" who, as he believed, had spawned the modern spirit—Renan and Taine. Renan he castigates for having made man a rival of God, and Taine for his preposterous theory that he could unearth the secret of genius by utilizing scientific methods to explain history and human creativity. The same themes and attacks are considerably expanded upon in the description that he would give of French society as being seriously (if not terminally) ill. In the very long essay "Concerning the Grippe" Péguy, recuperating

in bed from that illness, adroitly invents an imaginary dialogue between a doctor and patient and weaves into it an extended critique of
the "romantic sickness" of writers of the earlier period, along with
many allusions to current political matters and issues. Romantics (and
again his arch-enemy Renan) have, he claims, discredited work by their
false claims and facile reliance on the mystical illumination of the spirit. Such elitism, he claims, has drained young people of their natural
inclinations to give of themselves in the social order through hard and
honest labor, for the social order can only be changed through such
meticulous efforts. He further states that "to pray is not to work," and
French society would be much better off if clergymen had relied less
on private prayer and more on practical and sustained good works.[21]

Péguy's rejection of the spirit of the modern age is generally accom-
panied by a romantic evocation of "old France," of the days of his
boyhood. In one of his most personal and moving essays ("L'Argent,"
1910), he makes a sharp distinction between the "artisans" of the past
who have become the "workmen" of the present:

We knew workers who each morning when they got up would think of nothing else but their work. They arose (and at what a time) and they sang at the
thought that they were going to work. At eleven o'clock they were still sing-
ing when they went to get their soup. . . . Work was their very joy and the
profound root of their being. . . . There was an incredible honor in work, the
most beautiful of all honors, the most Christian, the only one that is
sustained.[22]

Other important topics developed in the essays are the call to defend
France against what Péguy (who lost his life at the front in the first
months of the war) saw as far back as 1905 as the threat of German
militarism ("Notre patrie," 1905); the general inadequacy of French
university education because of its preoccupation with filing cards,
doctrinaire methodology à la Durkheim, and the debased quality of
thought resulting from this preoccupation ("De la situation faite à
l'histoire et à la sociologie et de la situation faite au parti intellectuel
dans le monde moderne," 1907); and a strong defense of Bergson's
philosophy ("Note sur M. Bergson et la philosophie bergsonienne,"
1913) from attacks leveled at it by such critics as Julien Benda.

Ten years older than Péguy, Maurice Barrès (1862–1923) is another
prime example of the committed French intellectual of the period who
used his writings to develop and expound upon his political views and

aspirations for his country. An active politician (he was a member of the *Chambre des députés* for more than twenty-five years and a leading spokesman for the Right), this novelist, essayist, and propagandist evolved a program that he believed would bring France out of the moral morass brought about by the debacle of 1871 and the political turmoil of the Dreyfus years. In his first major literary production (a trilogy of novels published between 1888 and 1891), he brought to national attention his celebrated program of the *culte du moi*. By this program he proposed a search for one's own personal truth, the laws conditioning one's being, and the elementary forces that control it. The goal of such a question would be a kind of exaltation of the self or, as he further described it, the ability to realize one's deepest feelings through the most effective use of analysis possible (*"sentir le plus possible en analysant le plus possible"*). In this way Barrès sought to discipline the romantic impulse by orchestrating and controlling the diverse and contradictory forces that make up the reality of the person.

From this first stage of what might be called a form of directed narcissism he eventually proposed to harness this exaltation of self and the knowledge acquired therein to a national program for renewal of all aspects of French life. This harnessing he endeavored to accomplish by inculcating in his fellow citizens increased patriotic fervor for their country's traditions in general and an enhanced feeling and appreciation for their own original roots in particular. Along with these changes (though not an orthodox believer himself) he urged a renewed respect for and adherence to France's national form of religion, Catholicism. Only through these means, he argued, could the nation tap the strong sources of national energy needed in its present rivalry with, and possible future military involvement against, an increasingly menacing Germany.

Barrès's major essay collections were written almost exclusively to forward one or both of these ideals of the "cult of the self" and service of "national energy." The first major series, *Du sang, de la volupté, et de la mort* (1894) applies travel experiences and impressions to the process of developing a heightened sensitivity to his own inner life and to exaltation of various facets of his emotional makeup rendered possible by contact with the outside world. In the work he identifies sites in Spain, Italy, and his native Lorraine as symbolizing moral attitudes or approaches to life. Spain personifies a violence and passion that nevertheless exult in deliberate ascetic renunciation (exemplified by a Don Juan); hence the country is a strong and living model disposing man to subsume contradictory passions and psychological states in the same manner.

Expressing much the same reaction as Albert Camus would register in similar travels several decades later, Barrès finds that Tuscan Italy trivializes passion because of its striking but impassive, somewhat inhuman beauty, and by its relaxed sensuality and appeal to dilettantism.[23] In Ravenna, a kind of "magnificent tomb," he reaches the nadir of life experience in which even death, neutralized by boredom, has lost its force.

The third phase of his travels, through Lorraine, delivers him from the tedium experienced in Italy. When he visits a zoo (in "Le crépuscule chez les animaux"), he is buoyed up by a new sense of affinity with fellow human beings who, having evolved beyond animal life, find solace in the fragile bonds of human love. The essays on various aspects of nature (animals and trees) that follow seem to reconcile him with the reality that what is human must die. In a meditation on Gounod's funeral while he was walking through the gardens of the Grand Trianon ("Sur la décomposition") Barrès exclaims: "Here I accept death. Only dismal November frightens me, so dark and without desire to please."[24]

The next major collection, *Amori et dolori sacrum* (1903), marks a turning point in Barrès's evolution from the ideal of personal self-realization to that of championing various aspects of national "rootedness." By far the most memorable of these essays, "La mort de Venise" describes the city in magnificent lyrical terms as the very incarnation of the decadent spirit. But this same Venice, so often associated with those "beautiful souls" (Goethe, Chateaubriand, Byron, Taine, Sand, and Wagner) who succumbed, even if only temporarily, to its many temptations, Barrès claims to see for what it is: a beguiling trap for the emotions, a "courtesan," a "magician." Though the city's strange beauty cannot be contested, one must, he maintains, go beyond the worship of a beautiful artifact and find some kind of energy (presumably animal) with which to activate and channel one's vital forces. Venice, as one critic claims, thus taught Barrès to preserve the best attributes of romanticism: constant openness to new possibilities for experience as well as the constant vigilance against being frozen or mesmerized by passions and sentiments no matter how tantalizing.[25] That this resolution led him to a new shift in focus is manifested in the last essay of the collection, "Le 2 novembre en Lorraine." In it he clearly gravitates from the "cult of beauty"—now viewed as a prison of narcissist solitude—to the "cult of the dead"—here a positive gesture of solidarity with one's ancestral roots.

The third collection, which closes the circle in Barrès's intellectual and political evolution (*Les Amitiés françaises,* 1903), is in reality a tract on education in which he indicates how a youth should be formed in order to recognize his patriotic obligations to serve the national effort. Barrès's subject in the book is his son Philippe, who, as a member of the next generation, is taken as emblematic of the destiny of France. In the early pages of the essay the spectacle of children of many nationalities playing together on a European beach allows Barrès to meditate on how each will be dominated or influenced by moral and political forces that are infinitely varied. Thinking of his own son, he asks of the process of education that "it facilitate for each individual the fullest enjoyment of powers accumulated through the hereditary series."[26] Philippe, with his "weighty Lorraine heredity," should, Barrès declares, be educated in a system emphasizing in children "their innate faculty for growth . . . so they may draw from what they possess at birth." Above all, he concludes, all care should be taken that a child not become "an artificial being, a lying adult."[27]

Henri Massis (1886–1970) was a leading Catholic apologist and important member of the neo-Thomist revival led by Maritain. As an essayist he is perhaps best known in French circles for a long treatise defending Western civilization and values against what he considered, after World War I, to be a wave of "orientalism and Germanism" threatening the Western liberal tradition (*Défense de l'occident,* 1927). Earlier he wrote a memorable and influential essay on the state of French education at the turn of the century: *Agathon, ou l'esprit de la nouvelle Sorbonne—la crise de la culture classique; la crise du français* (1911). Still smarting from his own educational experience at the Sorbonne, Massis mounted in this essay a sharp criticism of what he regarded as the new and dangerous threat that the scientific method of Durkheim and the sociologists (a form of "Germanism") now presented to the teaching of the liberal arts. With arguments that could easily be adapted to debates now raging on the aims and method of education in our own computer age, he registers his fear that the universal application of the scientific method will lead to "a progressive debasement of general culture," to the end of the liberal arts tradition, and the formation of a new kind of person: not the *honnête homme* of the Renaissance tradition but the *esprit spécialiste.*[28] In fact, the concept of the liberally educated person nourished by the classics and trained in moral judg-

ment is, Massis contends, now considered an outmoded form of dilettantism; and in its place there has been established a new kind of moral
categorial imperative, that is: "Prepare yourself to be useful and to fill
a definite function." The new intellectual model, then, is not morally
sensitive human beings but rather "good cogs that fit in the general
mechanism."[29]

Taken as a whole, Massis's essay is one of the strongest defenses of a
general liberal arts education to have been written by anyone this century. In fact most of what is found therein of a general nature—lucid
arguments against education conducted only for professional utility,
solid reasoning to counter the fear of parents that a liberal-arts education will seriously disadvantage those entering the job market, and an
eloquent defense of the concept that students also need to know and
appreciate unproductive ideas (that they should not be formed to be
simple technocrats but thinking individuals)—is perhaps even more
pertinent today.

Though an agnostic, the essayist, journalist, and political theoretician Charles Maurras (1858–1952) was early allied with right-wing
Catholic intellectuals by his hatred for republican forms of government. One of the earliest adherents to *Action française* (originally a
republican antidreyfusard group), he was the chief architect in trans-
forming it into a movement dedicated to the overthrow of the republic
and to the restoration of a strong hereditary monarchy. He also founded
the journal *Action française* to popularize his political philosophy and
program for change; and at one time this persuasive propagandist had
grouped around him such prominent writers as Bourget, Lemaître,
Barrès, Bernanos, and Maritain. Appalled by the narrowness and rigidity of his views, his virulent anti-Semitism, and nascent fascism, most
thinkers gradually turned away from him, yet not without some regret
at having lost such a powerful spokesman for the Right.

One of the most cogent and provocative political essays written during this century is Maurras's early assessment of France's political condition and how it should be remedied, *L'Avenir de l'intelligence,*
published in 1905. In the essay he sets out: 1) to trace the demise of
the French state as an effective governing body—this tragic situation
caused, he claims, by the subversion of intellectuals and writers, and
2) to suggest a way out of the present crisis engendered by the weak,
ineffectual government of the republic. As regards the first, Maurras
develops his belief that the writers and intellectuals of the Enlightenment period, who were largely responsible for the destruction of the

monarchy, secretly lusted after that power which they had claimed should be vested in the people. When royal authority disappeared, legal sovereignty, rather than devolving to the people, was diverted to the real successors to the Bourbons, the men of letters. Incapable of understanding or of coming to grips with the "force" of events inherent in any political system, these writers (particularly with the advent of the romantic movement) progressively lost control of the reins of power and became instead a kind of subculture; "intelligence" was therefore dethroned from places of power and became progressively alienated from the real course of events and issues. With such figures as Baudelaire and Huysmans (precursers of modernism) literary people had virtually become victims of their own alienation and personal excentricities. As a result, the general public had come to regard their works as "bizarre and incomprehensible." On the other hand, the nineteenth century had witnessed the rise of a new power structure and allocation of money; immense fortunes had been made by a few families through industry, change, and speculation. Hence the earlier "elementary simplicity" had forever been altered and "French power" was now totally manipulated by an aristocracy of money.

Faced with this modern totalitarianism of wealth, the writer-intellectual could only survive by selling his services in the role of a parasite. This "selling" or conversion of intelligence for money in the marketplace represents for Maurras, "the real peril to contemporary intellectualism." To break up this combine of wealth and power in the hands of a few (mostly non-French or Jewish) families, Maurras suggests a program in which "intelligence" be directed to promote the cause of "force" in a powerful authoritarian state.[30] In this system, intellectuals and writers, long at odds with the concept of a strong French government, would no longer have to oppose national interests because of their bondage to "foreign gold." For with the reinstitution of a hereditary monarchy, the natural law of blood would replace the venal mercantilism of the socialist system, and French "intelligence" would finally have triumphed over the tyranny of money.

Another major essayist and political thinker who was Maurras's contemporary Julien Benda (1867–1956), could not be more diametrically opposed to the former's proposal for subordinating the role of the intelligence to political ends. In fact, as the very incarnation of the professional thinker, Benda devoted his whole life and writings to exactly the opposite principle, that the proper role of the intellectual is precisely to remain disengaged, even to be an adversary of political institutions and of the social order itself. Born of a wealthy Jewish family he early devoted himself to the life of a scholar-thinker. His intellectual temperament revealed a strong mathematical turn of mind and a marked preference for rational, abstract philosophical thought based on the Greco-Roman ideal of order. Historically Benda believed that the rationalism of the Enlightenment represented a high-water mark in the development of the mind, and he viewed with antipathy romantic (and postromantic) literature as well as most forms of modern philosophy (he was early an ardent critic of Bergson).

During his career Benda wrote several important cultural/philosophical essays, among the most significant of which are *Belphégor* (1918), an attack on the decadence of modern French society and the cult of subjectivism and vagueness in modern arts and literature; *Le Bergsonisme ou une philosophie de la mobilité* (1912), in which he takes the philosopher to task for indulging in "lyrical rhapsodies" and for replacing a philosophy of reason with feeling; and *La Trahison des clercs* (*The Betrayal of Intellectuals*), his most famous writing and that for which he is principally remembered. Published in 1927, the essay attained almost immediate and universal attention and was hotly debated in intellectual circles in Europe and America. And its title has subsequently become almost a cliché to express what continues today to be a controversial point of view.

Very difficult to present in any short summary, the essay is essentially a sharp attack on the modern world and the role that intellectuals play in it. Modern societies can be characterized, Benda believes, by nationalist sentiments that evolved in the nineteenth century during the rise of democratic systems. Endemic to these sentiments is an irrational, patriotic principle teaching that a citizen must uphold his country's interests whether they be right or wrong; the result of this view, he claims, is a devastation of the tradition of honor and justice underlying the older systems of monarchy or parliamentary rule.

One of the leading causes for this drastic change in attitudes toward the social order Benda sees as the changed role of the modern *clerc,* or intellectual. In its medieval sense the term meant one who "urged his fellow beings to other religions than that of the material."[31] Today, however, the modern "clerk" has lost his moral sense, has left his ivory tower, and plays an exactly contrary role. He has, in fact, descended to the market place with a vengeance and now places himself at the service of national passions. Essentially the sin of the intellectual consists, then, in the betrayal of a trust. Bending to the pressures of the times, the modern thinker has emphasized the emotional, the particular, or the practical at the expense of truths that are universal and spiritual. He has thus largely effected the subordination of intellectual humanism in favor of a murky sentimental humanitarianism (or love of human beings in the concrete). From this aberration there has stemmed a multitude of modern heresies: nationalism, pragmatism, utilitarianism, emotionalism, jingoism, debasement of philosophy, logic, and so on. In fact Benda seems absolutely convinced that modern society is, in all its manifestations, essentially corrupt and evil. Among the most prominent of the modern "Clerk"-betrayers Benda lists Bergson, Barrès, Bourget, Maurras, Péguy, d'Annunzio, Kipling, Brunetière, and William James, who, as the apostle of pragmatism—the religion of the "new order"—is perhaps the most dangerous.

The Essay as World Mirror

Whereas major essayists of the early part of the century give most of their attention to problems relating to France in the modern world, French writers after World War I undergo a decided change in emphasis and content. Subsequent generations of writers, whether in their prime of life in the 1920s (for example, Bernanos, Claudel, Valéry, Gide, and Duhamel), or just then arriving at maturity (Sartre, Camus, Weil, and Beauvoir), provide a series of essays more cosmopolitan in point of view and more universal in application. No longer intent solely on deploring the modern state of things or regretting a lost past, major essayists (who are also the most influential literary figures of the first half of the century) offer penetrating analysis and voice strong (often anguished) concern on a broad range of topics relating to the state of man and society viewed globally. Some of the more common variations and subtopics on this major theme include the following: spiritual, political, and economic appraisals of present-day society; concerns expressed at the rise of totalitarianisms; the erosion of spiritual values and resulting dehumanized social structures; the threatening vision of European society in the approaching era of advanced technology; fascination with, but apprehension of, American society as a harbinger of the new social and economic order; critiques of communism and capitalism; particular topics written on such perceived modern injustices and problems as racism, prejudice, colonialism, bourgeois hypocrisy, conformity; and various studies on art, literature, and aesthetics, with particular emphasis on reevaluating the creative process as it now applies to the total dimensions of man in the world of the twentieth century. What follows then is a summary introduction to the kind of serious formal essay written in France during the last fifty years (and roughly up to 1960). This presentation is obviously not intended to be exhaustive but rather representative of some of the best and most important works written during this time span.

Georges Bernanos (1888–1948) is (along with Mauriac) the most influential Catholic writer and novelist of the century. Yet he also wrote a number of essays that reveal him to be a powerful visionary figure with keen political sense. His anguished and often repeated message is the grim warning that modern Europe, in the last stages of dechristianization, is floating toward dehumanized, totalitarian forms of government in which human beings will be systematically transformed into kinds of robots. The two most important and substantial essays that reveal the evolution of Bernanos's political theory and his increasingly bitter indictment of contemporary religious and social institutions are the book-length works *La Grande Peur des bien-pensants* (*The Great Fear of Conservative Catholics*), 1931, and *Les Grandes Cimetières sous la lune* (*Vast Cemeteries under the Moon*), 1938. The first is reminiscent of the spirit and even the manner of Péguy's writing through its sentimental and nostalgic re-creation of the atmosphere of an earlier Christian past. In it Bernanos purports, initially at least, to be writing the biography of Edouard Drumont, (1844–1917) a rightwing Catholic, member of the monarchical political action group *Camelot du roi,* and author of the notoriously anti-Semitic pamphlet, *La France juive* (1886). Far from being a biographical account, however, the work is in reality a requiem for a period that has passed, and more especially for the demise of the "true" Catholic activism exemplified by Drumont and the antirepublican partisans of the early *Action française* groups. Bernanos seems, in fact, to be indulging in a refabrication of the "golden days" of his youth; and to his role model and tutor Drumont Bernanos gives titanic dimensions that allow him to tower over his ideological adversaries (Jews, Dreyfusards, and republican parliamentarians) as well as compromising and timid conservative Catholics of all stripes: insincere priests, diplomatic bishops, cowardly politicians, and the venal petite bourgeoisie.

In the more substantial part of the essay, Bernanos relates his change in attitude to World War I (in which he had served as a common soldier). Regarding it (while it was being waged) as a "sacred war," he now views this conflict with horror because it has filled Europe's cemeteries with the broken bodies of young soldiers who died defending the cynical interests of the wealthy and powerful. Bernanos further observes that Christianity lies groaning on its death bed, and he declares that the poor of this world are again to be sacrificed for nationalistic and mercenary interests in a terrible new war that is now being prepared. And the primary cause for this state of moral chaos he declares to be the betrayal of the Gospel teachings by the solid mass of practicing middle-class Catholics (the "reactionary" *bien pensants* of the political Right). He seems to be remarkably accurate when, in another part of the essay, he prophesies the rise of multinationals and the increasing bureaucratic control that these would exert on economic and social aspects of the individual's life in the Western democracies of the future. He declares for example, in the conclusion of the work:

The powerful capitalist democracies of tomorrow organized for the rational exploitation of man for the profit of the rich, with their frenetic statism, inextricable network of institutions of insurance, of trusts, will end up by erecting between the individual and the church an administrative barrier that even a Vincent de Paul will not be able to bridge.[32]

The equally long and impassioned essay *Sous les Grandes Cimetières* continues the author's lamentations on the vain sacrifice of the dead in the Great War (to which the work's title alludes). It has for its major theme, however, an indignant exposé in the most polemical terms of Franco's brutal repression of the Nationalists as he (Bernanos) had witnessed it on the island of Majorca, where he was then living with his family. Though at first a supporter of General Franco's cause, Bernanos became disgusted and appalled by what he had learned or seen with his own eyes. Despite his natural right-wing sympathies, Bernanos was finally forced to conclude that the Franco regime constituted a repugnant form of terror.

The essay is written in an even more disillusioned, pessimistic tone than the previous one. For Bernanos no longer sees any way to overcome the collusion of the "pious" conservative Catholics who place order and their own material interests before the spiritual and charitable ideals of the church. He further puts himself on record as opposed to the fascisms of Hitler and Mussolini; and the power of the press, of money, and of the modern heresies that have combined to destroy the concept of a Christian society. There is in fact, he concludes, no society left in the sense of a community of people, but only a solid phalanx of the bourgeois, drawn up on the Right and Left, and both possessing equally sordid interests at heart.

With the rich and extremely varied works that make up his prolific essay production, Paul Claudel (1868–1955) clearly reveals himself to be a modern virtuoso of the genre. His essay collection run the gamut from penetrating articles on art criticism, and particularly of the Dutch masters (*L'Oeil écoute*); to articles on poetic theory, poets (Jammes and Rimbaud), religious art, liturgy, music, and decorum in church (*Positions et propositions*); a series of dramatic dialogues (*Conversations dans le Loir-et-Cher*); short meditations on Scripture in which the author lets his imagination rewrite or complete biblical texts (*Figures et paraboles*); and many incidental journalistic essays written during his years as French diplomat on three continents—including an appointment as French ambassador to the United States—(*Contacts et circonstances*).

Taken as a whole Claudel's works testify to the omnipresence of the Divine Word in both the physical and human dimensions of the universe, as revealed in Scripture and interpreted by the Catholic Church. As a poet, dramatist, and writer, Claudel constructed a symbolism that attests to another world beyond that of appearances, a world that, as the deepest of human aspirations, defines and constitutes the very core of the human person. Claudel's literary mission was therefore to keep alive and intensify by use of symbol and analogy man's understanding of the spiritual destiny for which he has been created.

To varying degrees the essays bear out unmistakably those intentions. For whether they are cast in scholarly discourses or recount the day-to-day experiences and reflections of their author, they bear witness to the Claudelian principle that man does not suffice in and for himself; that the physical universe, in its diversity, beauty, and moral chaos, is incomplete, even impenetrable, unless viewed as the extension and work of the Divine Artisan.

The four *Conversations dans le Loir-et-Cher* (1935) are assuredly Claudel's most imaginative essay creations. Cast in the form of imaginary conversations, they have been described by him as "a hazardous picnic of propositions of odds and ends, written in fits and starts." Composed during intervals between his diplomatic "seasons," the conversations allowed Claudel to give vent with total liberty to the free play of ideas and associations that came upon him during moments of leisure. As such they were exercises in which he could give full rein to his lively imagination and *esprit fantaisiste*. Thus it is interesting to note that, like Diderot two centuries earlier, Claudel found the "conversation" form of the essay to be the most congenial for spinning out in dazzling array ideas and concepts still germinating and incomplete.

Extremely diffuse and tentative in their patterns of thought, the conversations are virtually impossible to summarize and are better read and meditated upon than described. Essentially they consist of four gatherings of groupings of people occasioned by every-day experiences common to any reader: The first three occur in the vicinity of a non-existent river/stream located in the department of Loir-Cher. Entitled *Jeudi, Dimanche,* and *Mardi,* they involve a cast of six characters (four men and two women). The men have Latin first names, which to some extent characterize their temperaments and opinions (Acer, Civilis, Flaminius, and Furius), and the women, Florence and Palmyre, are designated respectively as a musician and an actress. The first conversation takes place in the month of July on a terrace before the stream; the second, in August, is occasioned by a boat trip undertaken by the party on the river; the third occurs on a levee of the Loire somewhere between Chaumont and Amboise when the auto transporting the group breaks down. The Fourth conversation (*Samedi*) marks a radical shift in locale and character. In it the reader finds himself somewhere between Hawaii and San Francisco on a Japanese ship returning from the Far East. The participants are two urbane and experienced world travelers, Saint-Maurice and Grégoire.

The first three conversations are linked by the preoccupation their interlocuters have for such topics as the nature and quality of life in modern society, the increasing isolation of the individual despite increased means of communication, the changing face of the modern city, no longer built on a human scale but as a megalopolis; good and bad examples of modern architecture; futuristic proposals for the city of tomorrow (with kitchens and workshops constructed on lower tiers and the recreational space above and "closer to Heaven"). Why Claudel gives so much attention to the city in its modern manifestations is made clear when he explains what it means symbolically to him:

A city is the sojourn for souls. It is not a place in nature where we are seated in the middle. It has been built and arranged expressly for our residence. Here man sees nothing around him which is not the work of man and which does not bear the mark of an intention (either effectual or limited. . . .) This is why religious writers always see the future sojourn of the blessed or damned in the form of a city, of a spiritual community. It's Sion or Henokhia. It's Saint Augustine's City of God. It's Florence of the quattrocento.[33]

The central theme of the three conversations is the thesis that the contemporary city (with its particular sociological disposition and architectual arrangement) prefigures in time man's earthly pilgrimage to the eternal city. By their efforts, human beings can thus abet or hinder this spiritual ascent according to the degree of concern and charity that they accord (within this urban living space) to the needs and aspirations of their fellows. (We must, Claudel insists, ever come to the aid of others when we hear their "cry in the night"—that voice of despair of those in need of comfort and solace.)[34]

The fourth conversation provides its author with the opportunity to express his views on the essential difference in philosophy and attitudes held by the Orient and West, respectively, in such matters as politics, nature, and art. Especially striking here is Claudel's thesis that the Asiatic concept of permanence (seen in Buddhist asceticism, in yoga, and Oriental art forms) in which "everything is calculated to prevent man from budging from place" can be seen as operative in the Russian Communist state:

These ties, this privation of freedom, this primordial necessity for not moving (which does not exclude, moreover, a certain nomadism, for there is no better way to acknowledge one's prison than to inspect all its walls), hasn't this always been characteristic of Russia? The Soviets have thought that they were influenced by the West, but in reality they have been obedient to the profound law of Asia that never creates a form except through compression.[35]

Paul Valéry (1871–1945) bends the essay form to its most esoteric expression in his many works on art, esthetics, and the principles of intellectual activity itself. A poet, critic, and one of the century's most original and universal thinkers, he both experimented in artistic creation through his poetic masterpieces (*La Jeune Parque, Charmes,* and *Le Cimetière marin*) and wrote speculative essays on the creative process and the means which the artist uses to achieve his ends.

Valéry resembles Montaigne by his strong introspective bent and intense efforts to clarify, refine, and put to paper his most intimate thought. From the age of twenty he dedicated several hours of each early morning in filling his notebooks with thoughts and reflections running the gamut from language, philosophy, mathematics, physics, poetry, religion, dreams, memory and the phenomenon of consciousness. These exercises—a kind of intellectual gymnastics that he called his "sport"—make up much of his celebrated *Cahiers* that extend to over twenty-nine volumes (only a portion of which has been published).

Valéry did not, in the main, follow Montaigne's project of self-revelation or of filling his musings with details "seized" from every-day life. Rather he seems, in comparison, to have followed just the reverse process—that of willed detachment from reporting the minutiae of life as experienced by himself and others. For Valéry the point of reference of his diurnal investigations was more rarefied and he describes his procedures and aims as follows: "I have never referred to anything but my pure I, by which I mean the absolute operation of disengaging oneself automatically from everything, and this everything includes our very person with its history, singularities, diverse powers, and particular complaisances."[36]

Valéry's prolific essay writings consist of the collection *Variété* (published in five volumes and divided into such topics as "Études littéraires," "Études philosophiques," "Essais philosophiques," "Essais quasi politiques," and "Théories poétique et esthétique"); his dialogue essays *Eupalinos ou l'architecte, L'Âme et la danse,* and *Dialogue de l'arbre*; the volume *Analects* (aphoristic sayings drawn from the *Cahiers*); and the collections *Regards sur le monde actuel* (oratorical statements or pieces written "on command" in which the author records his observations and opinions on contemporary matters of political, cultural, and personal import).

The essay pieces most characteristic of Valéry's thought patterns and major intellectual preoccupation are those in which he pursues his own speculative investigations on the nature and psychology of art—in particular his three essay series on Leonardo (*Introduction à la méthode de Léonard de Vinci* [1894], *Note et digression* [1919], and *Léonard et les philosophes* [1929]). A brief examination of this series gives some indication of the dynamic nature of Valéry's thought process and of several of his key ideas on the nature and end of the artistic process.

Valéry's Leonardo essays are also his most sustained treatises on aesthetics of any major consequence. In them he undertakes to analyze through a study of Leonardo's manuscripts what kind of person he was and the essential nature of his genius. Tracing the "interior drama" of Leonardo's development, Valéry finds that it consists in this artist's having found (as only the greatest minds can) "relations . . . among things whose law of continuity escapes us."[37] This is another way of expressing, he says, Leonardo's attainment of works of art allowing him to surpass the role of the philosopher, or rather, to fulfill its meaning.

For through his remarkable facility to pass from contemplation to creation of authentic art forms, he in fact, Valéry claims, reveals the futility of verbal philosophy; for he transcends the "vile matter" (the word) on which the philosopher blows by going on to create something out of nothing.[38] As such Leonardo appears, in the context of the modern age, to be a kind of monster, "a centaur, a chimera" because he opposes the modern tendency to restrict or divide the functions and nature of the artist into well defined compartments.[39] He, in contrast, grappled in his art (particularly in painting) with the means of synthesizing therein all the problems that nature proposes to the mind.

André Gide (1869–1951), dominated for much of his life the field of French letters. Through his novels, plays, translations, journals, travel books, and critical works he had, in fact, become at the time of his death the moral spokesman (one might even say mentor) for several generations of young Frenchmen and European youth in general. These he had consistently encouraged to rebel against their bourgeois background and traditional moral values through his own example, made legendary by him in his brilliant and self conscious literary works. Gide devoted much of the fifty volumes of his writings to literary articles and essays (collected primarily in the volumes he entitled *Prétextes, Nouveaux prétextes, Incidences,* and *Interviews*). It is possible to hold, in fact, that all of his literary output (even purely fictional works such as *L'Immoraliste* and *Les Faux-Monnayeurs*) can be regarded as an extended form of criticism; and this is because it had for him the supreme function of applying moral criticism to the analysis of human values. This is not to say that Gide regarded literature as a moralizing exercise, or even that it should necessarily be edifying. (In one of the most quotable of his literary maxims he declares: "Bad books are made from noble sentiments.") He held, rather, that authentic literature had moral value in the therapeutic sense that it can aid its reader to gain a greater measure of self-knowledge and a deeper appreciation for values through the insights, even revelations provided by authors imparting their own point of view in works reflecting their particular psychological and physiological makeup.

Gide's most memorable volume of criticism is that entitled *Prétextes.* Not a simple work but a series of short essays written between 1903 and 1911, it resembles Baudelaire's views on criticism by its emphasis of a creative approach, its thematic compactness, and unitary vision. The pieces included there represent a compendium of some of Gide's most durable articles to have appeared previously in the periodicals

L'Ermitage and *Nouvelle revue française,* the eminent literary publication that Gide himself had launched in 1908 with a number of friends and disciples. In these various "Reflections on Literature and Morality" (as he describes the pieces in the volume's introduction), he explains his nonsystematic approach to criticism and expresses his intentional variance and distance from the "traditional" method employed by professional and university critics, whom he judges to be too rigid and abstract. In several of the articles ("Poplar Tree Quarrel," "Normandy and Bas-Languedoc," and "Imaginary Interviews") he takes strong issue with Barrès and Maurras on the issue of "rootedness" as a desirable feature of literature or even as a proper national goal in education. Calling, in fact, for just the opposite approach in education, he writes: "Taking root is for the weak, sinking into the hereditary habit that will keep them from cold. But for those who are not weak, who do not put comfort above all else, uprooting is called for in proportion to their strength, to their virtue."[40] And he further declares in no uncertain terms that art should have no other end than itself; thus every national requirement imposed on art and literature subjects these, he claims, to laws that are alien to their nature and function. He urges, as well, that an artist or writer, far from barricading himself in his own province or country, should instead travel widely so as to appreciate life in all its dimensions. In stating his own literary preferences, Gide assumes the stance of the cosmopolitan European who revels in his discovery of, and identity with, such universal minds as Racine, Shakespeare, Dostoievsky, Nietzsche, Goethe, and Claudel—geniuses whose art transcends the limitations of any national identity.

Throughout these articles Gide assumes the role of the rebel in regard to literary doctrines on form and content. One should, he claims, possess an open mind, and one untrammeled by the discipline or mentality of any school of thought. Neither should distinctions be assumed nor qualitative judgments made solely on the basis of the newness or venerable age of the modes of expression. Rather, he agrees with Baudelaire that beauty cannot be restricted to any certain time or place, since its forms are many. And the greater the initial revolt of the artist, often the more beautiful will be the work of art that results.

In other essays ("Nationalism and Literature," "Classicism," "Notes to Angèle") he defines a concept of classicism to which he aspires in his own creative works and which he also holds to be a legitimate, even a most desirable model for writers of the modern period. This he generally holds to be the fusion of "an individual with a universal means of expression." The elements in this fusion consist, he states, of a subject remarkable for its universal interest and purity of form rendered in a style revealing the deepest and most essential identity of the author. For Gide such a balance of the universal and the particular (previously struck by the great seventeenth-century classical writers Racine, Molière, and La Fontaine) also achieved within these writers themselves an admirable integration "of the totality of the ethical, intellectual, and emotional preoccupation of their times."[41]

The collection also contains a moving "In Memoriam" sequence featuring essays on Mallarmé and Oscar Wilde. In the finely etched portrait Gide gives to the English poet, Wilde is seen as emblematic of the bizarre and sensitive artist who, like Baudelaire before him, becomes the victim of bourgeois moral rigidity and narrowness of vision. Especially moving here are Gide's recollections of the conversations and meetings he had with Wilde in France just after the latter's release from his English prison. Gide describes him as a man broken by harsh experiences who seems a mere shell of his former self.

French curiosity about American society (viewed by many Europeans as the harbinger of the future) initiated a spate of essays written during the 1920s and 1930s. Certainly the best known of these contains the negative, vitriolic impressions of Georges Duhamel (1884–1966). Writing the essay *Scènes de la vie future* after a few months' travel in the United States about the time of the 1929 Stock Market Crash, this popular and influential French novelist and memorialist can hardly control his disgust at what he has witnessed. As he follows an itinerary from New Orleans, to New York, and then to Chicago, his basic theme can be reduced to what soon becomes an obsessive conviction: America resembles an experiment "conducted by some evil genius on animals in a laboratory."[42] He admits, moreover, to not being able to view this phenomenon dispassionately. For since this young and mechanized society is about to conquer the old world, Duhamel is convinced that "America thus represents the future for us [Europeans]."[43]

Duhamel's account of his voyage is like a veritable descent into hell. He lacerates America for its lack of culture and for the insipid yet dangerous control exerted by the state on all aspects of life: from degrading customs regulations for foreigners, to puritanical drinking laws, dietary habits, and health regulations (he was also a medical doctor), and invasions into the private life of its citizens. He prophesies that the country is on the verge of instituting "selective" regulation of births to enhance the species and judges the Americans whom he has encountered as already reduced to robotlike status. Observing, for example, people standing in line for a film, he writes: "They are patient, they have troubled looks and already are preparing for the hypnosis that will soon overcome them in this enchanted shadow."[44] He comments on the American form of ease and well being as "comfort for the rear end, a purely muscular and tactile one."[45] And the music that assails his ears in the cinema and other public places he calls "musical molasses."[46]

What Duhamel presents as "scenes" of American life are visits to a number of speak easies, the Chicago slaughter houses (emotionally described as "the kingdom of death"), sordid city slums, the "hysteria" of a college football game ("a quasi-religious rite") played in a massive stadium (or one of America's "new temples"), and lunch with black students and teachers in a Southern school where the author experienced his first direct contact with American racism ("this irreconcilable crime").

Apart from these colorful and emotionally charged outings, he resisted attempts by his hosts to have him visit educational institutions, hospitals, churches, art centers, and laboratories—sites that figured largely in travel accounts he had written a few years previous to this in voyages to Finland, Czechoslovakia, and the Soviet Union. Instead he apparently spent much of his time in hotel rooms, overcome by a feeling of desolation and appalled by the racket of the infernal automobile and the dirt of American cities.

Classifying American society in his concluding remarks as "entomological" rather than human, he sees in it "the same effacement of the individual, the rarefaction and progressive unification of social types, and the same submission of all to what Maeterlinck calls 'the genius of the hive and termitary.' "[47] He concludes also that Europe, "overwhelmed by astonishment, even horror," is now the anxious observer of two experiments: the Russian and the American; and he finds the Russian system, since it "is purely political and ideological," less threatening.[48] The American variety, however, is far more dangerous because its aims and effects transcend that of the Soviet Union. The American experiment is, in fact, manipulating morality, sciences, and religions to its own end; and its ultimate concern is not merely a governmental system but "a civilization, a way of life." Hence he predicts that even the Soviet Union will be colonized and changed by this all-engulfing American wave of the future.[49]

No French writer of this century has subjected the problematical nature of modern man and society to a more profound and anguished scrutiny than Simone Weil (1909–1943); nor, for that matter, has any writer been held in such veneration by so varied a group of admirers. Gide, for example, called her "the most spiritual writer of the century"; and Albert Camus, who aided in the posthumous editing of her works, regarded her as "the only great spirit of our time." Shortly after her premature death she had even been accorded a kind of unofficial canonization among religious and moral writers and thinkers (Leslie Fiedler regarded her as a special exemplar of sanctity for our time—the Outsider as Saint in the age of alienation).[50]

A contemporary of Sartre and Beauvoir (whom she knew in her student days at the Sorbonne), Simone Weil led during her brief lifetime a number of careers: that of a *lycée* teacher, factory worker, farm laborer, and political activist (in the Spanish Civil War and, later, in the Free French Movement). A brilliant scholar in philosophy and classical languages, she underwent an evolution in her philosophical and religious thought leading her from a state of indifference to her Jewish tradition, to a syncretic belief in God combining elements of Greek spirituality and Christian mysticism, and finally to the very brink of conversion to Catholicism. This final step she would not take because of her conviction that the hierarchical and temporal order of the Catholic Church was (like Judaism and the ancient religion of Rome as well) opposed in spirit to the renunciation of worldly power, material wealth, and total self-abandonment in God.

Pursuing her own brand of religious belief and practice, Simone Weil thus spent her adult life attempting to attain total detachment from the spirit and economic/political order of the world. In following this ideal she lived a form of ascetic renunciation and other worldliness as rigorous as that of any Trappist or Carthusian monk. The major cause of her death in London at the height of World War II was, in fact, a self-imposed, systematic form of starvation prompted by her determination not to eat any more than her fellow citizens under Nazi Occupation.

Far from separating her from contemporary concerns, then, Simone Weil's spirit of detachment and ideal of renunciation made her an even more committed and anguished critic of her times. In a number of major essays she offers acute and prophetic insights on "the miseries of this epoch" as she analyzes the actual situation of modern society from a number of points of view (spiritual, political, social, and economic, to mention the most important). Among the most well known and significant of these are *L'Enracinement* (*The Need for Roots*); *Oppression et liberté*; "The Iliad, Poem of Might," from the study *La Source grecque* (*Intimations of Christianity*); *La Condition ouvrière* (*Factory Work*); and her spiritual journals: *La Pesanteur et la grâce* (*Gravity and Grace*), and *Attente de Dieu* (*Waiting for God*).

The essay *Oppression and Liberty* (written in 1934), which Weil considered to be her principal political work, is a masterful summation of the dangerous trends and new forces that she saw as threatening the dignity and very existence of the individual at that period. And its concluding section, "Sketch of Contemporary Social Life," Camus praised as rivaling, through its insights on the economic and political condition of contemporary Europe, Marx's similar analysis of a century before.[51] In the essay she characterizes the social situation for all but a very few as a state of "destructive disequilibrium" that (as Hegel foresaw) results from the transformation of "quantity into quality."[52] In fact a slight difference in quantity suffices to change what is human into the inhuman. For example, human life, the body, and quickness of thought and act—hitherto identified as invariables—have now become regulated and controlled by a central authority or a collectivity. This means that the practical functions of life have taken on a more and more collective, restrictive character with the individual as such "playing a more and more insignificant role in this." Thus mass production, technological progress, and industrial concerns all have been allowed to reduce the manual worker to a passive role of that of a mere cog. Modern man, as a result, has lost the meaning of authentic life and thought and the dehumanized person is the end product.

Albert Camus (1913–60) also dedicated a significant part of his writing to the essay enterprise. Now considered by many to have been the most influential voice of the 1940s and 1950s in France and Europe (a kind of conscience for his age), he made extremely effective use of the essay as a means to develop and disseminate his political and ethical theories and opinions during those difficult years.

Camus's essays serve as admirable reflectors for the evolution of his thought through the principal phases (or cycles) that he himself describes in his *Carnets* as that of the absurd and of rebellion.[53] The pessimistic but never despairing patterns of thought of the absurd period are principally conveyed in the major essays *Le Mythe de Sisyphe* and *Lettres à un ami allemand* of the war years. The second stage of rebellion against menacing ideological systems is fully developed in the treatise

L'Homme révolté (1951) and in a number of journalistic essays and articles on the moral and political issues emerging from the intense rivalries and violence of the Cold War period of the late 1940s and 1950s: "Réflexions sur la peine capitale," "Le socialisme des potences," and "Le pari de notre generation" are among the most important.

As his first major essay, *Le Mythe de Sisyphe* (1942) laid the groundwork for what would afterward become Camus's celebrated "absurd" line of reasoning. Writing it several months after the publication of his novel *L'Étranger* and during the darkest hours of the war years, the young Camus anxiously tried to develop in it sufficient reason to justify (in ethical terms) the acceptance of life over suicide. In the first pages he diagnoses the reality of the human condition as that of an essential conflict between two irreconcilable and enduring factors: the first, the innate yearning by man for a universe governed by reason and justice; and the second, the world's constant denial and frustration of these profound human desires. The resulting confrontation between these two facts Camus designates as the state of the absurd; and he further calls it the essential starting point for a quest for meaning on any authentic human scale.

After this exposition Camus goes on to explore the two negative (or antihumanistic) responses to the problem of the absurd, which he designates as physical and philosophical suicide. Physical suicide cannot, he argues, be justified in any human way because it constitutes a capitulation to the absurd motivated by despair. Moreover, by becoming through this act an instrument of the absurd, the human agent annihilates not only his own consciousness but the very concept of the human itself. Intellectual suicide (which he defines as the refuge found in systems arguing for a leap to faith in the face of the absurd) must equally be rejected since it annihilates man's reasoning process and lucidity. Hence admirable as they may be in their desperate efforts to erect reasons for faith that the mind cannot justify, such thinkers and philosophers as Pascal, Dostoyevski, Kierkegaard, and Jaspers ultimately become poets of the irrational; for, instead of coming to grips with the nature of the universe as it is, they would justify what they cannot understand by recourse to a higher power or truth. It is rather, Camus claims, by the effort of rebellion (that is, the positive tension experienced by living against the absurd and for the human) that man can best develop his full human potential and be faithful to his nature. Thus like the mythological hero Sisyphus, who stole the secrets of the gods, modern man, Camus urges, should constantly confront the absurd through authentically human efforts allowing him to wrest a sufficient measure of meaning and fulfillment from the universe; and only by such apparently futile efforts can he, like Sisyphus, achieve a human measure of happiness. For, Camus concludes, "Sisyphus teaches the higher fidelity that negates the gods and raises rocks. He too concludes that all is well. . . . The struggle itself towards the heights is enough to fill a man's heart."[54]

Jean-Paul Sartre (1905–80) is unquestionably the most obvious and gifted continuer in the twentieth century of the tradition of encyclopedic essayist-writers established by such universal minds as Voltaire, Diderot, Renan, Taine, and de Gourmont. He was at once a philosopher, psychologist, novelist, dramatist, writer of film scenarios, and prolific essayist. Along with his universal scope of interests, he demonstrates throughout his works a remarkable stylistic ability to synthesize and popularize in the modern idiom concepts normally accessible only to professional scholars and intellectuals and to make those ideas understandable to the intelligent reader. As an enlightened commentator for the French on a vast range of philosophical, literary political, and social issues covering the period from 1945 through the 1970s, he had no peer in France, nor, very possibly, in the world at large.

Sartre's formidable essay output extends from book-length, serious philosophical treatises in which he develops his system of atheistic existentialism: *L'Être et le néant, Esquisse d'une théorie des émotions,* and *Critique de la raison dialectique*; three studies applying existential psychoanalysis to writers whose life situation (both as artists and human beings) serve to illustrate particular aspects of his concept of commitment and of the use that he believed the writer should make of it: Baudelaire (*Baudelaire*), Jean Genêt (*Saint Genêt, comédien et martyr*), and Flaubert (*L'Idiot de la famille*); moral, political, and literary treatises throughout which he develops as his particular point of view a kind of noncommitted but decidedly left-wing "existential" bias holding Marxism to be the matrix philosophy for "explaining" the world and changing it for the better: *Réflexions sur la question juive; Les Communistes et la paix, Matérialisme et révolution,* and *Qu'est-ce que la littérature,* to name several of the most important.

Sartre also ranks with Mauriac and Camus as a foremost writer of shorter journalistic articles. In fact, he had published from 1947 to 1976 a ten-volume series of essays entitled *Situations* containing articles most of which had previously appeared in the prestigious periodical *Le*

Temps moderne (which he founded in 1945 with Merleau-Ponty, Jean Paulhan, Simone de Beauvoir, and others). Grouped around such topical categories as "Critical Essays," "Portraits," "Colonialism," and "Problems of Marxism," they have been described as perhaps the most important collection of essays published in the present century.[55] In them one can follow the brilliant and complex evolution of Sartre's thought on philosophical, political, social, artistic, and economic issues in the post–World War II period. In many of them he deals with such leading authors as Faulkner, Dos Passos, Gide, Mauriac, Richard Wright, Camus, Paul Nizan, and the artists Tintoretto and Giacometti; there are also travel journals on his earlier trips to the United States ("New York, the Colonial City," "Individualism and Conformism in the United States"); through these pieces one can also chart Sartre's increasing estrangement from capitalist powers (the United States in particular), his skirmishes with policies of the French government and parties of the Right; his attacks against Soviet repression in Hungary and the resurgence of Stalinism; and his many interventions on the side of Third World nations (in particular, his partisan attacks against the "neocolonial forces" in Korean, Algerian, and Vietnamese wars).

Sartre's brilliant acumen for psychological analysis (as applied to sociopolitical problems) is strikingly exemplified in his philosophical essay on prejudice, entitled *Réflexions sur la question juive* (1947). In composing this essay Sartre had the primary intention of dealing with the Jew in *situation,* a word that for Sartre encompasses in meaning the sum total of the entire network of social, political, and economic forces that serve to form and define the individual. Sartre begins this investigation with the statement that the anti-Semite needs to be confronted by the Jew (in fact, he parodies Voltaire's reported commentary on the existence of God with his own declaration that for the anti-Semite, the Jew would have to be invented if he in fact did not exist already). The reason he gives for this statement is the deep resentment (and feeling of inadequacy) experienced by the hater of the Jew at the acknowledged ability of the latter to penetrate and succeed in French society through such typical Jewish means as intelligence, shrewdness in business, and skill in manipulating words. Unable to accept these as the logical result of applied intelligence and as a response to social barriers that had been in existence for centuries, the bigot must find a way to negate these qualities. This he does by denying to the Jew any place in the "traditional" values transmitted by French institutions. The Jew is thus judged to be an alien being, different, unassimilable, and a threat to the nationalist interests of France.

Anti-Semitism so described is, Sartre claims, an affliction especially common among the *petite bourgeoisie* in France. These lower-middle classes, though mediocre in intelligence, are hardly "humble or modest." Hatred of the Jew is therefore, Sartre says, the effort of average types to give value to mediocrity, or "to create an elite of the ordinary."[56] Since intelligence is identified as Jewish, the *petit bourgois* man or woman can now disdain it in all tranquillity. Hence, in an existentialist sense, anti-Semitism represents the fear of liberty and the refusal to accept the truth that man must be master of his own destiny and the creator of his own values. And such truths, Sartre declares, would also demand acceptance of other concepts: for example, that evil is an essential ingredient in the struggle to create values; that man is often the worst enemy of his fellow man; that good does not exist in any absolute state or form.

Constitutionally incapable of admitting such harsh truths or even of assuming personal responsibility for his own moral views, the bourgeois insists instead, Sartre claims, on viewing the world from a comforting Manichean perspective. In this scheme of things the Jew is conveniently elevated to assume an absolute personification of evil. All that is wrong with society, and indeed with the world, is ascribed to his sinister presence. He becomes, then, the menacing "Other" and wars, the class struggle, economic injustice, and all other evils stem from the fact "that the Jew is there, behind governments, breathing discord."[57]

The Jew, Sartre, says, thus lives with "a manufactured historical identity" imposed on him by the collectivity. To be authentic he must therefore abandon "the myth of the universal man" and assume his own Jewish condition. He must will himself into history as a historic and damned creature who, rejecting the myth of the "inauthentic Jew," asserts his being as "one who stands apart, untouchable, and scorned."[58]

A committed left-wing intellectual and close friend and disciple of Sartre, Simone de Beauvoir (1908–   ) belongs in the very first rank of contemporary French writers. She is also considered by critics to be the most influential woman writer to have appeared on the international scene since the early 1940s. Like her contemporaries Sartre and Weil, Beauvoir pursued graduate studies in philosophy; and after brilliantly succeeding at the *agrégation de philosophie* in 1929 (the same year as Sartre, she for the first time and he after a first unsuccessful try), she also began a career as lycée teacher. After holding a number of posts during the next fifteen years, she was finally suspended from her duties in 1944, apparently for being too controversial and unconventional in that role. By this time she had, through her now long association with Sartre, become well known in French intellectual and literary circles as a leading exponent of his existentialist thought. She therefore easily and quite naturally turned her formidable and increasingly independent intellect to a full-time career of writing. She has since become a prolific and important author, particularly in the areas of the novel, autobiography, and the essay.

She may very well be best remembered for her four innovative volumes of autobiography (*Mémoires d'une jeune fille rangée, La Force de l'âge, La Force des choses,* and *Tout compte fait*). In these she sketches her own evolution from a conservative, Catholic bourgeois background to her present eminent position as philosopher, writer, and left-wing activist known the world over for her support of the politically oppressed and downtrodden.

As an essayist she has written several notable philosophical treatises: *L'Existentialisme et la sagesse des nations, Pyrrhus et Cinéas, Pour une morale de l'ambiguité,* and the essay trilogy *Privilèges* directed against the belief that bourgeois values are based on moral absolutes. In one of the *Privilège* essays (*Faut-il brûler Sade?*) she writes a fascinating existentialist psychoanalysis of Sade, whom she presents as the victim of a value system that had been calcified and "canonized." There are also two travelogues of major journeys taken, one to the United States in 1947 (*L'Amérique au jour le jour*), and the other to China in 1957 (*La Longue Marche*), both providing solid and mostly impartial documentation of the daily life and color of these two nations.

In the earlier philosophical essays Beauvoir reveals herself to be a most perceptive, able, but largely derivative teacher and interpreter of Sartre's brand of existentialism. In the monumental essay *Le Deuxième Sexe* (1949), however, she has firmly established herself as the foremost (and certainly the most intellectual) spokesperson for the modern feminist movement. As Professor Konrad Bieber aptly remarks in an analysis he has written on this essay: "She has eventually equipped the combative champions of women's rights in our own day with the weapons to be used in the continued fight for equality and justice, and as it has turned out, not only for women but for all human beings treated unfairly."[59] Now universally regarded as a ground-breaking work for the movement, this more than seven-hundred-page essay is not intended by the author to be a purely objective, scientific work; rather it combines in tentative essay fashion facts of history, use of myth, and certain existentialist concepts applied to the woman. Beauvoir develops here, for example, the concept of the "Other" and applies it in much the same way as Sartre had done in his essay on anti-Semitism. Women have, she claims, also been denied their dignity as individuals and, through the biological division of the species, have been relegated to the subordinate position of servicing the needs of the male. Yet this situation is, she claims, even more degrading for the woman. For unlike repressed minorities such as the Jew, who is detested and made a pariah because of his superior traits, or the Negro who is denied human status, the woman has never been granted an identity of any kind. Rather she has ever been regarded as a mere appendage of man, inferior by nature and endowed with various attitudinal traits (such as being "lazy, impossible, scatterbrained, and frivolous") deemed natural to the female temperament.

To combat these prejudiced views Beauvoir considers women abstractly from three points of view: Her "destiny" as the weaker, child-bearing sex, her "history"—or how this biological form of dependence has been exploited to subject her to her permanent condition of social and political inferiority—and the "myths" that men have created to "explain" woman whom they see as goddess, virgin, temptress, and botched male. In a particularly memorable passage she states: "One is not born, but rather becomes a woman. No biological, psychological, or economic rate determines the figure that the human female presents in society; it is civilization as a whole that produces this creature, intermediate between male and eunuch, which is described as feminine.[60]

Chapter Six

Conclusion

From its initial form to its most recent manifestations in the present century, the French essay has never betrayed the humanistic aims that inspired its creation. Throughout the approximately four-hundred years of its existence it has, in fact, only broadened its original scope from that of a literary exercise for self discovery to more general commentary on all manner of topics of immediate concern to readers in the modern period. Indeed, if one should treat of or examine the French essay as if it constituted a single, continuous collection of serial pieces presented in separate volumes (much as Sainte-Beuve and Renan preserved their own works in the nineteenth century), one would find in its pages a comprehensive and faithful record of much of the intellectual, social, and moral history not only of France, but of Western society itself.

Primarily intended by Montaigne as a means to pursue self study and for developing the art of living well, the essay initially took for its ideal the rugged individualism that the early Renaissance humanists had adopted in their own works through their study of Seneca and other stoical writers of antiquity. When the emphasis on stoical self-sufficiency no longer provided a moral goal that was either accessible or feasible in an absolute monarchy, the great moralist writers adapted the form and content of the essay to the study of universal man embodied in the social concept of the *honnête homme*. In their essay musings Pascal, La Rouchefoucauld, and La Bruyère probed as deeply into the well spring of character and motive as any group of writers before or after them. They also fashioned the essential model which the subsequent manifestations of the French essay were, in varying degrees, to follow. Reacting against Montaigne's more untrammeled use of language and reluctant to indulge in self disclosure for its own sake, they recast the latter's familiar essay, making it impersonal in form but retaining its marvelous propensity to express the deep personal beliefs and convictions of the writer. Subordinating heart to head in their lucid and controlled prose, these moralist writers did not, nonetheless, attempt to disguise the intensity of conviction that lay directly beneath the surface of the new formal cast they had given the genre; and in their writings it is always possible to detect the pulse beat of the author through the essay's exterior framework.

As it emerged from the classical period, the essay form became in turn for the *philosophes* the favored literary genre by which they could forward their assault on the traditional citadels of power and prestige. Turning their attention to more concrete philosophical and social matters than the moral analyses that their moralist predecessors had given in their studies on the *honnête homme,* Enlightenment authors like Voltaire, Diderot, D'Alembert, and Rousseau attacked intolerance, oppression of mind and body, ignorance, and superstition under all the forms that these were to be found in the society of the *ancien régime.* Refined in the crucible of heated debates and polemical attacks, the essay soon became an excellent vehicle for combat. Now less abstract in content and more urgent and pressing through its attention to the burning issues and problems of the day, the essay constituted the primary means by which a committed writer could communicate his or her most deeply held ideas. The eighteenth-century essayists also achieved a conversational tone and delicacy of expression which would be identified as the hallmark of French writers in general and a model to be followed by the rest of Europe.

Little more need be said here regarding the path the essay would take in the nineteenth century. Building upon the serious intellectual aims and persuasive tone of the *philosophe* essayists, Sainte-Beuve, Renan, Taine, and de Gourmont, to name a few, achieved in the admirable "critical" essays of the period a felicitous amalgam of beautifully constructed prose and lucid, attractive presentation of matter that is often erudite and complex. Though almost exclusively devoted by Sainte-Beuve to literary topics and personalities, the critical essay soon came to be used by Renan, Taine, and de Gourmont to popularize in studies of extremely high quality the new knowledge and ideas of the golden age of scholarship and research that the last half of the nineteenth century certainly represented.

As it entered the intellectual mainstreams of the twentieth century, the essay had thus become a distinctly scholarly and eclectic kind of literary genre—and one supple enough to be adapted to the many individual styles and varied purposes for which it would be used by many of the leading French writers and intellectuals of the present century. Occupied in the main with philosophical, political, social, and moral

concerns, the French essay of the modern period has served primarily
as a quite serious vehicle for presenting humanistic themes and defending human values; and it has also become an admirable springboard for
speculation and commentary on crises and issues that have profoundly
shaken or at least affected belief and confidence in traditional values
and institutions not only for the French, but for Europeans as a whole.
As such, the modern essay has very often constituted a strong, resonant
voice pleading or arguing for the preservation of the human in a world
that seems increasingly hostile and menacing to all such concerns.

Because of the marked preference they have always had for serious,
and intellectual topics and issues, French essayists have consistently
cultivated the formal, serious essay to the detriment of the familiar
form. They themselves are, in fact, the first to admit that the familiar
essay is not one that is congenial to them. Taken as a whole, then, the
French essay possesses little of the informality, whimsicality, or the
playful use of the language that are frequently found in British and
American varieties of the genre. Unlike their Anglo-American counterparts, the French essayists have not been prone to let themselves go,
to indulge in fantasy, whimsy, even silliness. Rather, their reticence to
share any but serious intellectual and cultural concerns with their readers and their desire to convince by brilliant use of rhetroic and logic
have rarely allowed them to write without ceremony and in a minor
key. Yet even though we may regret the absence of the particular
warmth and intimacy so characteristic of essays written by Leigh Hunt,
Stevenson, Chesterton, Emerson, Twain, or Benchley, to name only a
few, we must also admire the distinctive cast and tone that the French
have given to their essay—that brilliant, serious, and moving voice of
an extremely intelligent, morally sensitive, and perceptive people.

Notes and References

Preface

1. Richard M. Chadbourne, *Ernest Renan as an Essayist* (New York, 1957), xix.
2. "Essai," in *La Grande Encyclopédie* (1973), 4541–42.
3. Ibid., 4542.
4. Ibid.
5. Hector France, "Essayist," in ibid., 384.
6. Pierre Villey, "La fortune des *Essais,*" in *Les Essais de Montaigne* (1932; reprint, Paris: Nizet, 1946), 158–82.
7. Gustave Lanson, *Les Essais de Montaigne, étude et analyse* (n.d.; reprint, Paris, 1948), 321–65.
8. "Essay," in *Cassell's Encyclopedia of Literature,* ed. S. H. Steinberg, (1953), 163.
9. Ibid.
10. David Daiches, ed., "Reflections on the Essay," in *A Century of the Essay British and American* (New York, 1951), 1–8.
11. Ibid., 3
12. Ibid., 5.
13. Chadbourne, *Ernest Renan,* xix.

Chapter One

1. *Bacon's Essays with Annotations,* ed. Richard Whately (Boston, 1871), xxxvii.
2. Ibid., xv.
3. Hugo Friedrich, *Montaigne,* trans. Robert Rovini (Paris, 1968).
4. Ibid., 371–74.
5. Ibid., 69–72.
6. In the chapter "Tradition et culture," ibid., 42–104, Professor Friedrich provides an excellent and concise treatment of Montaigne's cultural interests, and particular approach to reading classical texts. I am deeply indebted to this work for much of what I say of Montaigne's scholarly habits and interests.
7. François Rabelais, chapter 21 ("How Gargantua Was Educated by Ponocrate in Such a Method that He Never Wasted an Hour or a Day") and chapter 22 ("How Gargantua Spent His Time When the Weather Was Rainy") in *Gargantua,* ed. M. A. Screech (Geneva, 1971).

8. *The Complete Essays of Montaigne,* trans. Donald M. Frame (Stanford, 1948), 110. All references to the essays in this chapter are taken from Frame's translation and the page numbers are cited in the text.

9. Donald M. Frame, *François Rabelais* (New York, 1972), 40.

10. Villey, *Les Essais de Montaigne,* 36.

11. Pierre Villey, *Les Sources et l'évolution des essais de Montaigne,* 2 vols. (Paris: Hachette, 1908).

12. Professor Villey succintly develops this thesis of evolution in chapters 4–7 of *Les Essais de Montaigne,* 29–76.

13. Ibid., 29–76.

14. Donald M. Frame, *Montaigne's Discovery of Man: The Humanization of a Humanist* (New York, 1955). See also Professor Frame's valuable introduction in *The Complete Essays,* v–xiv.

15. Seneca, *Ad Lucillium Epistulae Morales,* trans. Richard M. Gummere, 3 vols. (London and New York, 1925).

16. Ibid., 1:329.

17. Ibid., 1:125.

18. Villey, *Les Essais de Montaigne,* 49.

19. In the essay "Let Business Wait till Tomorrow" (2:4), Montaigne records his pleasure at receiving the translation of the *Moralia.* Of Amyot he says: "But above all I am grateful to him for having had the wit to pick out and choose a book so worthy and appropriate to present to this country. We ignoramuses would have been lost if this book had not picked us out of the quagmire" (262).

20. For a detailed study of Plutarch's commanding influence on French humanists, see Friedrich, *Montaigne,* 84–93.

21. *Plutarch's Moralia,* trans. Frank Cole Babbitt et al., 14 vols, (London and New York, 1927).

22. Ibid., 1:5–69.

23. Villey, *Les Essais de Montaigne,* 61–62.

24. *Sextus Empiricus: Outlines of Pyrrhonism; Against the Physicists; and Against the Ethicists,* trans. Rev. R. G. Bury, 3 vols. (Cambridge, Mass. and London, 1936). Rev. Bury provides an extensive survey of the skeptical movement in Greek philosophy in his introduction, 1:vii–xlv.

25. Friedrich, *Montaigne,* 362.

26. Ibid., 354.

27. The essays that best illustrate this transformational stage in content and style are "Of the Education of Children," 1:26; "Of the Affection of Fathers to Their Children," 2:8; "Of Books," 2:10; "Of Cruelty," 2:11; "Of Presumption," 2:17; and "Of the Resemblance of Children to Their Fathers," 2:37.

28. Henri Peyre, "Literature, Nonfictional Prose," in *The New Encyclopedia Britannica: Macropaedia,* 1974, 1078.

Chapter Two

1. Antoine Adam, *Grandeur and Illusion: French Literature and Society, 1600–1715,* trans. Herbert Tine (New York, 1972), 264.
2. Pierre Charron, *De la sagesse, trois livres,* 2 vols. (Paris: Chez Chassériau, 1820).
3. Adam, *Grandeur and Illusion,* 71.
4. An excellent overview of the salon as a social phenomenon is provided by Prof. P. J. Yarrow in his *A Literary History of France: The Seventeenth Century* (New York, 1967).
5. Adam, *Grandeur and Illusion,* 71.
6. Jacques Bénigne Bossuet, "Sur les conditions nécessaires pour être heureux," in *Sermons choisis de Bossuet* (Paris, 1882), 404–5.
7. Antoine Arnauld, *La Logique ou l'art de penser* (1661; reprint, Paris, 1773), 341–42.
8. H. V. Routh, "The Origin of the Essay Compared in French and English," *Modern Language Review* 15 (1920):33.
9. Ibid., 35.
10. Jean-Louis Guez de Balzac, *Les Entretiens (1657),* ed. B. Beugnot, 2 vols. (Paris, 1972).
11. Ibid., 1:7.
12. Ibid., 2:413.
13. Ibid., 2:290.
14. Mme de Sévigné, *Lettres,* ed. Henri Baudin (Paris: Edition Bordas, 1968), 64–65.
15. Ibid., 226.
16. Charles de Saint-Évremond, *Oeuvres en prose,* ed. René Ternois, 4 vols. (Paris, 1962–69).
17. Ibid., 4:21.
18. Ibid., "Considérations sur la religion," 4:150.
19. Ibid., 152.
20. Ibid., "Goût et discernement des Français," 3:125.
21. La Rochefoucauld, *Réflexions ou sentences et maximes morales* (Paris: Chez Barbin, 1665). All references to the maxims in the text are taken from the edition *Maxims,* trans. L. W. Tancock (Baltimore, 1959). They are identified not by reference to page but to their standard entry number in the collection.
22. Adam, *Grandeur and Illusion,* 266–67.
23. Blaise Pascal, *Pensées sur la religion et sur quelques autres sujets,* ed. Louis Lafuma, 3d edition (Paris: J. Delmas, 1960). All references to the *Thoughts* in the text are taken from *Pensées,* trans. H. F. Stewart (New York, 1947). The page numbers are cited in the text.
24. All references in the text to La Bruyère's work are taken from *Char-*

acters, trans. Henri Van Laun (London and New York, 1963).

    25. Ibid., 89.

    26. Ibid., 89–90.

    27. La Bruyère stated in his introduction: "In reading the work, one should not lose sight of my title and forget that I am describing the characters and mores of the century; for though I often draw from the court of France and men of my nation, they [the characters] cannot be restricted to a single court and country . . . for I have attempted to paint man in general." La Bruyère, *Oeuvres complètes,* ed. Julien Benda (Paris, 1951), 62.

    28. Benda, ed., *Oeuvres complètes,* xix.

    29. Jean de La Bruyère, *Characters,* 206.

    30. Benda, ed., *Oeuvres complètes,* pp. xix–xxii.

Chapter Three

    1. Robert Niklaus, *A Literary History of France: The Eighteenth Century, 1715–1789* (London and New York, 1970), 20.

    2. Ibid., 36.

    3. Ibid., 55.

    4. Ira C. Wade, *The Clandestine Organization and Diffusion of Philosophic Ideas in France from 1700 to 1750* (Princeton, N.J., 1938), 5.

    5. Ibid.

    6. Arthur M. Wilson, *Diderot* (New York, 1972), 71.

    7. Voltaire, *Mélanges* (Paris, 1961), 14.

    8. Ibid., 12.

    9. Ibid., 58.

    10. Ibid., 28.

    11. Ibid., 97–98.

    12. Ibid., 104.

    13. Ibid., 107.

    14. Wilson, *Diderot,* 55.

    15. Denis Diderot, *Oeuvres philosophiques* (Paris, 1956), 13.

    16. Ibid., 14–15.

    17. Ibid., 25.

    18. Ibid., 23.

    19. Among the most remarkable examples of this form are Diderot's *Lettre sur les aveugles pour ceux qui voient* (1749) and Rousseau's *Lettre a M. D'Alembert sur son article Genève* or *Lettre sur les spectacles* (1758).

    20. Jean-Jacques Rousseau, *Essai sur l'origine des langues* (Paris, 1974), 174.

    21. Jean Le Rond D'Alembert, *Oeuvres complètes de D'Alembert* (Paris, 1821), 1:122.

    22. Voltaire, *Oeuvres complètes de Voltaire* (Paris, 1878), 13:177.

    23. Ibid., 180.

24. Paul-Henri Thiry, baron D'Holbach, *Essai sur les préjugés* (Paris, 1795), 5.

25. Ibid., 7.

26. Ibid., 315–16.

27. Pierre Carlet de Chamberlain de Marivaux, *Journaux et oeuvres diverses de Marivaux* (Paris, 1969), 114.

28. Ibid., 115.

29. Ibid., 278.

30. Ibid., 281.

31. Denis Diderot, *Oeuvres esthétiques* (Paris, 1968), 471–73.

32. Ibid., 547–52.

33. Ibid., 471.

34. Ibid., 484.

35. Among the more interesting and provocative entries are: *Athée* ("Atheist"), *Ame* ("Soul"), *Bien* (*tout est*) ("Everything is Good"), *Catéchisme chinois* ("Chinese Catechism"), *Genèse* ("Genesis"), *Guerre* ("War"), *Lois* ("Laws"), *Moïse* ("Moses"), *Messie* ("Messiah"), *Tolérance*, and *Religion*.

36. Voltaire, *Philosophical Dictionary*, trans. Theodore Besterman (Harmondsworth, Middlesex, England, 1971), 177.

37. Otis Fellows, *Diderot* (Boston, 1977), 98–100.

38. Diderot, *Oeuvres philosophiques*, 278.

39. Ibid., 282.

40. Ibid., 282.

41. Ibid., 314–15.

42. Ibid., 377.

43. Jean-Jacques Rousseau, *Oeuvres complètes* (Paris, 1971), 1:504.

44. Ibid., 504.

45. Ibid., 506.

46. Ibid., 509.

47. Ibid., 515.

48. Ibid., 523.

49. Rémy G. Saisselin, *The Literary Enterprise in Eighteenth-Century France* (Detroit, 1979), 7.

Chapter Four

1. Chateaubriand, *Essai historique, politique, et moral sur les révolutions anciennes et modernes*, 2 vols. (Paris, 1826), 2:412.

2. Ibid., 2:409.

3. Ibid., 1:40.

4. Ibid., 2:422.

5. Edmund Burke, *Reflections on the Revolution in France* (Indianapolis and New York, 1955), 17.

6. *The Works of Joseph de Maistre,* trans. Jack Lively (New York, 1971), 47.

7. Ibid., 55.

8. Hughes de Lamennais, *Essai sur l'indifférence en matière de religion,* 4 vols. (Paris, 1822), 1:10.

9. Ibid., 4:311.

10. Stendhal [Marie Henri Beyle], *Love,* trans. Gilbert and Suzanne Sole (New York, 1977), 45.

11. Ibid., 61.

12. Ibid., 57.

13. Ibid., 143.

14. Ibid., 147.

15. Ibid., 164.

16. Ibid., 192.

17. Barbey d'Aureyvilly, *Du dandysme et de Georges Brummell, oeuvre de Barbey d'Aureyvilly,* (Paris, n.d.), 23.

18. Ibid., 26.

19. Ibid., 28.

20. Ibid., 98.

21. Ibid., 100.

22. Chadbourne, *Ernest Renan as an Essayist,* xx.

23. Sainte-Beuve, *Extraits des causeries de lundi* (Paris, 1894), 20.

24. Ibid., 93.

25. Ibid., 266.

26. Ibid., 58.

27. Ibid., 115.

28. Ibid., 206.

29. Ibid., 116.

30. Ibid., 119.

31. Ibid., 59–60.

32. Ibid., 597–98.

33. Enid Starkie, *Baudelaire* (London, 1971), 166–69.

34. *Oeuvres complètes de Baudelaire* (Paris, 1961), 814.

35. Ibid., 815.

36. Ibid., 827.

37. Ibid., 877.

38. Ibid., 879.

39. Ibid., 956.

40. Ibid., 958.

41. Ibid., 1041.

42. Ibid., 1072.

43. Ibid., 1077–78.

44. *Oeuvres complètes de Renan,* ed. Henriette Psichari, 10 vols. (Paris, 1947–61), 7:11.

45. Ibid., 7:15.

46. Chadbourne, *Ernest Renan as an Essayist*, 55.

47. Psichari, ed., *Oeuvres complètes de Renan*, 2:11.

48. Ibid., 2:247.

49. Ibid., 2:249.

50. Ibid., 2:258.

51. Ibid., 2:294ff.

52. Hippolyte Taine, "Sainte-Beuve" in *Derniers essais de critique et d'histoire*, (Paris, 1894), 58–59.

53. Hippolyte Taine, *Essai sur Tite-Live*, 6th ed. (Paris, 1896), vii.

54. Ibid., 330–31.

55. Hippolyte Taine, *Essai sur les fables de La Fontaine* 16th ed. (Paris, 1903), iv.

56. Ibid., 7.

57. Ibid., 9.

58. Paul Bourget, "Lettre autobiographique" in Victor Giraud, *Paul Bourget* (Paris, 1934), 38–39.

59. Paul Bourget, *Nouveaux essais de psychologie contemporaine* (Paris, 1894), v.

60. Ibid., 133.

61. Ibid., 173.

62. Anatole France, *La Vie littéraire*, 4 vols. (Paris, 1888–92), 1:4.

63. Ibid., 2:ii.

64. Ibid.

65. Ibid., iv.

66. Ibid., 2:335.

67. Ibid., 2:7.

68. Rémy de Gourmont, *Promenades littéraires* (Paris, 1922–27), 6:87.

69. Ibid., 6:128–34.

70. Psichari, ed., *Oeuvres complètes de Renan*, 2:940.

71. Matthew Arnold, *Culture and Anarchy*, ed. J. Dover Wilson (Cambridge, 1935), 70.

Chapter Five

1. Florian-Parmentier, "Les essais" in *Histoire de la littérature française de 1885 à nos jours* (Paris: E. Figuière et Cie., 1914), 536.

2. In particular, Henry de Montherlant and Albert Camus. Montherlant's principal collection of lyrical essays, *Un Voyageur traqué*, composed from 1927 to 1929, consists of a trilogy of travel journals entitled *Aux fontaines de désir, La petite infante de Castille*, and *Un Voyageur solitaire est un diable*. In them he describes his inner feelings and increasing disillusionment in life played out before sites in Italy, Spain, and North Africa. Camus wrote three cycles of lyrical essays: *L'Envers et l'endroit*, 1935–36; *Noces*, 1936–37; and *L'Été*,

1939–54. These introduce and develop the dialectic (love of life and the experience of despair) that lies at the heart of his artistic vision.

3. Some of the essayists considered in this chapter who have written well-known autobiographies are the following: Alain (*Histoire de mes pensées*); Mauriac (*Mes plus lointains souvenirs*); Benda (*La Jeunesse d'un clerc*); Duhamel (five volumes of which the first is *L'inventaire de l'abîme*); Sartre (*Les Mots*); and Simone de Beauvoir (four volumes of which the first is *Mémoires d'une jeune fille rangée*).

4. Philippe Lejeune, *L'Autobiographie en France* (Paris, 1971), 33–34.

5. Henri Peyre, "Literature, Nonfictional Prose," in *New Encyclopedia Britannica: Macropedia*, 1974, 1079.

6. Robert E. Taylor, "Essay," in *Dictionary of French Literature*, ed. Sidney P. Braun (New York: Philosophical Library, 1958), 114.

7. Alain, *Propos sur le bonheur* (Paris, 1964), 218.

8. André Suarès, *Voici l'homme* (Paris, 1948), 16.

9. Ibid., 266.

10. Ibid., 120.

11. Ibid., 34.

12. Ibid., 33.

13. Jean Rostand, *Pensées d'un biologiste* (Paris, 1954), 9–10.

14. Ibid., 10–11.

15. François Mauriac, *Le Bâillon dénoué après quatre ans de silence* (Paris, 1945), 162–63.

16. Léon Bloy, *Oeuvres de Léon Bloy*, (Paris, 1968), 8:86.

17. Ibid., 106–7.

18. Ibid., 133.

19. Gonzague Truc gives an excellent introduction to Péguy and his importance in the Catholic Renascence in *Histoire de la littérature catholique contemporaine* (Paris: Casterman, 1961), 158 ff.

20. Charles Péguy, *Oeuvres en prose 1909–1914* (Paris, 1961), 517.

21. Charles Péguy, *Oeuvres en prose 1898–1908* (Paris, 1959), 157.

22. Péguy, *Oeuvres en prose 1909–1914*, 1105.

23. The essay "Death in the Soul" from the collection *L'Envers et l'endroit* (*The Wrong Side and the Right Side*) (Paris, 1965).

24. Maurice Barrès, *L'Oeuvre de Maurice Barrès*, (Paris, 1967), 2:177.

25. Anthony Greaves, *Maurice Barrès* (Boston, 1978), 108 ff.

26. Barrès, *L'Oeuvre de Maurice Barrès*, 5:475.

27. Ibid., 5:478.

28. Henri Massis, *Agathon, ou l'esprit de la nouvelle Sorbonne* (Paris, 1911), 70.

29. Ibid., 72.

30. Charles Maurras, *L'Avenir de l'intelligence* (Paris, 1905), 89.

31. Julien Benda, *The Betrayal of the Intellectuals*, trans. Richard Addington (Boston, 1956), 89.

32. Georges Bernanos, *Essais et écrits de combat* (Paris, 1971), 345.

33. Paul Claudel, *Oeuvres en prose* (Paris, 1965), 751.

34. Ibid., 728–29.

35. Ibid., 787.

36. Paul Valéry, "Letter to R. P. Rideau," in *Lettres à quelques-uns* (Paris, 1952), 245–46.

37. Paul Valéry, *Oeuvres*, (Paris, 1962), 1:1160.

38. Ibid., 1:1257.

39. Ibid., 1:1261.

40. André Gide, *Prétextes-Reflections on Literature and Morality,* trans. and ed. Justin O'Brien (Freeport, N.Y., 1959), 79.

41. Ibid., 202.

42. Georges Duhamel, *Scènes de la vie future* (Paris: Mercure de France, 1930), 18.

43. Ibid., 19.

44. Ibid., 48.

45. Ibid., 51.

46. Ibid., 53.

47. Ibid., 224.

48. Ibid., 240.

49. Two other important essays on the United States of this period are *Etats-Unis d'aujourd'hui* (1927) written by the eminent sociologist-historian André Siegfried, and Madeleine Cazamian's *L'Autre Amérique* (1931), which she composed to contest the grim and harsh portrayal of the United States presented in Duhamel's *Scènes*. In particular she wished to study "the other America"—the private sector, and the possibilities it offered for the human, aesthetic, moral, and social development, and betterment of its people.

50. Leslie Fiedler, "Simone Weil, Prophet Out of Israel, Saint of the Absurd," *Commentary,* January 1951, 36–46.

51. Albert Camus, in the preface that he wrote to Weil's *Oppression et liberté* (Paris, 1951), 8.

52. Simone Weil, *Oppression and Liberty,* trans. Arthur Wills and John Petrie (Amherst: University of Massachusetts Press, 1973), 108.

53. Albert Camus, *Notebooks (1942–1951),* trans. Justin O'Brien (New York, 1965), 158.

54. Albert Camus, *Essais* (Paris, 1965), 198.

55. Peyre, "Literature, Nonfictional Prose," 1079.

56. Jean-Paul Sartre, *Anti-Semite and Jew,* trans. George J. Becker (New York, 1948), 23.

57. Ibid., 40.

58. Ibid., 316–17.

59. Konrad Bieber, *Simone de Beauvoir* (Boston, 1979), 114.

60. Simone de Beauvoir, *The Second Sex,* trans. and ed. H. M. Parshley (New York, 1968), 269.

Selected Bibliography

PRIMARY SOURCES

Alain [Chartier, Emile]. *Propos sur le bonheur.* Paris: Gallimard Collection Idées, 1964.

Alembert, Jean Le Rond D'. *Essai sur les élémens de philosophie ou sur des connaissances humaines, oeuvres complètes de D'Alembert.* Vol. 1. Paris: A. Belin, 1821.

Arnauld, Antoine. *La Logique ou l'art de penser.* 8th ed. Paris: Chez Guillaume Desprez, 1773.

Aureyvilly, Barbey d'. *Du dandysme et de Georges Brummell, oeuvre de Barbey d'Aureyvilly.* Paris: Alphonse Lemerre, n.d.

Bacon, Francis. *Bacon's Essays with Annotations.* Edited by Richard Whately. Boston: Lee & Shepard, 1871.

Balzac, Jean-Louis Guez de. *Les Lettres diverses de Monsieur de Balzac.* 2 vols. Paris: Chez Jacques Le Gros, 1663.

————. *Les Entretiens (1657).* Paris: Librairie Marcel Didier, Société des textes français modernes, 1972.

Barrès, Maurice. *L'Oeuvre de Maurice Barrès.* 20 vols. Paris: Au Club de l'Honnête Homme, 1965–69.

Baudelaire, Charles. *Baudelaire as a Literary Critic—Selected Essays.* Edited and translated by Lois B. and Francis E. Hyslop. University Park: Pennsylvania State University Press, 1964.

————. *Oeuvres complètes de Baudelaire.* Paris: Gallimard Bibliothèque de la Pléiade, 1961.

Beauvoir, Simone de. *The Second Sex.* Edited and translated by H. M. Parshley. New York: Alfred A. Knopf, 1968.

Benda, Julien. *The Betrayal of the Intellectuals.* Translated by Richard Addington. Boston: Beacon Press, 1956.

Bernanos, Georges. *Essais et écrits de combat.* Paris: Gallimard Bibliothèque de la Pléiade, 1971.

Bloy, Léon. *Oeuvres de Léon Bloy.* 11 vols. Paris: Mercure de France, 1964–70.

Bossuet, Jacques Bénigne. *Sermons choisis de Bossuet.* Paris: Hachette, 1882.

Bourget, Paul. *Essais de psychologie contemporaine.* Paris: Alphonse Lemerre, Editeur, 1893.

————. *Nouveaux essais de psychologie contemporaine.* Paris: Alphonse Lemerre, Editeur, 1894.

————. *Nouvelles pages de critique et de doctrine.* 2 vols. Paris: Librairie Plon, 1922.

Brunetière, Ferdinand. *Etudes critiques sur l'histoire et la littérature françaises.* 9 vols. Paris: Hachette et Cie., 1896–1925.

Burke, Edmund. *Reflections on the Revolution in France.* Indianapolis and New York: Library of Liberal Arts Press, 1955.

Camus, Albert. *Essais.* Paris: Gallimard Bibliothèque de la Pléiade, 1965.

————. *Lyrical and Critical Essays.* Translated by Ellen Conroy Kennedy; edited by Philip Thody. New York: Vintage Random House, 1968.

————. *Notebooks (1942–1951).* Translated by Justin O'Brien. New York: Harcourt Brace, 1965.

Cazamian, Madeleine. *L'Autre amérique.* Paris: Librairie Honoré Champion, 1931.

Charron, Pierre. *De la sagesse.* 2 vols. Paris: Chez Chassériau, 1820.

Chateaubriand, René de. *Essai historique, politique, et moral sur les révolutions anciennes et modernes.* 2 vols. Paris: Advocat Libraire, 1826.

Claudel, Paul. *Oeuvres en prose.* Paris: Gallimard Bibliothèque de la Pléiade, 1965.

Condillac, Etienne Bonnot de. *Essai sur l'origine des connaissances humaines, oeuvres complètes.* Vol I. Reprint. Geneva: Slatkine Reprints, 1970.

Diderot, Denis. *Lettre sur les aveugles.* Edited by Robert Niklaus. Geneva: Librairie Droz, 1951.

————. *The Encyclopédie of Diderot and D'Alembert: Selected Articles.* Edited by J. Lough. Cambridge: Cambridge University Press, 1954.

————. *Oeuvres esthétiques.* Paris: Editions Garnier Frères, 1968.

————. *Oeuvres philosophiques.* Paris: Editions Garnier Frères, 1956.

Duhamel, Georges. *Scénes de la vie future.* Paris: Mercure de France, 1930.

Empiricus, Sextus. *Outlines of Pyrronism; Against the Physicists; and Against the Ethicists.* Translated by Rev. R. G. Bury. 3 vols. Cambridge, Mass.: Harvard University Press; London: William Heinemann, 1936.

France, Anatole, *Le Jardin d'Epicure.* Paris: Calmann-Lévy, 1923.

————. *La Vie littéraire.* 4 vols. Paris: Calmann-Lévy, 1888–92.

Gide, Andre. *Prétextes-Reflections on Literature and Morality.* Edited by Justin O'Brien. Freeport, N.Y.: Books for Librairies Press, 1959.

Gourmont, Rémy de. *La Culture des idées.* Reprint. Mercure de France, 1964.

————. *Promenades littéraires.* 7 vols. Paris: Mercure de France, 1922–27.

————. *Promenades philosophiques.* 3 vols. Paris: Mercure de France, 1913–22.

Holbach, Paul-Henri Thiry, baron D'. *Essai sur les préjugés.* Paris: Chez Chambon, 1795.

La Bruyère, Jean de. *Characters.* Translated by Henri Van Laun. London and New York: Oxford University Press, 1963.

————. *Oeuvres complètes.* Paris: Gallimard Bibliothèque de la Pléiade, 1951.

Lamennais, Hughes de. *Essai sur l'indifférence en matière de religion.* 4 vols. Paris:

Chez Méquignon fils aîné, 1822.

La Rochefoucauld, François VI, Duc de. *Maxims*. Translated by L. W. Tancock. Baltimore: Penguin Books, 1959.

Lemaître, Jules. *Les Contemporains*. 8 vols. Paris: Société française de l'impri-
merie et de librairie, 1888–1914.

Maistre, Joseph de. *The Works of Joseph de Maistre*. Translated by Jack Lively.
New York: Schocken Books, 1971.

Marivaux, Pierre Carlet de Chamberlaine de *Journaux et oeuvres diverses de Marivaux*. Paris: Garnier Frères, 1969.

Massis, Henri. *Agathon, ou l'esprit de la nouvelle Sorbonne*. Paris: Mercure de
France, 1911.

Mauriac, François. *Le Baillon dénoué après quatre ans de silence*. Paris: Edition
Bernard Grasset, 1945.

———. *Bloc-Notes*. 5 vols. Paris: Flammarion, 1952–69.

———. *Oeuvres complètes*. 16 vols. Paris: Bibliothèque Bernard Grasset, 1950–
56.

Maurras, Charles. *L'Avenir de l'intelligence*. Paris: Albert Fontemoign, 1905.

Montaigne, Michel de. *The Complete Essays of Michel de Montaigne*. Translated
by Donald M. Frame. Stanford: Stanford University Press, 1948.

Montherlant, Henri de. *Essais*. Paris: Bibliothèque de la Pléiade, 1963.

Pascal, Blaise. *Pensées*. Translated by H. F. Stewart. New York: Modern Library College Editions, Random House, 1947.

———. *Pensées sur la religion et sur quelques autres sujets*. 3d ed. Edited by Louis
La Fuma. Paris: J. Delmas et Cie., 1960.

Péguy, Charles. *Oeuvres en prose 1898–1908*. Paris: Gallimard Bibliothèque de
la Pléiade, 1959.

———. *Oeuvres en prose 1909–1914*. Paris: Gallimard Bibliothèque de la
Pléiade, 1961.

Plutarch. *Plutarch's Moralia*. Translated by Frank Cole Babbit et al. 14 vols.
London: William Heinemann; New York: G. P. Putnam's Sons, 1927.

Rabelais, François. *Gargantua*. Edited by M. A. Screech. Geneva: Droz,
1971.

Renan, Ernest. *Oeuvres complètes de Renan*. Edited by Henriette Psichari. 10
vols. Paris: Calmann-Lévy, 1947–61.

Rostand, Jean. *Pensées d'un biologiste*. Paris: Stock, Delamain, et Boutelleau,
1954.

Rousseau, Jean-Jacques. *Essai sur l'origine des langues*. Paris: Aubier Montaigne, 1974.

———. *Lettre à M. D'Alembert sur son article sur Genève*. Paris: Garnier-Flam-
marion, 1967.

———. *Les Rêveries d'un promeneur solitaire, Oeuvres complètes*. Vol I. Paris: Aux
éditions de Seuil, 1967.

Sainte-Beuve, Charles, de. *Extraits des causeries du lundi*. 3d ed. Paris: Garnier
Frères, 1894.

Saint-Évremond, Charles de. *Oeuvres en prose.* 4 vols. Edited by René Ternois. Paris: Librairie Marcel Didier, Société des textes français modernes, 1962–69.

Sartre, Jean-Paul. *Anti-Semite and Jew.* Translated by George J. Becker. Reprint. New York: Schocken Books, 1948.

———. *Situations.* 10 vols. Paris: Gallimard, 1947–76.

Seneca. *Ad Lucillium Epistolae Morales.* Translated by Richard M. Gummere. 3 vols. London: William Heinemann; New York: G. P. Putnam's Sons, 1925.

Sévigné, Marie de Rabutin-Chantal, Marquise de. *Lettres.* Edited by H. Baudin. Paris: Les Editions Bordas, 1968.

Siegfried, André. *America Comes of Age.* Translated by H. H. and Doris Hemming. New York: Harcourt Brace, 1927.

Stendhal [Marie Henri Beyle]. *Love.* Translated by Gilbert and Suzanne Sole. New York: Penguin Books, 1977.

Suarès, André. *Voici l'homme.* Paris: Albin Michel, 1948.

Taine, Hippolyte. *Derniers essais de critique et d'histoire.* Paris: Librairie Hachette et Cie., 1894.

———. *Essais de critique et d'histoire.* 2d ed. Paris: Librairie Hachette et Cie., 1866.

———. *Essai sur les fables de La Fontaine.* 16th ed. Paris: Librairie Hachette et Cie., 1903.

———. *Essai sur Tite-Live.* 6th ed. Paris: Librairie Hachette et Cie., 1896.

Valéry, Paul. *Lettres à quelques-uns.* Paris: Gallimard, 1952.

———. *Oeuvres.* 2 vols. Paris: Gallimard Bibliothèque de la Pléiade, 1962.

Voltaire. *Essai sur les moeurs, Oeuvres complètes de Voltaire.* Vol. 13. Paris: Garnier, 1878.

———. *Mélanges.* Paris: Gallimard Bibliothèque de la Pléiade, 1961.

———. *Philosophical Dictionary.* Translated and edited by Theodore Bestermann. Harmondsworth, Middlesex, England: Penguin Books, 1971.

Weil, Simone. *Oppression et liberté.* Edited by Albert Camus. Paris: Gallimard Collection Espoir, 1955.

———. *Oppression and Liberty.* Translated by Arthur Wills and John Petrie. Amherst: University of Massachusetts Press, 1973.

SECONDARY SOURCES

1. General Works

Adam, Antoine. *Grandeur and Illusion: French Literature and Society, 1600–1715.* Translated by Herbert Tine. New York: Basic Books, 1972. Brilliant study of seventeenth-century French society and the literature it created.

Arnold, Matthew. *Culture and Anarchy.* Edited by J. Dover Wilson. Cambridge: Cambridge University Press, 1935.

Cassell's Encyclopedia of Literature. Edited by S. H. Steinberg. Vol. 1. London: Cassell, 1953.

Daiches, David. *A Century of the Essay British and American.* New York: Harcourt, Brace & Co., 1951. Gives an excellent survey of major essayists of the modern period and an invaluable definition of the essay as literary genre.

Dictionary of French Literature. Edited by Sidney D. Braun. New York: Philsophical Library, 1958. Provides a brief but insightful historical survey of the essay in France.

Florian-Parmentier. *La Littérature et l'époque: Histoire de la littérature française de 1885 à nos jours.* Paris: E. Figuière et Cie, 1914.

Fraser, Theodore P., and **Kopp, Richard.** *The Moralist Tradition in France.* Gaithersburg, Md.: Associated Faculty Press, 1981. Only general work extant in English that provides a critical study of the French moralist tradition and a survey of the major authors. Many of the moralist authors dealt with here are major essayists.

Le Grande Encyclopedie. Inventaire raisonné des sciences, des lettres, et des arts. Vol. 16. Paris: H. Lamirault et Cie, n.d.

La Grande Encyclopédie. Vol. 8. 1973.

Lejeune, Philippe. *L'Autobiographie en France.* Paris: Collection U-Librairie Armand Colin, 1971. Consult for the best historical survey of French autobiographers and selections from their major works.

Niklaus, Robert. *A Literary History of France: The Eighteenth Century 1715–1789.* London: Ernest Benn; New York: Barnes and Noble, 1970. An admirably compact yet complete critical survey of the century.

Peyre, Henri. "Literature, Nonfictional Prose." In *New Encyclopedia Britannica: Macropaedia.* 1974. A superb overview of the essay's origin and development in world literature.

Routh, H. V. "The Origin of the Essay Compared in French and English," *Modern Language Review* 15 (1920):28–40.

Saisselin, Rémy G. *The Literary Enterprise in Eighteenth-Century France.* Detroit: Wayne State University Press, 1979. An interesting and valuable study dealing with the emergence of the writer as a professional in his own right in eighteenth-century France.

Truc, Gonzaque. *Histoire de la littérature catholique contemporaine.* Paris: Casterman, 1961. An extensive but sometimes superficial survey of Catholic literature and thought of the past two centuries. Provides valuable biographical data for major essayists identified as Catholic.

Wade, Ira C. *The Clandestine Organization and Diffusion of Philosophic Ideas in France from 1700 to 1750.* Princeton, N.J.: Princeton University Press, 1938. Ground-breaking work on clandestine essays written in the early part of the eighteenth century.

Yarrow, P. J. *A Literary History of France: The Seventeenth Century. 1600–1715.* London: Ernest Benn; New York: Barnes and Noble, 1967. Invaluable as a general introduction to major authors and works of the period.

2. Works on Individual Authors

Bieber, Konrad. *Simone de Beauvoir.* Boston: Twayne Publishers, 1979. Contains a solid section on the author as essayist.

Burne, Glenn S. *Rémy de Gourmont: His Ideas and Influence in England and America.* Carbondale: Southern Illinois University Press, 1963. Consult for an excellent moral portrait of de Gourmont as well as for an extensive commentary on his writings.

Chadbourne, Richard M. *Ernest Renan as an Essayist.* New York: Cornell University Press, 1957. Brilliant study of Renan the essayist as well as of the form the French essay takes in the nineteenth century.

————. *Ernest Renan.* New York: Twayne Publishers, 1968. The best introduction to consult for Renan's essential thought and works.

Fellows, Otis. *Diderot.* Boston: Twayne Publishers, 1977. A brilliant introduction to Diderot the man and his writings by a distinguished Diderot scholar.

Fiedler, Leslie A. "Simone Weil: Prophet Out of Israel, a Saint of the Absurd." *Commentary* 1 (1951):36–46.

Frame, Donald M. *Montaigne's Discovery of Man: The Humanization of a Humanist.* New York: Columbia University Press, 1955. A lucid and convincing study of Montaigne's intellectual evolution. Does not impose rigid categories on his thought.

————. *François Rabelais.* New York: Harcourt Brace Jovanovich, 1972.

Friedrich, Hugo. *Montaigne.* Translated by Robert Rovini. Paris: Gallimard Biliothèque des Idées, 1968. Contains an invaluable study of the authors of classical antiquity who anticipate the essay form in their writings and how Montaigne adapts their tradition to his project.

Giraud, Victor. *Paul Bourget.* Paris: Librairie Bloud et Gay, 1934. Excellent psychocritical study of Bourget the author.

Greaves, Anthony A. *Maurice Barrès.* Boston: Twayne Publishers, 1978. Contains a substantial section on Barrès's essay writings.

Lanson, Gustave. *Les Essais de Montaigne, étude et analyse.* Reprint. Paris: Mellottée, 1948. Remains the best study on the posthumous existence of the essay in France after Montaigne and up to the nineteenth century.

Starkie, Enid. *Baudelaire.* London: Pelican Books, 1971. A readable critical biography.

Villey, Pierre. *Les Essais de Montaigne.* Reprint. Paris, Nizet, 1946.

————. *Les Sources et l'évolution des Essais de Montaigne.* 2 vols. Paris: Hachette, 1908.

Wilson, Arthur M. *Diderot.* New York: Oxford University Press, 1972. The most complete study of Diderot's life and works.

Index